# Toward an Understanding of Russia

## New European Perspectives

Edited by
Janusz Bugajski

A Council on Foreign Relations Book
New York

Founded in 1921, the Council on Foreign Relations is a nonpartisan membership organization, research center, and publisher. It is dedicated to increasing America's understanding of the world and contributing ideas to U.S. foreign policy. The Council accomplishes this mainly by promoting constructive discussions and by publishing *Foreign Affairs*, the leading journal on global issues. The Council is host to the widest possible range of views, but an advocate of none, though its research fellows and Independent Task Forces do take policy stands.

THE COUNCIL TAKES NO INSTITUTIONAL POSITION ON POLICY ISSUES AND HAS NO AFFILIATION WITH THE U.S. GOVERNMENT. ALL STATEMENTS OF FACT AND EXPRESSIONS OF OPINION CONTAINED IN ALL ITS PUBLICATIONS ARE THE SOLE RESPONSIBILITY OF THE AUTHOR OR AUTHORS.

From time to time, books, monographs, reports, and papers written by members of the Council's research staff or others are published as a "Council on Foreign Relations Publication." Any work bearing that designation is, in the judgment of the Committee on Studies of the Council's Board of Directors, a responsible treatment of a significant international topic.

For further information about the Council or this book, please write the Council on Foreign Relations, 58 East 68th Street, New York, NY 10021, or call the Director of Communications at (212) 434-9400. Visit our website at www.cfr.org.

# Contents

# Foreword

Over a decade after the end of Cold War and the disintegration of the Soviet empire, the initial optimism on the part of some that Russia would became a responsible, modern state integrated into the "New World Order" has been replaced by a sense of wasted opportunity among some Western as well as some Russian elites. A large number of American scholars and analysts have focused on Russia and accumulated enormous amounts of knowledge. In addition vast resources have been devoted to assisting Russia in its transition to democratic capitalism. But their overall impact on democracy and capitalism in Russia has been discouraging. One should, therefore, ask whether knowledge automatically brings understanding and whether a lack of understanding can be overcome through material help. The answer to both questions is apparently negative.

This project was intended to help understand Russia better by bringing together the perspectives of American analysts with those of scholars who were much closer to Russia due to geography and history. Therefore, we invited 12 analysts from Central and Eastern Europe to share their views on issues ranging from Russia's structure of power and President Vladimir Putin's foreign policy goals to Russia's energy policy. We hoped to learn from the differences between these perspectives.

Several of them are worth mentioning here. American analysts examined Russia's potential to be a global actor that could challenge the United States, while analysts from the former Soviet empire concentrated on Russia as a European actor and its potential to influence that region.

More often than not, the majority of American analysts focused on Russia episodically, rather than systematically. This is the reason why extremely contradictory evaluations of Russia emerge in times of major political change in Russia, or during a crisis in Russian-U.S. relations. Bismarck's dictum that Russia is never as strong as one is afraid and never as weak as one hopes is largely forgotten in Washington. Central and Eastern Europeans tend to have a more nuanced view of Russia and in their analyses, they seek to identify the essence of Russia's self-identity and its policies rather than to rely on ad hoc analysis of short-term political turbulence in Moscow.

We hoped that bringing these different viewpoints to bear could enhance U.S. analysis of the roots of the Russian situation, as well as help make American policy planners take a longer view in shaping policies toward Russia. The U.S. policy-planning structure invariably focuses on short-term policy timetables. But, as the "lost decade" has demonstrated, the emphasis on achieving goals rapidly in Russia may have to be tempered with an understanding of how time is viewed halfway across the world. This Central and Eastern European focus on long-term trends inside Russia, and their impact on Russian foreign policy, is especially valuable in light of the recent reorientation of Putin's policy toward America. Indeed, one needs to ask in observing the transformation of Russian foreign policy since September 11, whether the changes, which depend primarily on Putin's decisions, are not too fresh to serve as a basis for long-term U.S. commitments in its relations with Russia.

*Lawrence J. Korb*
Maurice R. Greenberg Chair, Director of Studies
Council on Foreign Relations

# Acknowledgments

This volume is the result of a Council on Foreign Relations project "Toward an Understanding of Russia," which was supported by the Smith Richardson Foundation. The analyses in this volume were presented during a conference in Washington, D.C., on September 6–7, 2001. The views expressed are those of the authors alone.

The project director, Janusz Bugajski, as well as the project coordinator, Marek Michalewski, are grateful to all those who attended the conference, especially to our guests from Central and Eastern Europe. We are greatly indebted to the Smith Richardson Foundation, especially to Nadia Schadlow and Marin Strmecki for their assistance during the early stage of the project. We are also greatly indebted to Paula Dobriansky, who was the initiator of this project when serving as director of the Council's Washington office. We would like also to thank David Kramer for his advice regarding the selection of conference topics.

Gratitude should also be extended to Council intern Karolina Kotwica, who was of invaluable help during the preparation of the conference for over 100 participants. Last but not least we would like to thank those involved in the production of this volume, especially Patricia Dorff, director of Publications at the Council.

# Preface

*Janusz Bugajski*

On September 6–7, 2001, the Council on Foreign Relations organized an innovative international conference in Washington, D.C. The two-day meeting was truly international in its scope and content, not simply because Europeans were present but because the conference itself was designed as a forum for Central Europeans from the new democracies to analyze Russia and to help Americans better understand developments under President Vladimir Putin.

The conference was the key component of a project sponsored by the Smith Richardson Foundation and intended to expose U.S. policymakers and analysts to central and east European (CEE) insights on Russian domestic and foreign policy. The conference organizers gathered a broad array of speakers representing a number of prominent policy institutes from Ukraine, Slovakia, Poland, Lithuania, Hungary, Estonia, and the Czech Republic—countries that neighbor Russia and have experienced Moscow's policy more directly than their west European counterparts. This report is a product of the initial papers produced by the panelists, the ensuing discussions and inputs from conference participants, and important updates since the proceedings concluded.

The Council's conference had two specific objectives. The first was to encourage and promote central and east European input into U.S. policymaking toward Russia and toward the wider region. Such an input is both timely and important given the new administration in Washington and the necessity of gaining a clearer focus on the nature of the Putin government.

The second objective was to help in the development of closer ties between scholars, policy analysts, and policymakers on both sides of the

Atlantic. Such interchanges can encourage new research agendas, common projects, and the strengthening of research institutions in the eastern part of Europe where there is a wealth of knowledge and experience on the "Eastern question."

Because of time constraints, the conference simply could not cover every issue pertaining to Russia's evolution. Hence, certain significant questions such as Russia's national identity, demography, and ecology were set aside for another occasion. The focus was twofold: on key domestic and international issues that had a direct bearing on U.S. policy.

On the first day panelists and moderators concentrated primarily on domestic Russian questions and discussed, in turn, Putin's politics, the state of the economy, the energy issue, and the security question. The extent and limits of President Putin's power and influence were explored in relation to the role of the security services, regional leaders, the military, business people, and parliament.

It transpired that there were no viable political alternatives vying for power in contemporary Russia but several political and industrial lobbies that sought to evade Kremlin controls or influence its policies. Putin's Russia was defined as a hybrid system. It combined features of both democracy and centralism as the Kremlin endeavored to counter the disintegrative and anarchic trends visible in the Russian polity during the 1990s but was not prepared to impose an authoritarian regime. Some participants at the first session believed that Putin was simply simulating democracy and imitating liberalism while at the same time recognizing that it would be counterproductive to try and establish a strong dictatorship. The Kremlin would be more likely to pursue a tougher approach if Putin's power was endangered because of an economic downturn or a social breakdown.

Civil society in Russia was viewed as weak and fragile and often at the mercy of state institutions and oligarchic interests. Indeed, Putin's call for a "partnership" between government and civic society underscores that state leaders have little understanding of the role and independence of a genuine private social sector. If civic activists and media figures are simply co-opted to serve state interests and to promote government policy then civic society loses its independence and impact.

In discussions on the state of the Russian economy, a lively debate ensued between two schools of interpretation: the optimistic and the skeptical, the former represented by an American participant, the latter by a central European panelist. Optimists believe that a package of reforms pushed through the Russian parliament in summer 2001 heralds a major commitment by Putin to market reform and liberal economics. Changes in banking laws, the land code, ownership rights, the legal system, pensions, and taxation are crucial structural measures that will eventually stimulate economic growth.

But skeptics point out that much of the reforms exist on paper only and it is the implementation of laws that will test Putin's commitment and resolve. Moreover, the Kremlin is intent on introducing a "dictatorship of law" rather than the "rule of law," whereby legal measures are instrumentalized to promote a particular political agenda. Russia still lacks a secure class of property owners, has an inadequate financial and investment system, is dependent on primary commodities such as energy production, is uncompetitive in the global economy, and remains at the mercy of reactionary local authorities and corrupt officials.

In the energy field, panelists and participants discussed several pertinent questions. They considered how energy is used as a foreign policy tool to engender Russia's economic expansion and political influence in neighboring regions. Relations between the energy sector and the Russian authorities were also debated with differing perspectives on the degree of control Moscow exerts over the gas and oil industry and on whether the latter's foreign policies are synchronized at the center.

The Central European participants concurred that energy has been manipulated by Moscow for over a decade to influence neighboring countries. In the early 1990s, the Kremlin exploited the energy dependency and vulnerability of Eastern Europe to exert pressure on these states through threats and cutoffs in supplies. However, in recent years a more sophisticated approach has been adopted. Russian energy companies purchase strategic sectors of the local economies and evidently seek to gain political leverage through their economic influence. The intriguing question arises, whether this is simply an economic calculation by energy companies to make profits and gain revenues or a deliberate instrument of long-term Kremlin policy.

The security dimension was comprehensively covered at the conference by examining Russia's national security concept, its military doctrine and posture, and the progress of military reform. Moscow continues to define the North Atlantic alliance (NATO) as a threat to its national security and national interests. Meanwhile, the country's security documents seek to expand and consolidate Russian influence in several nearby regions as the country's elites still view Russia as a global power.

Conflicts have been evident within Russia's military elite and the political leadership over the extent and nature of essential force restructuring. Military reforms during the 1990s were largely unsuccessful but Putin is proposing a more ambitious approach that could meet with significant resistance against cutting force numbers in the creation of a professional military.

The second day broadened the scope of the conference by examining Russian policy toward its neighbors, toward the European Union (EU), and toward NATO and the United States. For Moscow, the member countries of the Commonwealth of Independent States (CIS) are considered to be in

Russia's sphere of "vital national interests." In the European CIS, Russia manipulates pan-Slavism and Soviet nostalgia in order to bring both Belarus and Ukraine into a tighter political orbit but without paying a high economic price by incorporating them inside the Russian Federation.

In Central Asia and the Caucasus, Moscow has promoted regional alliances dependent on Moscow for military support, energy, and transportation. Lacking stable state structures or strong economies, many of these countries are open to Russian influence. Moscow thrusts itself forward as the regional patron, it exploits local conflicts to place its own troops in these territories, and it favors local strongmen who stifle democracy but pursue a predictable foreign policy line.

With regard to the EU, Putin's policy is unlikely to return to the pro-Western approach of the early Boris Yeltsin years. Moscow is not seeking a full-fledged partnership and has limited chances of EU accession over the next decade. It is also concerned about the potentially negative consequences of EU enlargement into Central Europe. Specifically, the process may isolate Russia by limiting trade and investment with Moscow and block the movement of labor across expanded EU borders.

A great deal of discussion centered on the "wedge thesis," according to which Russia is purportedly intent on creating or deepening divisions between Europe and America in order to gain strategic advantage. While one Central European panelist viewed the theory as having only limited analytical value, the ensuing debate revealed that it generates significant interest and concern on both sides of the Atlantic. EU integration and moves toward developing a distinct European security identity may become useful vehicles for widening divisions in the alliance. Indeed, the Kremlin has been seeking an institutional link between the EU and Russia in the security arena—a policy clearly designed to weaken NATO.

The Russia-America panel proved lively and wide-ranging. It examined the feasibility of the NATO-Russia Charter, the mixed role of Russia during the Kosovo conflict, and the question of Russia's future membership in the alliance. Above all, would the latter prospect serve to undermine the rationale and purpose of NATO's existence and could a viable "Eurasian-Atlantic" security structure be devised or would it dilute and divert existing security institutions?

The two international panels also provoked a lively discussion over Moscow's objectives and policies toward the central and east European states. Several participants provided concrete examples of how Russian policy toward the region has involved attempts to pressurize indigenous governments, to purchase strategic sectors of the local economy, and to exert influence over political decision making in line with Russia's interests. The breadth and success of such a strategy was a subject of dispute, opening up the intriguing question of whether the Russian authorities, intelligence network, business interests, and criminal godfathers were working in tandem throughout the region.

The final session of the conference proved to be an innovative approach by posing to each analyst from Central Europe three specific questions on the future of Russia and asking for appropriate American responses. The three questions were germane to the preceding discussions.

There had been general consensus that Putin's Russia was a hybrid system combining democracy and authoritarianism, pluralism and centralism, legalism and statism, a market economy and a mafia economy. However, one cannot be sure how long such a hybrid can survive especially in conditions of economic uncertainty and growing security threats. Russia could sooner or later veer either toward a more consolidated democracy or a more severe dictatorship. If the first ideal scenario is set aside, presumably because in such an instance there would be little for international actors to fear, we are left with the second possibility. This would prove challenging not only for Russia's neighbors but also for the United States. The three questions therefore revolved around two potentially negative scenarios.

The first question considered what scenario would prove more destabilizing for the region, Russia's reimperialization or disintegration. The panelists differed in their responses. While each believed that either possibility seemed unlikely, some considered disintegration as more dangerous because of fears over a loss of control over Russia's nuclear arsenal. Others claimed that neo-imperialism in a new guise is a bigger menace to all neighbors as it could destabilize these states or impede their progress toward European and transatlantic integration.

The second question—how should the United States assist the neighboring independent states in protecting themselves against the negative impact of Russia's rise or further decline—evoked a variety of responses. The focus would evidently need to be on stabilizing Russia and thereby preventing any negative spillovers. For example, Moscow should be engaged in all global fora, Soviet-era debts should be forgiven, and Russia must be assisted in becoming a functional state through the development of legal institutions and civil society. With regard to Central Europe, there was consensus that both NATO and EU membership would help secure the region and anchor each state politically, economically, and militarily in a stable international structure.

Answers to the third question—what should be the priorities of the central and east European states in their dealings with Putin's Russia—supplemented the previous responses. For instance, EU and NATO membership were viewed as a priority, a coordinated "Eastern" policy should be adopted in the region, and a common energy policy must be pursued. Each state could also do more to encourage Western investment but, ultimately, they have limited tools in influencing Russian foreign policy.

In sum, several participants asserted that it was essential for the Central Europeans, working in tandem with the EU and the United States, not to allow Russia to create new zones of influence in the region. Such observations confirmed that the conference addressed issues and provided insights on questions that will preoccupy policymakers and analysts on both sides of the Atlantic for many years to come.

# 1

# Who Rules Russia and How?

*Katarzyna Pełczyńska-Nałęcz*

Power in Russia is often identified with the country's president. Discussion about the future of the Russian Federation is dominated by questions about the scope of power enjoyed by Vladimir Putin, his beliefs and plans, and about the Russia he intends to establish. However, the answer to the question "Who is Mr. Putin?" allows us to understand only a part of the Russian reality. Although Vladimir Putin is undoubtedly the most important and, currently, the most influential person in Russia, he constitutes only one of many forces decisive for the direction of the country's development and future.

In this chapter, I will try to show that, despite the visible reinforcement of presidential power and an almost complete disappearance of organized public opposition, there is no "one-person-rule" in Russia. There are deep institutional (between particular governing structures) and personal (between unofficial groups based on professional, regional, or familiar relations) divisions in the Russian ruling elite. These divisions make it difficult for the Kremlin to develop a coherent vision of the country's future, and they call into question the implementation of possible social and economic reforms.

While answering the question put forward in the title above, "Who is ruling Russia and how?" I would like to avoid presenting a "Putin-centric" view of Russia. My aim is to provide a description of the complex governmental structure in that country, as well as relations (i.e., areas of cooperation and conflict) among particular influential groups. However, it is difficult to discuss Russian mechanisms for exercising authority without considering the influence of society upon the decisions of government. Although ordinary people are still an object rather than a subject of policy, they exert a certain influence on decisions and actions taken by the ruling elites.

The above-mentioned issues, including the characteristics of the specific centers of government and the influence of society upon the decisions of Russian elites, constitute the core of the first part of this chapter. In its second part I attempt to distinguish the principal features of the Russian system of government. The third part is devoted to the problems of such a system. I try to answer the question: What kind of social, political, and economic reforms may be carried out in Russia taking into consideration the current existing structures and mechanisms of authority?

## KEY CENTERS OF GOVERNMENT

*Federal Executive Power.* The president, presidential administration, and government constitute the most influential center of power in the country. They set the objectives for both the internal and external policies of Russia, and they develop projects for political, social, and economic reforms. The president—the head of the federal executive authority—is definitely the person who holds the strongest position in the country. His power stems mostly from the fact that he makes the final decision on appointments to all of the most important state posts (i.e., the prime minister, members of the government and presidential administration, and the president's representatives in the seven federal districts). The president's agenda is supported by the administration and the Security Council (officially a consultative body). He also exerts extensive control over the government. However, the constitutional prerogatives set out only a possible framework for the activity of federal executive authorities. The real areas of competence of the specific structures and the manner in which they will be used are determined to a great extent by individual resources and the predispositions of the highest state officials and, above all, of the president.

Under the rule of Boris Yeltsin the specific stages of the system's evolution were closely related to the changes in the mental and physical condition of the president.[1] The personalization of power became particularly visible after Vladimir Putin was elected president on December 31, 2000. The appearance of a new politician at the highest state post implied important changes in the manner of activity of both the government and presidential administration. First of all, the influence exerted by the president within the scope of his federal executive power was considerably strengthened. At the same time, the Kremlin was provided with new opportunities to affect the decisions of other authorities (e.g., regional leaders, the parliament). The relations between representatives of businesses and the most important state officials changed too. Although certain financial potentates are still favored by the government, their political influence was seriously restricted.

Despite significant strengthening of presidential power, Putin cannot be regarded as omnipotent. One of the important factors weakening his position is the lack of homogeneity in the federal executive bodies. Although, in a formal sense, both the government and presidential administration are loyal to the president, in fact, they are deeply divided. Before he was appointed to the post of prime minister, Putin was a state official unconnected with any political party or movement. While taking over the highest post in the country, he was not supported by any organized political force that could have helped him develop his own agenda and team. As a result, Putin's closest advisers have been rather "eclectic" from the very beginning. The divisions in the administration and government are not associated with membership in the different political parties. They are formed primarily on the basis of familiar and regional bonds or friendship between people who have worked or studied together.[2] Due to the informal character of these divisions the composition of particular groups and factions is highly mutable. This makes it much more difficult to identify correctly the real affiliation of particular politicians. Currently we can distinguish at least three such groups in Putin's circle:

- The first faction consists of so-called liberals declaring their strong support for free-market reforms. It includes, among others, the president of the largest state enterprise—Joint Power Systems of Russia (RAO JES Rossii)—Anatoli Chubais, and German Gref, the main author of the "Development Strategy for Russia until 2010," a study developed at Putin's request.
- The second faction, called "Petersburg," is made up of a group of Putin's confidential agents whose careers are owed to Putin. Membership in that faction depends not only on one's geographical origin (namely, from St. Peterburg) but is also awarded to former KGB members. This group is convinced of the need to create a strong state that would take control over the economic sphere. In the majority, they are devoted to the struggle against their political opponents and people criticizing Putin. The most influential representative of the above-mentioned group is a retired general of the Federal Security Service, currently the minister of defense, Sergey Ivanov.
- The third group of people surrounding the president comprises representatives of the old team of Boris Yeltsin, loyally cooperating with the current president. This group includes Alexandr Voloshin (the head of the presidential administration), Mikhail Kasianov (the prime minister), and Vladimir Ustinov (the general public prosecutor).

In May 2000, Putin issued a decree under which the Russian Federation was divided into seven federal districts governed by the president's representatives. The establishment of these districts has changed neither the number nor the status of the existing administrative units. The new structure is aimed at increasing the influence of the Kremlin in the country and securing implementation in the regions of decisions made by central authorities.

In order to sum up the activities of Putin's representatives, it may be said that the establishment of the federal districts has undoubtedly increased the amount of information received by the Kremlin about the processes taking place in the Russian provinces. The districts, however, did not improve the efficiency of the implementation of decisions made by the federal centers.[3] Introduction of another level of the state administration has made relations among Russian executive authorities even more complex.

The duties of the president's representatives, which had not been defined well enough, appeared to constitute a major problem here. According to the decree, their main task was supposed to be the "organization of the implementation by the state authorities of basic principles of internal and foreign policy by following the president's instructions."[4] The decree did not specify, however, the manner in which such a purpose was to be achieved, nor did it provide the representatives with any specific executive power. The failure to define the scope of responsibilities of the president's representatives brought about three main consequences in federal district functions:

- First, it resulted in conflicts between the representatives and the presidential administration (in particular, with its administrative and territorial department) on the one hand, and the governors on the other.
- Second, in order to exert real influence, the president's representatives could not rely on the regulations imposed by supreme authorities and they had to establish their own mechanisms for influencing the regional authorities and federal district departments. In effect, the manner of activity and the efficiency of the particular representatives depended upon their individual predispositions, as well as contacts they maintained with people in the country and in Moscow.
- Third, the position of the representatives was made dependent, to a considerable degree, on the position held by the president himself. Due to the lack of institutional mechanisms regulating actions of the federal districts' heads, their basic trump card was the personal support of the president. In other words, both people in regions and the federal structures showed certain obedience to the president's representatives not because of the legal provisions but because of their respect for the Russian president. Such a situation means that the current position of the representatives may depend on the country's political climate. Any possible loss of influence by the president (e.g., caused by a drop in his social popularity) will, most probably, immediately affect the position and operating efficiency of his representatives.

*Regional Executive Power.* In mid-2000, out of the president's initiative, the parliament of the Russian Federation adopted legal acts, which significantly reduced the influence of regional authorities upon decisions made by the center. Among other things, the principles for forming the upper house of the Russian parliament, the Council of Federation, were changed. Beginning in 2002, the council does not include heads of the regional legislative and executive authorities (as had been the case previously), but only the representatives appointed by them. Under the approved legal acts, the president has also obtained the right to dismiss heads of the regional executive authorities. However, this procedure has become subject to court supervision.

In 2000, some additional actions were taken in order to restrain the power of the heads of local administrations—e.g., the amount of centrally reallocated funds was increased at the expense of local budgets, and the control of central authorities over local federal departments was made more strict. The position of governors also became considerably weaker due to the improved cooperation of the president with special services that, at any time and at the request of the Kremlin, are ready to supply materials compromising the particular regional leaders.

Despite all the changes described above, the heads of the regional administration still have considerable power. First of all, they have maintained significant influence in their regions. Their authority is based both on official capacity and on expanded networks of private connections with local business, courts, and managers of federal departments. As a consequence, heads of local executive departments have at their disposal funds included in local budgets (and it should be remembered that those budgets spend about 50 percent of the resources of the consolidated Russian Federation's budget).[5] They fix the prices of electric energy for regional receivers, and they decide about the allocation of preferential credits or licenses for carrying out economic activity. Governors and presidents of the citizens of the Russian Federation usually exercise control over local courts and the media.

While regional leaders have very limited means to affect decisions being made in Moscow, they do have some very effective tools for exerting influence on the actual enforcement of those decisions. The power they have at the regional level provides many opportunities to circumvent, ignore, or boycott the Kremlin's decisions. In that context, the way in which political, social, and economic reforms being prepared by the Kremlin will be carried out in the future depends to a great degree upon the regional leaders.

The position of the country's elites becomes stronger due to the fact that Moscow's capability to appoint governors, presidents, or mayors is still extremely limited. The procedure for removing regional leaders, which was introduced last year, is so complex that, so far, it has not been used even once. The only case where a governor was dismissed before the end of his term of office resembled more of an informal barter transaction than an official dismissal of a state employee by the president. In exchange for his resignation as governor of Primorskii Krai, Jevgenii Nazdratenko obtained a profitable post as the head of the Fishery Commission. The dozens of elections of governors held within the last several years have also revealed the limited capabilities of the Kremlin to influence the outcome of local elections. Contrary to expectations, the administration of Vladimir Putin did not carry out any revolution among the governors. Incumbents won almost 70 percent of the elections. Only a few winners owe their success to the president's support, such as Vladimir Yegorov in the Kaliningrad district.[6]

In defining the position of regional leaders in the Russian governmental system, one should take into account the fact that the governors have many diverging aims although in some cases they also have some common interests. The most important dividing lines run between the rich and poor regions (e.g., the latter, as opposed to the former, support the idea of increasing the amount of funds reallocated from the center), and between the republics and other regions (e.g., the republics are defending their privileged status in the Russian Federation). These conflicts overlap with both personal and geographical antagonisms. The lack of a homogeneous character among the regional elites makes it more difficult for them to participate in joint initiatives, and it allows for the Kremlin's manipulations and intrigues.

*Federal and Local Legislative Authorities.* The only legislative authority actually affecting the situation in Russia is the federal parliament and, in particular, its lower house, called the Duma. The role of local legislative assemblies is marginal.

Currently, there is no anti-presidential opposition in the Duma. The political orientation of the particular groups may be defined as less (CPRF, Yabloko, Right Force Alliance) or more (Unity, Home Country–All Russia, People's Deputy, Regions of Russia) loyal to the president. The lack of opposition does not, however, mean the bills submitted by executive authorities are approved automatically without being discussed or negotiated. The bills considered controversial by the particular groups of deputies are subject to long-lasting consultations, which often result in extensive amendments. In certain extreme cases (e.g., as regards the act on land ownership) the legislative procedure may even get postponed. Most of the discussions on such bills are held behind the scenes and quite frequently before the act is officially submitted. As a result, there are not many public confrontations in the parliament.

*Courts.* Officially, the Russian courts are bodies fully independent of other governmental institutions. In reality, they are subject to various political pressures, and the situation is the worst in the case of courts at the lower level. Due to their actual financial dependence on regional authorities (local budgets often include additional payments to the remunerations of judges, and local authorities also usually decide on allocating flats to court employees), courts are often almost entirely dependent on executive authorities of a given administrative unit.

Higher-ranking courts, including the Supreme Court and Constitutional Court, are also susceptible to political influence. However, they are usually subject to a more subtle pressure. An example of such a situation may be the amended act on the Constitutional Court, recently adopted by the Duma, which provides for the prolongation of the judges' terms of office and exempts judges aged over 70 from the obligation to retire. The act was most likely aimed at winning the support of Constitutional Court judges and, in particular, the court's chairman, Marat Baglay. (It may not be a coincidence that the draft act was filed with the Duma one year before the chairman would reach retirement age).

*The Army and Special Services.* The Russian power sector does not constitute an autonomous center of government. Neither the special services nor the army aspire to take over power in the country. However the position of armed services in the Russian Federation is strong enough that the Kremlin sometimes has serious difficulties maintaining complete control over these structures.

The most vivid example of this situation is the war in the Chechen Republic. Thanks to the military operation in the Caucasus, a completely unknown person, Vladimir Putin, became, within only several months, the most popular politician in Russia and won the presidential elections in the first round. However, the Chechen war was not a single event, but rather it initiated a process in which control over one of Russia's regions became fully dependent upon the presence of the army and other power structures. It cannot be excluded that currently the armed forces purposefully use the situation in the republic (e.g., they fail to catch Chechen leaders, do not prevent terrorist acts, etc.) in order to maintain the status quo. The army's power in the northern Caucasus gives its officers the opportunity on the one hand to lobby their interests in Moscow, and on the other to take profits from the illegal businesses that flourish in the region.

The growth in importance of the security structures is largely connected with the greater representation of those sectors in the governing structures. This trend may be illustrated by the fact that five out of seven of the president's representatives in Federal Districts have connections with the army or security services.[7]

## POWER, SOCIETY, AND REFORMS

While watching the Russian decision-making mechanisms, one may say that the society does not take part in the process of ruling the country. The above statement may be supported by the fact that there have been no actions taken by citizens for the last year and a half (e.g., lobbying actions of nongovernmental organizations, strikes, or manifestations), which would force the government to change its adopted political orientation. The fact becomes particularly important if we realize that during this time a military operation was initiated and carried out in one of Russia's regions, an administrative reform was implemented, and the Media-Most holding (made up of one of the most popular Russian TV channels and a number of widely read newspapers and weeklies) was liquidated.

The minimal or nonparticipation of the Russian society in decision-making processes does not mean that it is completely ignored by the authorities. Rather, the situation is quite opposite of this. Peoples' preferences and expectations are one of the key factors influencing the policies of the government. Both federal and local authorities are appointed in the Russian Federation based on the results of general elections. Although such elections do not meet all of the democratic standards, the results are usually not forged so they most probably reflect the preferences of voters. The need to confirm the mandate obtained as a result of the elections makes the authorities take into consideration at least some of the citizens' expectations. Peoples' support is also necessary not only for re-election but also as an important political trump card in the period between the elections. For example, the impressive popularity of Putin (for the past year and a half it maintained the level of 60–70 percent) considerably increases his ability to exert influence on regional leaders. The most recent local elections have revealed that governors obtain more votes if they are loyal to the president, whereas their insubordination makes people reluctant to vote for them.

As politicians are aware of the fact that strong social support is important political capital in Russia, it makes them scramble for popularity among ordinary citizens. The specific nature of the situation in Russia is based on the fact that actions taken to win the voters' support are not connected with any attempt to involve them in decision-making processes. In their efforts to gain the support of voters, politicians mostly manipulate public opinion (e.g., by promoting their views in the media, or by making demagogic statements or actions). The fact that Russian politicians fear losing voters does not make them account for their achievements in a more overt or responsible way. On the contrary, it results in the intensification of manipulation. Such a relationship between the government and society becomes an obstacle to the development of civil society in Russia. By trying to maintain maximum support from ordinary people, the authorities (both federal and local) deprive citizens of access to reliable and correct information about the situation in the country, and they promote xenophobia. According to an analysis of the contents of messages transmitted by the Russian media, the media loyal to the authorities and, in particular, RTR and ORT TV stations not only avoid criticizing the Kremlin but they consistently implement a well-considered information strategy. Such a strategy includes among other things the creation of a positive image of the authorities and, above all, of the president, while stressing the weakness and hostility of Western democracies (in particular, the United States) toward Moscow.[8]

The system of government currently existing in Russia considerably restrains the possibility of carrying out reforms in a quick and efficient way. The institutional and personal divisions of governmental structures result in a situation where, after a year and a half of the new president's rule, the authorities have not managed to develop any coherent vision of planned changes. No complete reform program has, so far, been developed and approved. The "Development Strategy for the Russian Federation until 2010," drawn up at the president's request and regarded as a presentation of the reform program of the Kremlin, has never been accepted by the government nor has it been published as a whole.

Lack of a complete program for reforming the country can be seen in almost all of the program statements made by the president.[9] His presentations often included contradictory statements (e.g., Putin keeps supporting liberal reforms by stressing, at the same time, the need to maintain social guarantees currently existing in Russia). The declared objectives clearly differ from the authorities' practices (e.g., the principle of the dictatorship of the law, promoted by the president, does not seem to be an obstacle to his using informal or even illegal pressure mechanisms). The lack of a coherent vision of what kind of political and economic system should be established in Russia is reflected in the character of already implemented changes as well as in currently prepared reform projects. Many of these projects try to merge the elements of the existing hybrid system with the new, more democratic and liberal regulations.

The inefficiency of the government is revealed not only at the general planning level, but also during the preparation of specific reforms. It refers mainly to transformations that would introduce sweeping social and economic changes. The legislative process is usually rather languid and confused. Most often, several projects are being developed at the same time (e.g., by the government and by governors). Then the projects are submitted for numerous consultations resulting in many amendments. If the reform project receives approval by the government or by the president, it becomes grounds for preparation of the specific acts. At that stage many long negotiations and discussions are usually held. Sometimes, before submitting it to the Duma, the deputies additionally discuss the bills. Due to this procedure, most of the essential projects of socioeconomic reforms are still at the initial stage of development. For example, the process of restructuring Gazprom, which has been forecast for many years, has not yet been included in any homogeneous and complete project, nor have the ideas of a retirement pension or municipal or health service reforms been agreed upon. The decision on the manner of resolving the important issue of agricultural land ownership has not yet been made either.

The divisions of governmental structures as well as the corruption of people in power may slow down the process of preparing the reforms, as well as the implementation of approved legal acts. The execution of reforms is largely dependent on the activities of local authorities. Most of the regional leaders are unwilling to support any liberal reforms. Such changes would significantly weaken their influence (i.e., they would not be entitled to control the issuance of all types of concessions or reliefs). Moreover, governors would be made responsible for counteracting any negative social effects of such changes (such as an increase in the price of electric energy or rents, etc.). Therefore, local leaders are likely to make an effort to prevent the reforms, and such sabotage may prove very efficient considering their strong influence in the Russian regions.

## CONCLUSIONS

On the basis of the description of the Russian authorities provided above, we may distinguish features of the existing Russian system of government. A closer look at the Russian system makes it obvious that the practice of governing differs from the existing constitutional and legal rules. Both the competence and manner of activity of the particular institutions are derived to a considerable degree from informal relations and patterns developed by the ruling elite on one hand, and from individual resources and predispositions of an official occupying a given post on the other. Although there are constitutional provisions, there is no official or organized political opposition in Russia. Power is concentrated exclusively in the hands of executive authorities. Certain influence on the situation in the country is exercised also by the federal parliament and, in particular, the Duma. Other legislative bodies (regional parliaments), as well as territorial self-government and courts, do not constitute autonomous centers of government affecting the country's situation. Often such structures are used by the people in power as tools to serve certain political purposes.

The lack of true opposition and an almost complete monopoly of executive bodies by the president and his administration do not, however, mean that there is a uniform structure of authority in Russia. Paradoxically, the pluralism of the authority of the Russian Federation does not manifest itself in the existence of an opposition to the government, nor are there any mutually independent government institutions (e.g., courts, self-governments, etc.). The heterogeneous character of the Russian authorities stems mainly from: 1) conflicts among particular governmental structures (i.e., between governors and the president's representatives controlling them or between the president's representatives and his administration); and 2) the existence of various informal parties and influence groups, the majority of which originate in the executive power structures.[10] The divisions among such groups are unofficial, as they do not result from differences in political programs but from differences in strictly private interests. It can be said that, in today's Russia, official competition between various political options has been replaced by a hidden rivalry of informal governmental groups.

This phenomenon is connected with another feature of the Russian system of government—an advanced privatization of the state.[11] Lack of divisions based on the difference in political programs in the Russian political arena results from the fact that officials do not accept positions in state posts for public good, but rather they treat these posts as private "assets" allowing for the implementation of one's own political and economic interests. Thus, people in power quite often take actions aimed at obtaining occasional benefits adjusted to the needs and expectations of a given official rather than for a general vision of the state's development.

Another feature of the political regime in the Russian Federation is the personalization of authority. The competence of a particular governmental body is so vague that the actual manner of functioning for a given structure is determined to a considerable degree by the individual predisposition of the official in power.

Russian governmental practices are very different from democratic standards. This does not, however, mean that power in Russia does not depend in any way on society's will. Quite the opposite: due to the fluent character of the rules of the political game, social support is an extremely important argument in the competition among the ruling elites in Russia. However, such support is obtained mainly by means of manipulating public opinion and not by the participation of citizens in the country's government.

It seems that the current system of government will not be reformed radically in the near future. Neither Putin nor his advisers have a clear vision of the political and economic system to be built in Russia. Therefore, currently realized reforms are not part of a coherent strategy but rather a result of compromises and clashes between different groups and institutions. The Russian government poses many obstacles to profound political and economic changes. It is still difficult to determine to what extent such obstacles may slow down the country's reforms. Now it seems certain that the reform process will last for a long time if such changes are made. Due to numerous unavoidable compromises and attempts to adapt the reforms to serve the individual interests of particular officials, the results of such changes may differ considerably from the expected ones.

## NOTES

1. Wlodzimierz Marciniak, *Rozgrabione Imperium* (Krakow: Arcana, 2001).

2. Witold Rodkiewicz, "Postsowiecki feudalizm we wspólczesanej Rosji. Próba postawienia problemu," in W. Materski, ed., *Państwo w transformacji w perspektywie XXI wieku* (Warsaw: ISPPAN, 2000).

3. Bartosz Cichocki, "Przedstawiciele prezydenta—personalizacja wladzy w Rosji," www.osw.waw.pl (2001).

4. "Polozenie o polnomocnom predstawitielie Priezidienta Rossijskoj Fiedieracii w fiedieralnom okrugie?" www.rg.ru/oficial/doc/ykazi/.

5. "Russian Economic Trends," April 18, 2001, www.recep.org.

6. Bartosz Cichocki, "Wybory gubernatorskie w Rosji," www.osw.waw.pl.

7. Nikolai Petrov, "Russia Under Putin," *Russian Regional Report,* vol. 6, no. 23, 2001.

8. Jadwiga Rogoz'a, "Oblicza państwowej propagandy," in *Tydzień Na Wschodzie,* February 8 (Warsaw: OSW, 2001).

9. Such statements include the program presentation, "Russia at the Edge of the Millenium," of December 29, 1999, during the conference of the post-Kremlin Unity movement; "Open letter of Vladimir Putin to the Russian Electorate" published on February 25, 2000; or two annual proclamations addressed so far to the Federal Assembly by Vladimir Putin.

10. Siergiej Karaganow, *Stratiegia dla Rosii. Powiestka dnia dla Priezidienta* (Moscow: Wagrius, 2000).

11. Igor Klamkin and Timofiejew Lew, *Tieniewaja Rossija* (Moscow: RGGU, 2000).

# 2

## Civil Society in Russia

*Hryhoriy Nemyria*

For some reason, the question "Who is Mr. Putin?" has gained much more attention in the West than the question "What is Russian society?" While the first question is important, especially in assessing Russia's short- to medium-term horizons, an adequate answer to the second question is of greater importance for the long-term perspective. Also, it is necessary for our understanding of informal societal constraints vis-à-vis Vladimir Putin's political and institutional creativity.

Developing a democratic culture and civil society takes time, no less than it does for restructuring the economy. In a mutually reinforcing equilibrium, "norms and networks of civic engagement contribute to economic prosperity and in turn [are] reinforced by that prosperity."[1]

To what extent has Russia developed a civil society? What forces are shaping civil society in Russia? What are the emerging patterns of interactions among civil society, the public sphere, and the state? How can reciprocal linkages among political culture, economic development, and stable democracy manifest themselves in the Russian context? What role, if any, can Putin play in fostering or impeding the development of civil society? What role, if any, can the West play in facilitating or inhibiting the development of civil society in Russia?

In the mid-1990s, the European Commission's Forward Studies Unit identified five reference scenarios for Russia's future:[2]

1) A policy based on improvisation;
2) Enlightened authoritarianism;
3) Hard-line authoritarianism;
4) Weakened central power; and
5) Gradual democratization.

What we observe today is enlightened authoritarianism that may muddle through or else evolve either into hard-line authoritarianism or gradual democratization. Which one prevails will depend not just upon Putin, but also on the quality of civil society.

This chapter starts with working definitions of civil society. It then proceeds with descriptions of two paradigms of Russian society and their relevance to the current domestic environment, underlines emerging patterns of interactions between the state and society, and finishes with short policy recommendations based on the analysis of dominant trends.

## CIVIL SOCIETY

*Civil society* is a concept that goes deep below the mechanisms of government into the culture and traditions of society at a more private level. It gained immense popularity in the 1980s and 1990s as a "conceptual code of the epoch" and was "one of the principal hermeneutic keys" to an understanding of relations between the modern state and modern society, especially those undergoing transformation.[3]

According to Gellner, "civil society is that set of diverse nongovernmental institutions, which is strong enough to counterbalance the state and, whilst not preventing the state from fulfilling its role of keeper of the peace and arbitrator between major interests, can nevertheless prevent the state from dominating and atomizing society."[4] Cohen and Arato offer a more detailed definition of civil society as "a sphere of social interaction between the economy and state, composed above all of the intimate sphere (especially the family), the sphere of associations (especially voluntary associations), social movements, and forms of public communication. Modern civil society is created through self-constitution and self-mobilization. It is institutionalized and generalized through laws. In the long run both independent action and institutionalization are necessary for the reproduction of civil society."[5] Habermas underlines communicative connections between civil society, the public sphere, and the state: "Civil society is composed of those more or less spontaneously emergent associations, organizations, and movements that, attuned to how societal problems resonate in the private life sphere, distill and transmit such reactions in amplified form to the public sphere. The core of civil society comprises a network of associations that institutionalizes problem-solving discourses on questions of general interest inside the framework of organized public spheres."[6]

## TWO PARADIGMS FOR CIVIL SOCIETY IN RUSSIA

After ten years of transformation one can discern two clusters of thought about Russian civil society. The first is "path dependence"—where you can get to depends upon where you are coming from. History matters, and the weight of Russian history is too great. Zinaida Golenkova has suggested that "in Russia, unlike the countries of the West, another type of social system had evolved historically, and this system was based on the effectiveness of power and not the effectiveness of property. Relations between property and power were inverted."[7] With enforced homogenization gone, a number of constraints going back to the Soviet past continue to restrict the articulation of interests. Yuri Levada, the patriarch of Russian sociology, concludes that "'Homo sovieticus' as a social type has proved to be ... much more stable, [and] capable of adapting to the change of circumstances than it seemed ten years ago."[8] The old communist system collapsed from above *before* civil society had grown sufficiently strong enough to challenge it effectively from below. Civil society existed in the old system in a very embryonic form. One of the most extreme conclusions belongs to Tatiana Zaslavskaya: "When we say that civil society is a society of free people we must admit that there is no such society in our country and nothing is possible ... in the near future."[9] Thomas Dine shares the opinion that "economic growth by itself will do little to create a civil society where it has not existed in the past."[10]

The second school of thought presents contrasting views of the relevance of history for the development of civil society. Despite its importance, history does not preclude a significant change in Russian culture. Thus, based on their analysis of grassroots attitudes, Timothy Colton and Michael McFaul challenge an established wisdom of comparative politics, which portrayed the process of democratization as a top-level elite affair aimed at the establishment of new institutions, thus facilitating democratic change. They argue that the Russian people "have assimilated democratic values faster than the elite [have] negotiated democratic institutions" and that "Russian society seems more transformed ... than the political structures governing it."[11]

Within the framework of this school of thought, special attention is paid to the set of contemporary factors blocking the potential for the development of civil society in Russia. Those factors are mostly attributed to the degradation of Russia's human capital and to the nature of Putin's regime. The following items are the most frequently mentioned: 1) *growing poverty*—more than 40 million people, or about 30 percent of the population, are living below the subsistence level on less than U.S.$1 a day, and more than 70 percent of Russian children are living in poor families; 2) *deepening income disparities*—the biggest income gap of all East European transition economies (incomes of the wealthiest groups are more than 14 times higher than those of the poorest); 3) *growing number of disabled*—close to 10 million or about 7 percent of the population; 4) *excess mortality*—the Russian population is shrinking by 750,000 every year; 5) *soaring infectious diseases*—the 1999 death toll from tuberculosis was about 15 times the toll in the United States, or nearly 30 times greater when measured as deaths per 100,000 persons in both countries; 6) *skyrocketing unemployment*—about 25 percent; 7) *declining provision of public services*—education, social services, etc.; 8) *escape through substance abuse*—alcohol and drugs; and 9) *rampant corruption*.[12] Needless to say, these factors severely limit social activities. Everyday survival eats up almost all time and energy and produces an apathetic citizenry, whose mobility is additionally constrained by such relics of the past as the residence-permit system, or *propiska*.

Those who follow the path-dependency school differ on their interpretation of Russia's future. Some observers share the view that Russia is unique and will always be different from the West. Others believe that Russia is capable of modernization and adaptation but that the process will take longer. Both subgroups believe, however, that the way out of Russia's multifaceted path dependencies should be "a homegrown affair" with a marginal role for the West to play. As William Odom put it, "adapting U.S. policy accordingly does not mean slamming the door on Russia, but it does suggest fewer U.S. efforts to shape Russian political developments through economic and technical assistance programs."[13]

To some extent, these two schools of thought are somewhat rigid on a conceptual level, which means their conclusions have limited relevance on a policy level. What is lacking here is an analysis of the relationships between state institutions and those of civil society. Interactions *internal* to political, economic, and societal developments in Russia could help analysts understand, for example, the nature of the current debate on Russia's "return to Europe." Does it mean accepting a whole set of political and economic norms (and societal values) that together transform society in a way that is democratically desired, but is not so easily achievable in new democracies without commitment to an extremely fixed rulebook of *acquis communautaire*? Or is it just a rhetorical exercise without significant practical meaning, because if implemented it would contradict the "Russia's own way" paradigm?

There is no doubt that throughout the 1990s civil society in Russia became stronger. However, it remains rather weak on an institutional level, even though the Justice Ministry's registry of nonprofit organizations is about 350,000. About 70,000 of these are actually operational. Every year they create up to one million jobs and provide free services to 20 million Russians—worth 15 billion rubles a year.[14]

As Table 2.1 shows, Russia, classified in the category of "hybrid/transitional states,"[15] and featuring characteristics of "at best an illiberal democracy"[16] with a predominantly closed policymaking procedure, has emasculated legislatures, inefficient and corrupt governmental agencies, weak and unpopular political parties, backward courts, oppressed media with growing habits of self-censorship, and a fragile civil society. Together with the continuation of warfare in Chechnya, Russia firmly occupies a place between the new "democracies with competitive market economies," like Poland, Hungary, and Lithuania, and the new "consolidated autocracies with fully statist economies," like Belarus, Uzbekistan, and Turkmenistan.

**Table 2.1: Nations in Transit 2001: Selected Ratings Summary[17]**

| Country | CS | IM | PP | GPA | DEM | CLJF | CO | ROL |
|---|---|---|---|---|---|---|---|---|
| **Russia** | 4.00 | 5.25 | 4.25 | 5.00 | **4.63** | 4.50 | 6.25 | **5.38** |
| Azerbaijan | 4.50 | 5.75 | 5.75 | 6.25 | **5.56** | 5.25 | 6.25 | **5.75** |
| Belarus | 6.50 | 6.75 | 6.75 | 6.25 | **6.56** | 6.75 | 5.25 | **6.00** |
| Uzbekistan | 6.50 | 6.75 | 6.75 | 6.00 | **6.50** | 6.50 | 6.00 | **6.25** |
| Georgia | 4.00 | 3.50 | 4.50 | 4.75 | **4.19** | 4.00 | 5.00 | **4.50** |
| ======= | === | === | === | === | === | === | === | === |
| Bulgaria | 3.50 | 3.25 | 2.00 | 3.50 | **3.06** | 3.50 | 4.75 | **4.13** |
| Slovakia | 2.00 | 2.00 | 2.25 | 2.75 | **2.25** | 2.25 | 3.75 | **3.00** |
| Lithuania | 1.75 | 1.75 | 1.75 | 2.50 | **1.94** | 1.75 | 3.75 | **2.75** |
| Poland | 1.25 | 1.50 | 1.25 | 1.75 | **1.44** | 1.50 | 2.25 | **1.88** |

CS=Civil Society; IM=Independent Media; PP=Political Process; GPA=Governance and Public Administration; DEM=Democratization; CLJF=Constitutional, Legislative, and Judicial Framework; CO=Corruption; ROL=Rule of Law.

Ratings are provided on a one-to-seven scale, with 1 representing the highest and 7 the lowest level of democratic progress. The ratings for Civil Society, Independent Media, Political Process, and Governance and Public Administrations subsections are averaged to determine a Democratization score; the Constitutional, Legislative, and Judicial Framework and Corruption ratings are averaged to provide an overall Rule of Law score. The 2001 scores and ratings reflect the period July 1, 1999, through October 31, 2000.

Organized groups are necessary for people to be able to act independently of or in opposition to the state authority in a sustained way. It is a well-known fact that *organizational membership* is much lower in post-communist countries than in either the older democracies of the West or in the post-authoritarian countries of southern Europe, Latin America, Asia, and Africa. A country's prior communist experience has a strong negative effect on contemporary organizational membership.

Data from the Post-Communist Organizational Membership Study, a representative survey that was conducted in 1999 in Russia, eastern Germany, and western Germany, shows that three factors have a mutually reinforcing negative effect on public participation in post-communist Europe: 1) a legacy of mistrust of organizations; 2) the persistence of vibrant friendship networks; and 3) the widespread disappointment with the new systems.[18] It means that in order to curb the above-mentioned negativism, organizations (trade unions, political parties, advocacy nongovernmental organizations [NGOs], etc.) should be perceived as efficient and trustworthy institutions able to undertake autonomous and independent actions, and that standards of living should visibly improve. Both conditions scarcely exist in Russia today and this situation is not likely to be improved in the near future. An immediate implication of this social dynamic would be a negative impact on the process of personal learning, because learning requires a liberal public space, "an arena in which interested parties can communicate and test hypotheses."[19]

Table 2.2 demonstrates the extent to which civil society is able to undertake autonomous and independent actions and meet important criteria on a personal level. A growing majority of Russians prefers the Soviet model of a very modest but guaranteed income. Only 6 percent would opt for the full risk of "ownership of your own business." A relatively higher portion, almost 25 percent, would choose "high work and high earnings," even without guarantees for the future. It means that approximately one-third of Russians value risk-bearing strategies to achieve economic success. Though a dominant majority continue to prefer stability, the figures nonetheless present an encouraging picture of emerging active social groups, which could add value to Russia's social capital. This conclusion is also supported by an observation that the proportion of those valuing "hard work and hard earnings" includes as much as 32 percent of respondents between the ages of 25 and 40.

**Table 2.2: Guarantees and Risks: A Choice of Priorities**
**("What Would You Prefer if You Could Choose?")[20]**

| What would you prefer if you could choose? | 1989 | 1994 | 1999 |
|---|---|---|---|
| Low wages, but more free time and easier work | 10 | 4 | 3 |
| Low but guaranteed wages and confidence in tomorrow | 45 | 54 | 60 |
| Hard work and high earnings, even without guarantees for the future | 26 | 23 | 23 |
| Ownership of your own business, with all the risk and rewards | 9 | 6 | 6 |
| Difficult to say | 10 | 19 | 8 |

## A WEAK STATE AND A WEAK CIVIL SOCIETY IN RUSSIA

We understand "weak state" to mean inefficient state institutions with a weak performance. However, this does not make them less visible. In fact, the situation is just the opposite. In Russia, the state is very inefficient but still excessively visible and "heavy."

Even under the ideal conditions of a strong and vibrant civil society, the state has limited significance if it is weak and inefficient. In a social context, when new "trust networks" or "risk-bearing networks" do not exist or at least are very fragile, the ineffectiveness of the state forces people to resort to—and then refashion and adapt—the familiar networks, such as labor collectives, which are outside public politics.[21] Therefore, what looks familiar may have new causes. What may seem to be "restorations" of familiar socialist patterns may be responses to new conditions, "produced *by* them, rather than remnants of an older mentality." If one cannot rely upon proven capacities of the government to meet its commitments, there are few incentives to develop civic associations or to lobby respective social interests. The state must be able to implement policies in order to encourage people to shift the locus of their interpersonal networks to partial dependence on governmental agents. If the state becomes more effective, it becomes reasonable to put sustained pressure on it, which might empower civil society and facilitate its healthy input into public politics. If Putin's reform program produces better governance, then pressure from civil society would increase rather than decrease, thus building trust in the sustainability of change. Citizens always have some power, even in illiberal democracies, because elites must compete for citizens' favor.

However, it seems that like Mustafa Kemal in Turkey, Putin is inclined to create political institutions and promote social-economic change without broadening political participation and relying on a loyal bureaucracy as a main modernizing force. Avoiding a *blitzkrieg* strategy, he is carefully implementing a special sequence of reforms—national, political, and economic.[22] In some way Russia's reform process seems similar to what David Kelly and He Baogang wrote on China. They pointed to a "new authoritarianism" offering an "express train to modernization" in which democracy would be for the elite only, and in which it would only be the new rich, property-owning middle class who would enjoy the rights of participation in civil society.[23]

According to Adam Przeworski, when the legitimacy of democracy becomes detached from its efficacy and it is unconditionally accepted by large majorities, we have *prima facie* evidence of normative consolidation. Before achieving this stage of democratization, government authorities are perennially tempted to replace politics with administration, anarchy with discipline, to do the moral or the rational—in other words, to resort to authoritarianism. "The temptation is fueled by several ideologies. Nationalism provides one, religion another. *Organic* views of the nation are incompatible with the tolerance of partial interests. If the nation is an organism, it is not a body that can breed divisions and conflicts.... Individualism and dissent are manifestations of not belonging.... Political forces do not appear as parties representing partial interests against other partial values or projects.... Democracy is then just an *interim moment* of competition for the monopoly in representing the national interest."[24]

Russian post-communist nationalism compounded by persistent nostalgia about lost greatness is on the rise. A set of personalized historical "markers" proves this convincingly. The first five most remarkable people of all time for Russians were in listed in 1989 as Lenin (75%), Peter I (41%), Pushkin (27%), Lomonosov (22%), Suvorov (18%); in 1994, Peter I (41%), Lenin (34%), Pushkin (23%), Stalin (20%), Suvorov (18%); and in 1999, Peter I (46%), Lenin (42%), Pushkin (42%), Stalin (35%), and Gagarin (26%).[25] It is no surprise therefore to see a portrait of Peter the Great in Putin's office.

Despite many signs of the rebirth of Russian nationalism as one of the forms of adaptation to post-imperial trauma, its usefulness as an effective long-term mobilization tool is limited. As Table 2.3 demonstrates, the Russian people have a very low opinion of the social and economic situations in Russia and a very high opinion of the most developed Western democracies, most notably the United States. The same phenomena would also limit external expressions of nationalism in Russia's foreign policy, including its relations with the United States. After the tragic events of September 11, that becomes even more difficult.

### Table 2.3: In What Country?

| In which of the following countries...? | Do not know, but definitely not in Russia | Russia | Germany | Great Britain | United States | Undecided |
|---|---|---|---|---|---|---|
| More guarantees for freedom of speech | -10 | 8 | 8 | 7 | 41 | 26 |
| People are more equal | -11 | 9 | 15 | 11 | 29 | 28 |
| People are more free from state intervention in their personal lives | -10 | 8 | 11 | 9 | 35 | 25 |
| People have more rights and opportunities | -10 | 5 | 12 | 8 | 43 | 26 |
| State cares more about citizens | -12 | 3 | 23 | 12 | 28 | 21 |
| People have more opportunities to influence state politics | -14 | 5 | 12 | 12 | 30 | 16 |
| People are more prosperous | -11 | 1 | 23 | 10 | 40 | 22 |

Source: All-Russian Center for the Study of Public Opinion (VTsIOM) nationwide poll of adult Russians conducted in June 2001 (N=1600) available at: www.wciom.ru/vciom/new/public/public_own/010610 _mancountr.htm.

Institutional patterns (the rules of the game in a society) are self-reinforcing, even when they are socially inefficient. It is almost always easier to adapt to the existing rules of the game than to seek to change them. Informal norms and culture change more slowly than formal rules, and tend to remold those formal rules, so that the external imposition of a common set of formal rules will lead to widely divergent outcomes.[26]

As long as Putin is perceived as an embodiment of stability and apostle of order, he and the current regime are safe. But what if he ceases to be perceived as a guarantor of order and positive, albeit gradual, change? His current high approval rating does not in itself guarantee future loyalty and support of society. In fact, it could be even double-edged, as it produces excessive expectations and inherently holds a risk of extreme disillusionment. Gorbachev and Yeltsin learned this well. Any events that could fuel those feelings of disillusionment could produce pressure to strengthen authoritarian practices. That would bring back the risk of a legitimate crisis, eroding trust and opening space for both civil disobedience and pathologies.

According to Lilia Shevtsova, one of the mechanisms of bureaucratic stabilization used by Putin's "elective monarchy" is imitation. Another one is co-optation. If the process of "nativization" of the idea of democracy is really under way in Russia,[27] one may not exclude the possibility that the elites are experiencing a kind of perverted nativization. While in foreign policy Putin's Russia is shifting from a "redline" language to a "pipeline" language, in communication with intelligentsia authorities are becoming familiar with the language of civil society. Not incidentally, one can therefore observe previously unthinkable phenomena, such as a roundtable in the Kremlin entitled "Power and Civil Society: Perspectives of Cooperation." A special meeting between Putin and carefully selected leaders of the NGO community was held in June 2001. There an agreement was made to organize a civic forum of NGOs, which was held in November 2001. The NGO Advisory Council under Chairman of the Russian State Duma Gennady Seleznev had been established earlier. In a similar move and in parallel to the authorities, a controversial oligarch, Boris Berezovsky, launched an ambitious Foundation for Civil Liberties with a mission to "provide resources for civil society to defend rights and liberties."[28]

Some observers interpret these moves as an attempt to mobilize and exploit civil society's energy and structures for the Kremlin's ends. In other words, recent "civic forum brainwaves" are about co-opting, controlling, and managing civil society.[29]

Speaking at the meeting with the leaders of pre-selected NGOs, Putin specifically expressed his concern that "many nongovernmental organizations exist on foreign grants.... It does not give us dignity, our civil society should be developed on its own base.... Power in Russia has already strengthened enough to provide support and defend rights and the liberty of citizens. I wish we would become allies."[30] This is Putin's original answer to the question, "What role, if any, can the West play in facilitating the development of civil society in Russia?" If we take note of these nuances in Putin's vision of partnership between the Kremlin and NGOs, and bear in mind the still unfriendly legal framework for their operation in Russia, it is difficult to avoid feelings of déjà vu: Putin's remarks consititute a vivid reminder of the practice of "building developed socialism" under the slogan *"Narod i Partiya Ediny."* There is a danger that the new campaign, "Building civil society," could well serve as an ideological justification for the emerging "neo-authoritarianism with a human face." It would mean that Russia is moving from enforced homogenization of the Soviet past through enforced change of the Gorbachev *perestroika* and enforced adaptation of the Yeltsin era to enforced civil society as a by-product of Putin's "modernization by order."

Putin himself responded to his critics at the opening session of the Civil Forum at the Kremlin's Palace of Congresses on November 21, 2001, saying that he regards "any attempts to impose a civil society from above as absolutely counterproductive, practically impossible, and even dangerous."[31] Whatever happens after the Civil Forum should be considered a test for the new Russian pattern of interaction between the state and society and viewed through the lens of Putin's clear-cut statement. Further organizational maturing of the Civil Forum type of activities would mean strengthening the pattern of "controlled democracy" with an emphasis on the civil society networks and organizations loyal to Putin. If, on the other hand, Russian society really is more transformed than the political structures governing it, then we would observe more modern and less hierarchical patterns of interactions.


## CONCLUSIONS AND RECOMMENDATIONS

It would be a mistake to follow a "pendulum pattern" in designing technical assistance programs—that is, shifting from a top-down approach that supports the institution-building of "political society" to a narrowly understood opposite approach of "empowering civil society." It does not mean simply seeing a distinction between supporting the third sector of NGOs and a broader network of civil society. What is more important is to design programs that will facilitate *interaction* between civil society and political society in order to "mobilize counter-knowledge and draw on its experts to make the pertinent translations of issues that administrative power may try to control"[32] and to organize the social learning process around a normative issue.

The same logic is relevant for considering a ratio of Moscow-centered and regionally based initiatives. To simply shift from the capital to the provinces and push each province to seek its oasis of civil society would be a mistake. What is required is a design of programs that will encourage networking and cooperation both among regional projects, as well as among capital-based groups and regional networks.

A vital civil society requires a political culture in which people actively participate in public debates. The West should do more fostering of communicative structures within *existing* institutions and public spheres. One of the most promising areas is the development of professional associations. Their agenda-setting and opinion-forming power in a society marked by growing differentiation and low respect for political parties should not be underestimated. Citizens' access to information, including such areas as implementation of freedom of information laws, development of freedom of the press, and citizens' watchdog groups in Russian regions, should be a priority. In this light it would be advisable to support programs aimed at improving the public's ability to make sense of policy options, by providing much better access to information and by helping the policy community and media make issues understandable to the public. The West could help in strengthening the ability of nongovernmental organizations and civil society groups to monitor government accountability, transparency, and respect for the rule of law, and to forcefully advocate measures which limit corruption.

Broadening space for civil society should be considered an important preventive countermeasure vis-à-vis temptations on the part of government to over-regulate in the post–September 11 environment. That would require continuous support in developing and implementing sound tax reform and charitable-giving laws, broadening links to grassroots membership, and ensuring effective civil society input into governmental decision-making.

Coping with isolationist and nationalist trends within Russian society requires constant external pressure from old and new transnational civil society networks. In addition to strategic, diplomatic, bilateral, and multilateral interaction and deepening economic interdependence within the current international system, this would help promote social and cultural interpenetration vital for Russia's reemerging civil society. The patterns of interaction, accountability, and learning that are developing within the framework of the Community of Democracies initiative and the World Forum of Democracy[33] could become an important instrument in ensuring the positive integration of Russian civil society actors into global civil society. Given the fragility of civil society in Russia and the specific understanding of the "partnership between the state and civil society" by some Putinists, this international link is crucial. Civil society forces neglected or silenced inside Russia may well gain a voice at the regional, if not global, level. They should not be sacrificed for the sake of presumably higher national security interests in the post–September 11 strategic geopolitical environment.

Putin's policy may well become an attempt broken by path dependency linked to a double legacy of imperialism and communism and to the legacy of failed early transition. Whether he will be able to play this historic role depends both on his ability to abandon Russia's ingrown systemic mistrust of society, and on the ability of civil society not to fall into the pattern of "controlled democracy," *a priori* loyal to the Russian state striving to restore its greatness.

Russian society is not a Sleeping Beauty, just passively waiting to be awakened. It is gradually becoming a Cinderella, resembling a story of human transformation and rebirth, and a change from poverty and neglect to personal fulfillment. Still, this process is not yet universal throughout the country. Moreover, the process contains both new oases of autonomous social life and old ghettos of authoritarian order within the regionally and culturally varied social fabric of the former empire. In some places it rather reminds one of the noble image of Don Quixote with his state of personal confusion, peculiar inability to see things clearly, and, alas, vulnerability to manipulations of rulers. Will Russia eventually become Joan of Arc, replete with her sense of leadership, freedom against oppression, and ability to act? It remains to be seen. At the same time, however, we hope Russia will be able to avoid Joan's tragic fate and remain alive.

## NOTES

1. Robert D. Putnam, *Making Democracy Work: Civic Traditions in Modern Italy* (Princeton, N.J.: Princeton University Press, 1993), p. 180.

2. "Shaping Actors, Shaping Factors in Russia's Future," http://europa.eu.int/comm/cdp/cahiers/resume/russie_en.htm.

3. Michael Emerson, *Redrawing the Map of Europe* (London: Macmillan, 1998), pp. 129–30; Zinaida Golenkova, "Civil Society in Russia," *Russian Social Science Review*, vol. 40, no. 1 (January/February 1999). Christopher Candland has rightfully observed that "as a result of its recent popularity, the concept has become somewhat detached from its intellectual roots. The term 'civil society' is now often used as an elaborate substitute for society, without any substantial difference in meaning." See Christopher Candland, "Civil Society," in *The Oxford Companion to Politics of the World*, 2nd edition (Oxford: Oxford University Press, 2001), p. 140.

4. Ernest Gellner, *Conditions of Liberty: Civil Society and Its Rivals* (London: Hamish Hamilton, 1994).

5. J. Cohen and A. Arato, *Civil Society and Political Theory* (Cambridge, Mass.: MIT Press, 1995).

6. J. Habermas, *Between Fact and Norms: Contribution to a Discourse Theory of Law and Democracy* (Cambridge, Mass.: MIT Press, 1996), p. 367.

7. Golenkova, *op. cit.*

8. Yuri Levada, "Soviet Man Ten Years After, 1989–1999," *Russian Social Science Review*, vol. 42, no. 1 (January/February 2001).

9  Tatiana Zaslavskaya and N. Mikhailova, "Social Structure and Civil Society," *Social Sciences,* vol. 31, no. 3 (September 2000).

10. Thomas Dine, "Free Media in Unfree Societies," *Harvard International Review,* vol. 23, no. 1 (Spring 2001).

11. Timothy J. Colton and Michael McFaul, "Are Russians Undemocratic?" Carnegie Endowment for International Peace, Working Paper No. 20 (June 2001), pp. 21, 22. See also *The Russia Initiative: Reports of the Four Task Forces* (New York: Carnegie Corporation of New York, 2001); *An Agenda for Renewal: U.S.-Russian Relations: A Report by the Russian and Eurasian Program of the Carnegie Endowment for International Peace* (Washington, D.C.: Carnegie Endowment for International Peace, 2000); and EWI Bipartisan Task Force, "How Should the United States Deal with Putin's Russia?" in *Toward the Common Good: Building a New U.S.-Russian Relationship* (New York: The East-West Institute, July 2001).

12. Tatyana Maleva, "What Sort of Russia Has the New President Inherited?" *Briefing Papers,* vol. 2, no. 4 (April 2000) at www.pubs.carnegie.ru/english/briefings/2000/issue04-00.asp; and Murray Feshbach, "Russia's Population Meltdown," *Wilson Quarterly* (Winter 2001) at http://wwics.si.edu/outreach/wq/WQSELECT/FESHB.HTM. See also Steven Rosefielde, "The Civilian Labor Force and Unemployment in the Russian Federation," *Europe-Asia Studies,* vol. 52, no. 8 (December 2000); Lincoln C. Chen, Friederike Wittgenstein, and Elizabeth McKeon, "The Upsurge Mortality in Russia: Causes and Policy Implications," *Population and Development Review,* vol. 22, no. 3 (September 1996); Lidia Prokofieva and Lolita Terskikh, "Standards of Living and Family Structure in a Period of Social Transformation: Russia in the 1990s," *Population: An English Selection,* vol. 10, no. 2 (1998); V. Shkolnikov, E. Andreev, and T. Maleva, *Inequality and Mortality in Russia,* at http://pubs.carnegie.ru/books/2000/02tm.

13. William E. Odom, "Realism about Russia," *National Interest,* no. 65 (Fall 2001), p. 65.

14. *Izvestia,* November 21, 2001.

15. Adrian Karatnycky, "Nations in Transit 1999–2000: From Post-Revolutionary Stasis to Incremental Progress," in Adrian Karatnycky, Alexander Motyl, and Aili Piano, eds., *Nations in Transit 1999–2000: Civil Society, Democracy, and Markets in East Central Europe and the Newly Independent States* (New Brunswick, N.J.: Freedom House and Transaction Publishers, 2001), pp. 10–11.

16. Colton and McFaul, *op. cit.*

17. Adrian Karatnycky, Alexander Motyl, and Amanda Schnetzer, eds., *Nations in Transit 2001: Civil Society, Democracy, and Markets in East Central Europe and the Newly Independent States* (New Brunswick, N.J.: Freedom House and Transaction Publishers, 2001), p. 25.

18. Marc Morje Howard, "Free Not to Participate: The Weakness of Civil Society in Post-Communist Europe," *Studies in Public Policy,* no. 325 (University of Strathclyde, Scotland: Center for the Study of Public Policy, February 2000).

19. Aaron Wildavsky, *Speaking Truth to Power: The Art and Craft of Policy Analysis* (New Brunswick, N.J.: Transaction Publishers, 1993), p. 263.

20. Yuri Levada, *op. cit.*

21. Risto Alapuro and Markku Lonkila, "Networks, Identity, and (In)action: A Comparison Between Russian and Finnish Teachers," *European Societies,* vol. 2, no. 1 (2000), pp. 65–90; Michael Burawoy and Katherine Verdery, "Introduction,"

in Burawoy and Verdery, eds., *Uncertain Transition: Ethnographies of Change in the Postsocialist World* (Lanham, Md.: Rowman and Littlefield, 1999), pp. 1–17.

22. More information in Samuel Huntington, *Political Order in Changing Societies* (New Haven, Conn.: Yale University Press, 1996), pp. 348–52.

23. Quoted in Bill Lomax, "Reviews," *Europe-Asia Studies*, vol. 45, no. 3 (1993), p. 559.

24. Adam Przeworski et al, *Sustainable Democracy* (Cambridge: Cambridge University Press, 1995), pp. 59, 61.

25. Yuri Levada, *op. cit.*

26. See Robert Putnam, *op. cit.*

27. Lilia Shevtsova, "Elective Monarchy Under Putin: Perspectives on the Evolution of the Political Regime and Its Perspectives," *Briefing Papers*, vol. 3, no. 1 (January 2001), available at http://pubs.carnegie.ru/english/briefings/2001/issue01-01.asp; "Power and Political Leadership in Russia under Putin," presentation at the conference "Russia: Ten Years After," June 2001, available at http://www.ceip.org/files/programs/russia/tenyears/presentatiom/shevtsova.htm.

28. See website of Berezovsky's foundation at www.kolokol.org.

29. Ian Traynor, "Putin plays the liberal," *The Guardian,* August 20, 2001.

30. See http://strana.ru/print/992355479.html.

31. See http://strana.ru/stories/01/11/16/2029/85321.html.

32. Michael Welton, "Civil Society and the Public Sphere," *Studies in the Education of Adults,* vol. 33, no. 1 (April 2001).

33. The Community of Democracies Ministerial Meeting was convened in Warsaw on June 26–27, 2000. At the meeting, 110 governments endorsed the Warsaw Declaration, which lays out a comprehensive set of democratic principles and practices that member governments commit themselves to uphold. A parallel, nongovernmental World Forum on Democracy called for support in establishing an alliance of open societies to "foster improved conditions for freedom and democracy within individual countries," to "promote an open society based on the rule of law," and to "ensure more effective cooperative development efforts focused on democratic change."

# 3

# Russia's Political Economy

*László Csaba*

This chapter discusses the sustainability of the Russian economic recovery of 1999–2001 and covers the short-term factors that brought it about: energy prices and the devaluation of the ruble. This chapter also advances the thesis that an activist presidency is not equivalent to the rule of law. The fight against the "oligarchs" implies a restructuring of economic power, but not a change in the modus operandi of Russia's version of a market economy. While much of the legislation approved after the Strategy of Economic Development of June 2000 points in the right direction, these measures definitely fail to address some key issues that determine economic development in the long run, such as financial intermediation, local power, the ability of corporations to finance their own growth, small business, and foreign direct investment (FDI). Russia's export performance is likely to diminish, even according to the government's three-year plan published in July 2001. Thus, Russia's ability to service debt will depend heavily upon successful agreements with the Paris and London Clubs.

The weak point in the Russian economic success story of 1999–2001 has been its continued reliance on exports of raw materials and the lack of improvement the manufacturing sector's competitiveness. The government's strategy for 2002–2004 rightly acknowledges that currency inflows and the inability to centralize them continue to put a severe limit on long-term economic growth. While economic growth in the front-runner transition countries has been export-led and thus sustainable, the Russian economic miracle will easily fall victim to weakening oil prices coupled with the limitations of an import-substitution industrial recovery, which has been the hallmark of the early Vladimir Putin years. Decelerating growth may force the new president to make some hard choices: either to radicalize the structural reforms, or to allow for a backtracking, which in turn will further weaken economic performance.

## BACKGROUND TO REFORMS

The collapse of the Russian ruble in August 1998 and the subsequent developments following the event have proven that the Russian economy is by no means peculiar. Indeed, it functions according to the logic of standard textbooks. If you liberalize the capital account prematurely, use short-term money to cover structural deficits in the fiscal accounts, and at the same time try to sustain a fixed exchange rate, you are heading for trouble. Only the timing is subject to chance. If you devalue the domestic currency to one-fourth of its original value, you create an enormous impetus for import substitution, protect your markets, and trigger a supply-side response, while the current account is likely to improve tremendously. Add to this oil prices that more than triple, where 53 percent of currency inflows are derived from the exports of fuel and energy. The surplus in the current account is likely to be substantial, and the fiscal account is likely to close with a surplus, while activity indicators will improve. Indeed, Russia's current account surplus of U.S.$2 billion in 1998 did grow to U.S.$18 billion by 1999 and U.S.$41 billion by 2000.[1] General government deficits, consolidated according to government fiscal statistics (GFS) standards, were 8.9 percent of gross domestic product (GDP) in 1997, 3.2 percent in 1998, and 1.0 percent in 1999, giving way to a surplus of 4.6 percent in 2000. Estimates for 2001 call for a surplus ranging from 0.25 percent to 1.5 percent of GDP.[2] All in all, there is nothing deviant in the way the Russian economy works; there are no grounds for talk about a miracle. Likewise all analysts agree that growth likely decelerated in 2001, from 2 to 4.5 percent on an annualized basis, with the consensus estimate being around or below 2 percent, strongly dependent, of course, on the actual level of world oil market prices. Actually, as econometric evidence suggests, the correlation between Russian industrial output and world oil prices is over 81 percent, allowing for a mere 1 percent increase in Russian GDP in the medium run.[3] This is certainly at odds with the overly optimistic assumptions of the Gref Plan (launched by Economic and Trade Development Minister German Gref), which aims at a steady 7 to 8 percent per year for a decade.

The above-cited numbers reflect a fairly mechanical process of adjustment to external disturbances, which could happen in any economy, regardless of its economic institutions and policies. When external shocks dominate overall macro performance, it is particularly important to discern which, if any, of the outcomes are attributable to policies and which are a result of circumstantial factors. If we take into account that Russia's terms of trade have improved tremendously, by 48.1 percent in 1999 and by yet another 66.3 percent in 2000, over 1998 actual figures, it is hard to overlook the enormous one-time windfall component in shaping the macroeconomic landscape in the country. The chief economist in President Putin's administration, Andrei Illarionov, a long-term observer of Russian macroeconomic policies, has provided the following table comparing the windfalls and macroeconomic performance and expressing them as percentages of GDP:[4]

**Table 3.1. Windfall and Macroeconomic Performance as % of GDP**

|  | 1997 | 1998 | 1999 | 2000 |
|---|---|---|---|---|
| Windfall | −1.1% | 3.3% | +1.1% | +12.7% |
| GDP | +0.9% | −4.9% | +3.5% | + 7.7% |

The author interprets the difference between the two elements presented in the table as a possible measure of *net contribution* that year (i.e., over and above the favorable windfall effects) of economic policies to the overall macroeconomic performance. Given that the Primakov and Stepashin periods saw a deceleration of reforms, and that the year 2000 was mostly spent on presidential elections and the establishment of the new power structure, the strongly negative contribution is anything but surprising. It also helps in explaining why the new president could have been convinced that further reforms were urgent, rather than being content with the status quo of dramatically improving short-term indicators (with the partial exception of unemployment). Moreover, half of the population lives under the World Bank poverty level of U.S.$2 per day. The level of development at the market exchange rate is below U.S.$1,900 at PPP (purchasing power parity), about U.S.$6,000, or two-thirds that of Hungary. All these factors have been rightly seen as stimuli for quick and radical action.

## YELTSIN'S LEGACY

Much has been written about this topic, which has grown in significance following the first-ever, successfully completed peaceful handover of power in Russia. The country's economic system was, beyond a doubt, a full-fledged market economy by the time Putin took power in March 2000.[5]

Today, prices mostly reflect scarcities. Money can buy any commodity including foreign currency, and allocation follows market signals, while dominant private owners maximize their asset value and switch their portfolios in response to financial incentives. Certainly the Russian variant of the market economy is not the same as the model set forth in introductory textbooks. Instead, it resembles the developing-country variants described in advanced courses on comparative and development economics. Still, introducing market order has been a remarkable accomplishment, especially if we consider the relatively low cost of reestablishing the market. (Costs of postcolonial wars, of course, should not be added to this bill.)

The fundamental feature of Russia's transformation has been conditioned by the weak state, which often leads to the strong presence of vested interests and the ensuing market failures.[6] With the major power struggle phase ended and new rules of the game established, inflation has never gone out of control, as many of us feared following the collapse of the ruble. In fact, annual inflation in 1998 was 84.5 percent, in 1999 it came down to the moderate level of 36.6 percent, in 2000 to 20.2 percent, and in 2001 is forecast in the range of 25 percent. This reflects a consolidation of power and also a common understanding by all those in power that hyperinflation is deadly for a modern economy and society alike. Also reflected in this remarkable outcome is the unwillingness to undergo yet another redistribution of wealth.

Thus, Boris Yeltsin managed to liberalize, stabilize, and privatize the Russian economy. However, he could not get the country over the transformational recession to sustaining growth. Thus, poverty became a predominant feature in large parts of the country, especially outside the metropolitan areas. Yeltsin also managed to preserve the unity of Russia's federal government, creating a situation in which the local governments stood to gain more by cooperating than by seceding.[7] This is no small accomplishment for a country whose "natural" or "historical" borders are anything but trivial. The bilateral deals, also anchored in Russia's constitution, strengthened and formalized the power of local organs and have been exerting a formative influence over the actual workings of the Russian market economy.

## PUTIN'S INPUT

There seems to be a near consensus among analysts that the accession to power of Vladimir Putin represented an attempt to redefine the name of the game as it emerged under the Yeltsin years. Quite in line with the mainstream view on development economics, it was understood that a strong state power, emancipated from the patronage of vested interests, is a necessary condition for achievement of meaningful policy reforms.[8] Thus, it is self-explanatory why the new president has been focusing so much attention on cutting the umbilical cord that ties him to the Yeltsin group and to constituent oligarchs. At present, it is too early to assess the extent to which this initiative will prove successful. However, the thrust of the initiative can, at least in theory, be interpreted as an attempt to emancipate Putin from dependence on vested interests.

In the first round of managed transition, the 1999 Duma elections produced a so-called floating party system with the emergence of three roughly equal blocks (left, centrist—i.e., pro-government—and right).[9] This allowed the president to have virtually any law passed. It also removed the powerful obstacle of communist domination, which hobbled Yeltsin in both his presidential terms. Moreover, as the parties seem to be more active in representing economic interests than ideological lines, policy compromises are easier to strike. A detailed analysis of the Communist Party indicates its ideological decay and growing opportunism: it can still create trouble, but it can no longer reverse policy in any major area.[10] Last but not least, the above-cited consolidation of regional power within Russia means that governors cannot secede and lack interest in doing so, thus making them vulnerable to centralizing tendencies.

In addition, certain side effects of the 1998 financial crisis worked to Putin's advantage. This crisis has forever crippled the oligarchs (i.e., those with vested interests based on financial assets rather than industrial holdings). Their vulnerability has come under the spotlight since the Primakov episode,[11] while energy sector corporations flourished.[12] Confiscation of bank assets in response to Kirienko crisis management measures left the state-owned banks—primarily Sberbank and Vneshekonombank—without competitors. Most of the surviving private banks are actually no more than financial departments of large industrial organizations. This, of course, allows for the takeover of previously held positions in various areas, as the takeover of the Berezovsky and Gusinskii media empires demonstrated.

In systemic terms, the above developments may be interpreted as a series of evolutionary and policy-led actions that allow for a redefinition of those institutions and of the rules of the game for maximizing wealth that emerged during the late Yeltsin period. In the following section, this chapter attempts to assess the extent to which this potential has materialized or will materialize as a consequence of actual policymaking under President Putin.

Putin has moved with conspicuous speed and deliberation to get rid of symbolic figures and features of oligarchic power. Such cases as the extradition of former Kremlin financial chief Pavel Borodin; the demotion of Viktor Chernomyrdin from Gazprom; the demotion of Rem Vyakhirev from his post of chief executive officer of Gazprom; and the erosion of Moscow mayor Yuri Luzhkov's standing in the presidential campaign, which led to the recent merger of his Fatherland movement with so-called "Bear" Unity party may be seen as milestones for this new drive. Changing Russia's constitution and the procedures for formation of the Council of Federation (the upper house of parliament), depriving local governors of their immunity and even allowing for their demotion, followed by a series of presidential measures that outlawed local regulations, send clear messages. Successful attempts to control the press, put in place "managed democracy,"[13] and give the state much more extensive roles than those of chief arbitrator and guardian of the rules of the game, are bound to have immediate repercussions on the way that economic rules and institutions function in reality.

In short, given Russia's current situation, talk of a strong state and "dictatorship of the law" is likely to be a far cry from *Rechtsstaatlichkeit,* (authorities being able to commit themselves to uphold property rights and enforce impartial, private contracts among parties).[14] This is certainly quite a different agenda from establishing one's own control over the oligarchs with new, uncorrupted followers who are loyal to the new bearer of supreme power.

In fact, such reverberations contribute to the overall feeling of insecurity and raise particular questions concerning acquired property rights. They objectively shorten the time horizon under which investors optimize their decisions. The investors are pushed to demand quick returns and to disregard any possible long-term consequences of their actions. Capital flight from insecure to secure places is not criminal, nor is it theft from the country itself, but is a sign of how capital, the world over, behaves in a rational manner, rationally expecting interventions that will destabilize its workings. A poor investment climate deters domestic and foreign investors alike, putting a severe limit on the development potential of domestic financial intermediation (banking and capital markets alike).[15]

Under the circumstances described above, it is understandable why the Strategy of Economic Development, based on the workings of the group surrounding Economic and Trade Development Minister Gref (also a member of the Petersburg Clan), aims primarily at securing high growth rates in a sustainable fashion. In order to attain that goal, the plan envisions a series of systemic measures.

It is important to note that the full text of the approved program has not been published.[16] The program seems to reflect a deal between two "marketer" approaches, i.e., a supply-side cum deregulation approach and a major tax cut approach. The concrete formulation of the plan is reflected in the eighteen-month program adopted for the period of 2002–2004. The main tasks or areas of action can be summarized as follows:

1. Tax reforms;
2. Fiscal reforms aimed at restructuring expenditures;
3. Deregulation and easing market entry barriers;
4. Protecting private property;
5. Decreasing and harmonizing customs duties;
6. Developing capital markets;
7. Reform of natural monopolies;
8. Social security reform, introducing the targeting of social benefits; and
9. Pension reform.

As can be seen, this is perhaps the first multi-year program that truly departs from the Soviet heritage. The program is not dominated by quantitative indicators or sectoral priorities. Rather, it reflects the conviction that structural adjustment is a matter of market process; it treats the diminishing of tax burden as its priority; it aims at creating the comprehensive institutional infrastructure that has been missing from previous reform packages; and it addresses some traditional sore points of Russian reforms, such as overregulation and the underdevelopment of capital markets. In short, the program seems to have addressed the bottlenecks that tended to plague reform efforts during the Yeltsin period. Coupled with a new strength and vigor regained in Moscow, the platform may be seen as promising. In the following section, this chapter tries to assess whether and to what extent these measures suffice for bringing about and sustaining high growth rates. This is the crux of the matter, regardless of actual attainments of the quantitative estimates (which seem to have been proven overly optimistic anyway).

As indicated above, the Strategy for Economic Development was conceived as a medium-term document whose goals are to be implemented primarily in the 2002–2004 period. However, experience with policy reforms throughout the world, especially in Russia, shows that changes must be front-loaded. This means that changes standing a better chance for implementation come first, while those slated to be enacted later often undergo substantive modification or may even be cancelled. Thus, early measures may also be treated as a kind of early warning system in economic policy assessments.

Tax legislation has been simplified significantly by the 2000 modification of the tax code. Further rate cuts are envisioned by the governmental proposal approved in the first reading by the Duma in June 2001: reduction of the corporate tax rate to 15 percent and the marginal income tax rate to 35 percent. The legislation also limits the power of local authorities to levy taxes not specified in federal legislation, or to apply higher rates than federally approved.

One of the problems of these stipulations has traditionally been that local power is often informal by nature, and is based on proprietary and regulatory interconnections between local authorities and locally dominant forms. Thus their deals are often covert and inaccessible to external observers.[17] Corporations take over or simply provide financial support for municipal social services and employ underpaid local officials. The latter, in turn, reschedule debts, tolerate regular nonpayment of taxes, allow for covert subsidies, and impose local customs barriers and other protectionist measures to keep "outsiders" at bay. "Moscow is far away," as the old dictum says. And indeed, despite changes in the balance of power, it would be naive to expect any central organ to be able to penetrate and even less to redefine the intricate interconnections. More likely, any central government representative would be quickly absorbed by the local social and economic networks, if for no other reason than the need for continuous on-the-spot crisis management.[18] This likelihood is very high in light of the first detailed empirical field research results on the implementation methods of President Putin's federal reforms.[19]

It would be hard to overlook that federal tax cuts are not supplemented by a radical rollback of entitlements, or that the practice of allotting but not funding federal tasks has been discontinued. Under these circumstances it is hard to conceive of local authorities adopting a hands-off strategy. They continue to be confronted with cumulative economic problems (crime, floods, blasts of pipelines, etc.). They cannot cut taxes in order to simply avoid over-taxation. Given that they too are elected officials, their incentive is to continue with the hidden ways of "taking care of" the area, including raising sufficient tax revenue and protecting "theirs" in the corporate sphere from outside "intruders," primarily foreigners. Incomplete fiscal reforms by definition constrain the effectiveness of any tax measure.

Given that more than 80 percent of output needs to be licensed, granting permits has developed into a profitable business for the authorities to secure their otherwise insufficient funding.[20] Thus, it is highly unlikely that the abolished rules would be immediately replaced by "appropriate" substitutes, partly due to tsarist and Soviet legal tradition, and partly out of sheer economic necessity.

Protecting private property is quite important. However, when violent methods of settling disputes have become the norm rather than the exception, the state has leaned toward further strengthening of its proprietary and managerial roles,[21] as well as setting an example by punishing "plutocrats" in political practice. Ongoing disputes over such well-publicized cases as those of Gazprom, Svyazinvest, and EES, to mention a few, all tend to end up with minority shareholders being marginalized, with their rights diluted. This tendency has been strengthened rather than weakened in 2000–2001.

It is important to recall that while the Duma finally enacted the law allowing private land ownership in June 2001, this law basically condones ongoing practices rather than creating new opportunities. In fact, nonarable land could be purchased for years, and even a modest turnover could be observed in some of the regions. In order to secure support from the communist factions, the law continues to retain most of its previous restrictions.

The issue of natural monopolies also tended to be high on the agenda of the Gref Plan. In the case of the gas industry, market-building measures have formally been postponed for 2002, at the time new leadership is nominated. In the electricity market, state control of prices and ongoing nonpayments make deregulation highly unlikely.[22] In the case of railways, any market reform would presuppose a partial recapitalization of the underinvested company, together with tariff increases. The latter might prove strategically impossible given the arbitrary location of many Russian industries and cities, while investments on this scale do not figure in the approved budget. In the case of pension reform, the underdeveloped state, as well as the shaken reputation of capital markets, makes the switchover to a partially funded system improbable. The ever-growing problem of aging and the lack of an affluent middle class also make such a change politically and economically risky. Moreover, if there is nowhere to invest, a funded system can easily degenerate into a costly gamble.

## UNADDRESSED ISSUES AND PROSPECTS

The strategy failed to tackle some important issues from the very outset. The issue of financial disintermediation, which has plagued Russia for a long time, is also known to be a headache for government officials.[23] It is a depressing sign that the Duma has indefinitely postponed even general debates over this issue when limited sustainability of growth is already on the policy agenda. The less the financial system is able to transform savings into investments, the higher the probability of ongoing capital flight, since domestic savings cannot earn good returns for the risk of staying home rather than fleeing abroad. The central government's ability to raise taxes is unlikely to improve once oil prices start to decline. Corporate expansion, based exclusively on retained profits, is likely to be sluggish over the long term.

Along the same lines, large corporations are trying to become self-sufficient, even in ownership terms, which further strengthens the ongoing tendency toward concentrated ownership patterns.[24] This means that corporate restructuring is likely to continue via mergers rather than closures and startups. Furthermore, bankruptcy continues to be an instrument used by authorities to punish disobedience rather than serving as a means to promote horizontal deals, including restructuring.

Legislation that covers joint stock companies trying to support creditor and property rights against managerial power was repeatedly dropped from the Duma's agenda in June and December 2000. Meanwhile, neither the privatization law that would discontinue the practice of listing salable and nonsalable firms, nor the nationalization law, which provides for compensation in the event of unilateral state actions, has been approved by the Duma. However, the Duma did adopt a communist-backed general ban on selling large corporations, stopping such obvious targets as Lukoil and Gazprom from listing on stock exchanges around the world.

Legal reform is also generally seen as a weak point. Though Russia regularly posts current account surpluses, a currency law requiring 75 percent home transfers—obviously not adhered to—is still in force. There are many

other examples, such as articles prohibiting speculation, or the recent
Academy of Sciences circular reintroducing Soviet regulations on contact
with foreigners. In sum, anybody can be criminalized, basically for anything. These measures do not create an environment that promotes long-
term investment.

The more people worry about Russia's long-term growth prospects being
constrained by the extreme poverty of close to half of its population (acting as a demand constraint), the more they see the overall climate as generally unfriendly to business. It is evident that red tape, uncertainty, and
lack of market prospects act as major deterrents for the small business sector.[25] Special incentive programs or the repetition of business-friendly slogans offer little help in overcoming this barrier. In turn, the domestic
demand-based growth path, which is slow but steady, may also prove hard
to enter.

The role of foreign direct investment, currently a favorite topic in international development literature, tends to be severely underrated in most
Russian policy debates. FDI is not just a means to attract technology or
cover current account deficits. In the broader international context it is
seen as a pace-setter, a small but vitally important ingredient for the
smooth functioning of a modernizing economy. For the time being,
investors, even in the energy sector, where it is easiest to survive, seem
rather deterred.[26] It is embarrassing to read that the president's chief economist (Illarionov) has said that Russia's investment absorption capacity was
technically a given[27] and that the problem was abundance of capital. This
is mixing up cyclical and strategic considerations. Absorption capacity is by
definition an "ex post concept" and is conditional upon factors influencing
the business climate. In Russia, more FDI could be a way of overcoming
the bottlenecks created by decades of underfunding in physical infrastructure, market-oriented production-line developments, and many other
areas. Moving away from the Kuwait syndrome is also contingent upon
FDI.

On the basis of what has been surveyed, we may venture to forecast that
the old *perestroika* slogan, "there is no way back," may be true. There is
no room for Russia to regress into totalitarian political and economic structures, as transformations have been too profound. Likewise, there is little
hope that Russia will be able to advance to the conditions of a normal
Western democracy and market economy, as has been hoped by the elite
of the country.

If oil prices remain high, they may help bridge the more obvious gaps
in the central budget. Thus slow growth is likely, in the range of 2-plus
percent in the medium term. This prediction is borne out by U.N. statistics,
which state that Russia's GDP is still around two-thirds of its pre-1989 level.
Thus, the room for quasi-automatic recovery is substantial indeed.

Institutional improvement is unlikely to be radical or robust, but slow and steady improvements are conceivable. They cannot be taken for granted. Thus, the revenue-generating and debt-servicing ability of Russia continues to be unilaterally dependent on oil and related revenues. The 1996 peak of export revenues was only surpassed in 2000; volumes decreased, which meant that price was the sole factor. This may create a problem, unless Russia uses most of its windfalls to amortize foreign debts or negotiate generous write-offs for the Soviet-era debt. Both possibilities look unlikely to happen. The most probable scenario is a continuous rollover of debt.

Russia's debt problem has several causes. First, Russia has assumed Soviet-era debt alone and has not shared the burden with any of the other Soviet successor states. Second, Russia's export performance is one of the worst among the transition countries: the Czech Republic and Hungary tripled their exports, Estonia nearly quadrupled exports, and even Poland nearly doubled exports. Russian exports grow and decline with oil prices. Russian exports peaked in 1996 at U.S.$86.9 billion, and then declined to U.S.$72.9 billion in 1999, growing, thanks to oil prices, to U.S.$105.6 billion. However, according to the official medium-term forecast of July 2001, exports are forecast to decline again to U.S.$94.6 billion by 2004. Thus Russia's economy has not experienced export-led growth in the way economic theory describes the concept; rather, it has simply harvested the windfall from favorable changes in the terms of trade, which is a world of difference.[28]

A third problem follows from the fact that current account surpluses, registered in statistics, are realized basically by private entrepreneurs rather than the state. Thus, despite these surpluses, total national debt has declined only slowly. Russia's gross foreign debt grew from U.S.$143.3 billion in 1996 to U.S.$166.4 billion by 1998 and declined, thanks to trade surpluses, to U.S.$150.1 billion by 2000, U.S.$144.4 billion by 2001, and an estimated U.S.$140.3 billion by 2002. In the same period, current account surpluses totaled U.S.$12.4 billion in 1996, U.S.$1 billion in 1998, U.S.$47 billion in 2000, U.S.$32.1 billion in 2001, and an estimated U.S.$21.4 billion in 2002.[29] Accordingly, the debt: GDP ratio was 34.3 percent in 1996, 60.3 percent in 1998, 72.8 percent in 2000, 58.7 percent in 2001, and is forecast at 50.6 percent for 2002. Therefore, Russian analysts do not consider the situation to be dramatic, especially if authorities can reduce capital flight and limit the money supply, while at the same time mobilizing hard-currency savings by creating lucrative placement opportunities in domestic banks.[30]

It is misleading to say that Russia would have no debt problem at all if all currency inflows, as reported in the official balance of payments statistics, had been used to amortize public debt rather than for investments based on capital flight. In fact, the accumulated surplus for the years

1999–2001 would have sufficed to pay back two-thirds of Russia's out-standing payments without any rescheduling or debt relief arrangements. Capital flight is a sign that obviously better informed domestic investors find it more rewarding and secure to invest their funds abroad than at home. If current account surpluses generally exceed foreign investment, this is a telling verdict of market players on the country's attractiveness to investors.

In sum, Russia seems to struggle with three problems: 1) inadequate exports due to antiquated export focus; 2) reliance on raw materials and capital flight; and 3) mismanagement, i.e., the central government seeking debt relief at a time when the country enjoys unprecedentedly large current account surpluses. The real option would be to reverse capital flight by a series of investment promotions and security measures.

Because the measures we surveyed do not seem to be adequate in the eyes of market players to reverse their attitudes, further loosening of the Central Bank of Russia's currency surrender requirement is unlikely to occur. There is no reason for us to believe that the ability of the Russian authorities to collect taxes and attract investments will be radically improved in the medium term. Rather, the three interrelated problems lying behind debt will continue, and a possible decline in oil prices will only exacerbate the debt situation.

On the domestic front the move toward more explicit forms of fiscal federalism seems unlikely, as it runs counter to most of the interests of those participating in it. Likewise, the most profitable parts of the Russian economy are under state regulation. Thus, bargaining with the state remains a major source of revenue. It may well be that a state dominated by oligarchs will be replaced by another system of oligarchs, nominated and dominated by the state.[31] Insider dominance continues to be a highly influential factor of Russian capitalism. True, this is still superior to no privatization at all (i.e., the Belarusian variant), but it also provides support for an overall business environment that is continuously hostile to foreign ownership and penetration.[32] Thus, the scenarios of large-scale modernization and industrial renewal cannot be seriously considered among the feasible options for the medium to long term.

Last but not least, the issue of Western involvement needs to be addressed. In the early 1990s the International Monetary Fund (IMF) and World Bank dominated Russia's financial scene—or at least they were the most visible means of Western leverage over Russia. However, this period is clearly over. As a large country Russia is more likely to be involved and included via such forums as the G-8, the Paris and London Clubs, or KFOR (Kosovo Force). Russia cannot be lost or gained.

As we have demonstrated in the preceding sections, the measures implemented so far are unlikely to foster dramatic improvement in conditions for private investment. The ongoing reforms do not address the fundamentals: i.e., connections with local governments and lack of meaningful financial intermediation. Large-scale state involvement is not the way to remedy these problems.[33] For domestic statist policies, the revenue base is simply missing; without it, the country will start down the road to hyper-inflation, which is not in the interest of any of the current players—a condition well understood by the reformist team around President Putin. Alternatively, Russia could try to attract more foreign money. Since this is unlikely to be private money (due to the lack of incentives and security), perhaps public money could be mobilized. But experiences with large-scale, publicly funded international projects in the developing world have been so depressing that nobody, even in the international financial institutions, would advocate such a step. Along the same lines, legislative bodies in any major donor country are unlikely to endorse such mega-projects.

In concrete terms, the current situation leads us to conclude that disengagement would be counterproductive. Russia continues to have a stake in world affairs, particularly, though not exclusively, in Europe. It continues to perceive itself as a major European power. Thus, it remains sensitive to confrontations with European norms, be they human rights conventions or the *acquis* of the European Union. World Trade Organization (WTO) membership is an attainable target that may help formalize reform measures, particularly in the trade sector. Involvement in various forums defining good fiscal practices, banking standards, and accounting and disclosure practices may slowly but steadily help Russian reformers to change the entire socioeconomic environment in which they function.

The economic potential that is likely to emerge under the conditions of our baseline scenario, excluding major catastrophes, puts severe limits on the medium- to long-term potential of ongoing revitalization plans for the Commonwealth of Independent States (CIS) as an economic and monetary union, or the reintegration of neighboring Slavic countries. On the other hand, a Russia that perceives itself as alienated and excluded still possesses a considerable nuisance capacity, as events in southeast Europe, the Caucasus, and Central Asia may equally demonstrate. Thus, continued inclusion of Russia within various global forums and agreements, like the follow-up to the Kyoto Protocol or agreements regarding the Internet, as well as various forms of fighting organized crime, will continue to remain on the agenda.

## CONCLUSIONS AND RECOMMENDATIONS

President Vladimir Putin has clearly given priority to reestablishing the independence of state authority, shaping the related economic interests, and even—during the late Yeltsin period—trying to dominate it. In a way, Putin has continued the effort begun by Yevgeni Primakov during his short premiership following the August 1998 financial crisis, though without the current statist, antimarket and anti-Western undercurrents. The "dictatorship of the law" has thus, by definition, little to do with the Western concept of the rule of law, since law continues to be seen as an instrument to attain power and policy objectives rather than an arrangement limiting lawmakers and various authorities in the context of checks and balances. In fact, the often reactionary-style balancing role played by the Duma and the Council of Federation, by elected local officials, and the "not free but independent and pluralist" Russian press, or the view of Western observers of various sorts during the Yeltsin years, has been steadily on the decline. This is quite in line with Putin's intentions.

New legislation, such as the Labor Law, Land Law, and Banking Law, all point in the right direction. However, these fail to address some of the fundamental problems rendering the propensity to save and invest less than adequate in Russia: insecurity of property rights, prohibitively high costs of contract enforcement, lack of impartial conflict regulation by an effective judiciary, and last but not least, a system of sound financial intermediation. Those banks that survived the August 1998 crisis and the campaigns of the authorities are either semi-state units or fully state-owned, like the dominant players Sberbank and Vneshekonombank, or are home banks, accounting departments of large corporations, or regional authorities. Intertwining between state and business at the local level continues to dominate. The incentives and concerns continue to assist building and maintaining local empires, closed autarkic units rather than the allocation and optimization of resources across sectors, regions, and activities.

Recent campaigns concerning natural monopolies, particularly Gazprom, but also EES and the railways, did increase control by top echelons of power. However, this was a poor substitute for market-building measures, for making these markets contestable, and for making their prices and tariffs realistic, which would have made them good objects for domestic and foreign investors alike. The grievances of minority shareholders have not been addressed by the ousting of those previously involved in wrongdoings of various sorts. Actually, the stronger central control is, the lower the probability that minority shareholders can, in case of conflict of interest, enforce their rights via an independent court ruling against the dominant parastatals or the outright state owners. Reforms aimed at introducing elements of competition have either been watered down, as in the electricity sector, or delayed to 2002, as in the gas sector, or not even seriously considered, as in the railway sector. The latter, together with the aging of Soviet-era pipelines, may turn into a severe bottleneck for economic development in the foreseeable future. The sums needed for the recapitalization of these industries are not earmarked in the budgets of the current fat years. Moreover, rearrangement of transport tariffs, essential for any private investment to make sense, are not even envisaged to any degree that would make a difference for an investor in his right mind.

It appears that the government will restructure, rather than discontinue, the intimate intertwining between the public and private spheres, so typical of Russia and much of the developing world. The balance of power between central and local powers and state and business may change, but the name of the game remains bargaining, rather than free competition among political and economic ideas and agents.

As we have seen, the emerging crisis management measures solidify autarkic structures and counter tendencies to reallocate resources, save, invest and grow, and adjust inherited production lines to external demand. Therefore, the sluggish export performance of Russia is systemic rather than caused by high oil prices. The latter may only overshadow deeper problems and allow for continued optimism in forecasting. True, the current medium-term plan, estimating a 3.5 percent growth for 2002, 2.6 percent for 2003, and 4 percent for 2004, is a realistic correction of the over-optimistic estimates of the Gref Plan. However, even this might prove overly ambitious, depending upon oil price developments.

As we tried to prove, limited progress in the economic sphere is directly related to the conceptual limitations of enlightened absolutism, where centralizing political tendencies are married to, more or less, market radicalism. In a comprehensive economy and society in Europe, where urbanization and literacy are dominant, there is no role for the developmental state of the coal and steel and textiles period. Lacking progress in political pluralism puts inherent limits on economic legislation and institution building, whereas the latter will constrain allocation efficiency and the propensity to invest domestically. And even in the most outward-oriented East Asian states, foreign direct investment could only complement, but not replace, domestic savings and domestic private investment as an engine of sustaining growth.

## NOTES

1. U.N. Economic Commission for Europe (UNECE), *Economic Survey of Europe*, no. 1 (2001).

2. Comparative estimates reported in *Voprosy Ekonomiki*, no. 3 (2001), p. 44; consolidated deficit figures, ibid., p. 61.

3. Clifford Gaddy and Barry Ickes, *Russia's Virtual Economy and Economic Rebound* (Washington, D.C.: The Brookings Institution, forthcoming) provides detailed econometric evidence.

4. Andrei Illarionov, "Ekonomicheskaia politika v usloviiakh otkrytoi ekonomiki so znachitelnim syrevim sektorom," *Voprosy Ekonomiki*, vol. 72, no. 4 (2001), p. 21, provides evidence and the numbers.

5. Described impartially in detail by *Economic Survey of the Russian Federation, 1999–2000* (Paris: OECD, 2000). For an insider view see the exhaustive analysis of Yegor Gaidar, ed., *Ekonomika perekhodnogo perioda* (Moscow: IEPPP, 1998).

6. For an explanation of the paradigmatic and practical significance of this circumstance, see V. Mau, "Politischeskaia priroda i uroki finansovogo krizisa," *Voprosy Ekonomiki*, vol. 70, no. 11 (1999), pp. 4–19; and László Csaba, "A Decade of Transformation: Russia and Hungary Compared," in Andrzej Brzeski and Jan Winiecki, eds., *A Liberating Economic Journey* (London: CRCE, 2000), pp. 99–140.

7. This point is circumspectly documented and explained in Alfred Stepan, "Russian Federalism in Comparative Perspective," *Post-Soviet Affairs*, vol. 16, no. 2 (2000), pp. 171–73.

8. See the summary chapters of these two authoritative collections, in which the editors highlight this particular point. Robert Bates and Anne Krueger, eds., *The Political Economy of Economic Policy Reform* (Oxford: Blackwell, 1992); and John Williamson, ed., *The Political Economy of Policy Reform* (Washington, D.C.: Institute of International Economics, 1994).

9. Richard Rose, Neil Munro, and Stephen White, "Voting in a Floating Party System: The 1999 Duma Elections," *Europe-Asia Studies*, vol. 53, no. 3 (2001), pp. 438–40. They highlight the low level of representation and lack of ideological orientation among the major factions.

10. Luke March, "For Victory? The Crises and Dilemmas of the Communist Party of the Russian Federation," *Europe-Asia Studies*, vol. 53, no. 2 (2001), pp. 263–90, offers a comparative perspective on the Euro-communist experience.

11. Acting on a law and order platform, Yevgeni Primakov, the first post-crisis premier, attempted to crush the power of the oligarchs by a series of anti-corruption and tax-law enforcement measures. He proved to be much more aggressive and also much more successful in political, if not macroeconomic, terms than any of his predecessors. His success and popularity at the time made him a powerful rival to Yeltsin, who was too slow to get rid of him by appointing the state security chief Sergei Stepashin to the premiership. Primakov then joined forces with Moscow mayor Yuri Luzhkov in forming the "Fatherland" movement, which was then seen as the most challenging opposition movement for the presidency.

12. According to Alexander Radygin, "Sobstvennost i integratsionniie protsessi v korporativnom sektore," *Voprosy Ekonomiki*, vol. 70, no. 5 (2001), p. 26, 64 percent of all profits originated from fuel companies in 1999 and 71 percent did in 2000.

13. See Masha Lipman and Michael McFaul, "'Managed Democracy' in Russia," *Press and Politics*, vol. 6, no. 3 (2001), pp. 117–28, highlighting the limitations this approach puts on any system of checks and balances.

14. See one of the harshest critics of Yeltsin's practices, Stefan Hedlund, "Property without Rights: Dimensions of Russian Privatization," *Europe-Asia Studies*, vol. 53, no. 2 (2001), pp. 234–35. The rest of his article provides extensive historical background to this argument. In a similar vein, see also László Csaba, *The Capitalist Revolution in Eastern Europe* (Cheltenham: E. Elgar, 1995), part I.

15. This point is highlighted strongly in an otherwise optimistic assessment of Russia in Anders Aslund, "Think Again: Russia," *Foreign Policy*, no. 127 (November 2001).

16. This was expressed by an insider in Vladimir Mau, "Ekonomicheskaia politika Rossii: v nachale novoi fazi," *Voprosy Ekonomiki*, vol. 72, no. 3 (2001), pp. 10–11, calling attention to the compromise nature of the strategy.

17. Aleksei Lavrov, John Litwack, and Douglas Sutherland, "Reforma mezbudzetnikh otnoshenii v Rossii: 'federalizm sozdaiuschii rynok'," *Voprosy*

*Ekonomiki*, vol. 72, no. 4 (2001), pp. 39–41, in their detailed empirical study of parallel fiscal policies conducted by local authorities.

18. For a similar argument, see Leonid Smiriagin, "Who Runs the Russian Regions?" at the conference "Russia, Ten Years After" hosted in Washington, D.C., by the Carnegie Endowment for International Peace, June 7–9, 2001. He calls attention to the very strong formal and informal power base of elected local leaders against presidential envoys, as well as to the arbitrariness of the newly created seven regions that are already crosscut by actual economic processes.

19. As documented in detail in a monograph by Matthew Hyde, defended as his Ph.D. thesis at the University of Essex and summarized in Matthew Hyde, "Putin's Federal Reforms and Their Implications for Presidential Power in Russia," *Europe-Asia Studies*, vol. 53, no. 5 (July 2001), pp. 719–43.

20. In their empirical study Auzan and Kriuchkova (pp. 80–81) discuss "lock-in phenomena" in which regulators and the regulated develop a joint interest in sustaining the status quo and excluding any new entrant. A. Auzan and P. Kriuchkova, "Administrativniie barieri v ekonomie: zadachi deblokirovaniia," *Voprosy Ekonomiki*, vol. 72, no. 5 (2001), pp. 73–88.

21. Tatiana Dolgopiatova, "Modeli i mekhanizmi korporativnogo kontrolia v rossiiskoi promyshlennosti," *Voprosy Ekonomiki*, vol. 72, no. 5 (2001), pp. 46–60, provides an empirical proof based on a survey of the three hundred largest firms in Russian industry.

22. Some Western analysts draw parallels to experiences of Organization for Economic Cooperation and Development countries where policy expediency and entrenched structures produced similar outcomes. See Martin Siner and Jon Stern, "Reform Electricity Market in Transition Economies: How to Avoid Traps of Deregulation?" *Transition* vol. 11, no. 6 (2000–2001), pp. 8–10.

23. V. Mau, "Ekonomicheskaia politika Rossii: v nachale novoi fazi," pp. 20–21, adds to this the problem of ongoing conceptual disputes between the government and Central Bank over the future role of banks.

24. A. Radygin, "Sobstvennost i integratsionniie protsessi v korporativnom sektore," pp. 36–38, provides empirical evidence for the process of multidimensional concentration.

25. Empirical cross-country evidence for this point (including Russia) is provided in Robert McIntyre and Bruno Dallago, eds., *Small Business in Transition* (Oxford: Oxford University Press for WIDER, forthcoming); and L. Csaba, ed., *The Hungarian Small Business in Comparative Perspective* (Washington: U.S. Agency for International Development, 1998).

26. J. Laurilla, "FDI and the Russian Energy Sector: An Ill Managed Partnership," BOFIT, *The Russian Economy: The Month in Review*, April 2001, cites profitability gaps due to low prices, high taxes, and nonpayments.

27. Absorption capacity is a technical economic concept, denoting the amount of money any economy is able to put into good use (i.e., producing high returns) in any particular period of time. It has been proven, especially during times of plenty, as in major oil-producing countries following the 1973 and 1979 shocks, that overinvestment can be welfare reducing, even in the long run. It should be obvious that a good investment climate allows for more investment and a bad climate for less, thus this capacity is never technically a given (i.e., by a mere reference to per capita GDP).

28. Anders Aslund, "The Soviet Transformation," *Financial Times*, September 11, 2001, argues forcefully in favor of interpreting post-Soviet growth as export-led and attributable to the new radicalism in reform policies all across the CIS region.

29. "Kreditanstalt," *Central European Quarterly*, no. 2 (2001), p. 53.

30. This argument is advanced by S. Alexashenko, A. Klepach, O. Osipova, and S. Pukhov, "Valiutnii kurs i ekonomicheskii rost," *Voprosy Ekonomiki*, vol. 72, no. 8 (August 2001), pp. 28–31.

31. This is the view expressed in the presentation by Sergei Vasiliev, "The Structure of the Russian Economy and Political Trends in Russia," at the Carnegie conference referenced in note 18.

32. Silvana Malle, "Russia After a Decade of Transition," in A. Brzeski and J. Winiecki, *op. cit.*, pp. 65–97, concludes by stressing both components of the same phenomenon.

33. An English language summary of the arguments for statist policies, still proliferating in the Russian academic and policy-making literature, is presented by Jacques Sapir, "The Russian Economy: From Rebound to Rebuilding," *Post-Soviet Affairs*, vol. 17, no. 1 (2001), pp. 1–22, without, however, addressing the two major points of our critique, i.e., nonavailability of funds and lack of administrative capacity to implement such projects.

# 4

# Russia's Energy Policy

*Jurgis Vilemas*

This chapter presents the various ways in which Russia's energy policy and foreign policy interacted with each other after the collapse of the Soviet Union and the subsequent consequences for developments in neighboring countries. In the difficult process of transition from central planning and state ownership to a market-oriented economy and private ownership, Russia efficiently exploited several newborn, semiprivate companies such as Lukoil, Gazprom, and United Energy Systems (UES) to expand its economic control and political influence. This chapter presents some concrete examples of that process. Vast reserves of natural resources are a very important factor in Russia's relations with the European Union and other Western countries. Russia's urgent need for huge investments in order to exploit its resources has a particular influence on those relations.

New discoveries of oil and gas around the Caspian Sea have fomented long-running strategic disputes among many countries, particularly in the area of transportation to the markets. The deposits are located between high-volume consumers—today Europe and Russia, China in the future, and Iran—and are of great geopolitical interest for all of them, as well as the United States.

The significance of Russia's vast natural resources, and especially energy resources, to Russian energy and foreign policy cannot be overemphasized. Russia controls the greatest oil, gas, coal, and uranium deposits on the globe. It has a comparatively well-developed technical infrastructure for exploration and development of those resources, and that infrastructure is backed by a cheap and experienced labor force. During its post–Soviet period, Russia used those assets not only to influence the former satellite countries' domestic economic and energy policies, but also as a very powerful instrument of foreign policy. This influence is particularly strong in

Russia's relations with all neighbors, but especially with the ex-Soviet and east European countries. Given the political and financial instabilities that Russia faced after the collapse of the Soviet Union, the oil, gas, and nuclear sectors performed reasonably (and surprisingly) well, particularly in sustaining export volumes. Thus, the energy factor, as a Russian policy instrument, has likely been underestimated in the West and the details of its mechanics not properly understood.

## ENERGY POLICY BACKGROUND

Russia inherited the Soviet Union's completely state-owned energy sector, which was managed by vertically integrated monopolies. The process of economic reorganization and privatization in Russia started just after the breakup of the Soviet Union. The oil sector, for example, consisted of more than ten vertically integrated companies and a series of independent regional producers. A vast majority of these companies were privatized and the state now owns only a small stake in a number of them.

The gas and electricity sectors have developed very differently. The vertically integrated monopolies Gazprom and UES still dominate, maintaining almost full control over each respective sector. Nevertheless, the Russian government has only a 38 percent stake in Gazprom and 52 percent of UES.

Never before had any society transferred such huge values from state to private ownership in so short a time, and the state encountered great difficulties in controlling the process. During that period very powerful and influential private owners or "oligarchs" arose, and they are very resourceful in seeking further enrichment and influence. Lack of proper legislation, a corrupt governing bureaucracy, and an underdeveloped banking sector (a significant part of which was controlled by the same oligarchs) created unprecedented possibilities for transfers of vast financial sums to accounts in foreign countries through establishment of numerous daughter companies or local affiliates, particularly in former Soviet and Eastern bloc countries. Indeed, most of Russia's biggest semiprivate energy companies, such as Lukoil, Gazprom, and UES, followed this strategy. The new companies not only conduct export operations, but also control a significant share of the refining and petrochemical businesses.

Broad involvement of newly born, aggressive, and inventive private companies in oil and gas exports made it possible over the past decade to maintain or even increase export volumes, even though production was gradually deteriorating. Evidently, the economic crisis and subsequent deep reduction in domestic consumption helped stabilize exports. But only the private sector was able to fully exploit the situation. Very low domestic prices (several times lower than the international prices) also helped encourage exports.

Oil and gas exports generate roughly 50 percent of Russia's hard currency revenues. In 2000 alone, sales of Russian oil companies exceeded U.S.$60 billion. But the owners of the largest companies are reluctant to share any income with the state. President Vladimir Putin clearly understands that without properly controlled "oil and gas money" it is impossible to start rebuilding and modernizing Russia's ailing industry and deteriorating infrastructure. Investments in each sector must be increased considerably even to maintain existing export capacity. Establishing more strict controls on the energy business is one of President Putin's most important near-term tasks. Recent replacements in the government and the appointment of a new chairman of the Gazprom board confirm this fact.

However, attempts to strengthen control of the powerful, private giants may only achieve short-term success. The long-term target should be basic restructuring and liberalization of the economy, a goal that may require a decade to achieve. Another big obstacle to substantial increases in oil and gas exports is that large-scale domestic consumption is dependent on energy-intensive industry and transportation. However, in Russia nearly all industries require more than twice as much energy than in modern economies. An extremely wasteful heat supply system, combined with a harsh climate and long distances for fuel delivery, needs more primary energy resources than a more developed system. Country-wide modernization will require enormous investments. Additionally, few new power plants were built in Russia during the last twenty years. And soon the country will face the enormous task of renovating the old generation of plants. Otherwise, the reliability of the heat and power supply will fall to an unacceptable level, as it happened in Russia's far east and in Siberia. Any cold winter, even in European territory, can be disastrous.

The government's "Russian Energy Strategy for the Period up to 2020" calls for 3 percent annual growth of electricity generation capacity, which will require huge investments: from U.S.$2.5 billion in 2001 to U.S.$6.5 billion in 2010. At least U.S.$2 billion are needed just to keep natural gas production at 2001 levels. According to the strategy, annual natural gas production will climb by 27 percent, to 750 billion cubic meters in 2020 from 590 billion in 2000. Oil industry expansion will also be expensive. About U.S.$15 billion is to be raised between 2001 and 2005, while total investment in the upstream oil industry between now and 2020 will be as high as U.S.$43 billion. Together with downstream investments, the figure could reach U.S.$115 billion to $135 billion.[1] Russia's urgent need for huge investments—to keep running the country's energy industry and to maintain oil and gas export levels—exceeds any realistic internal possibility even if oil prices stay high.

With output falling and gas exports set to rise, domestic customers should gradually switch to other fuels. Gazprom does not want to supply fuel for power plants for U.S.$12 per 1,000 cubic meters. Thermal power plants consumed 135 billion cubic meters in 1999, while Gazprom requires a 30 percent reduction of gas consumption in power generation.[2] The situation with fossil fuels can explain why Russian energy strategists revitalized a great idea of the 1980s: to use nuclear power as the main source to justify growing demand. In May 2000 the government of the Russian Federation issued a "Nuclear Power Development Strategy in Russia in the First Half of the Twenty-first Century," in which it postulated that nuclear power generation should grow from 15 percent of total generation in 2000 to 21 percent in 2020.[3] That means that production in NPP (net power production) should almost triple from 129 TWh (Terawatt hours) to 340 TWh (210 TWh in 2010). Taking into account that nuclear power plants require much bigger investments per unit of capacity and that foreign capital is difficult to attract, the program does not appear to be achievable. Many analysts have raised questions about whether Russia will be able to meet the rising demand for huge investments. Where will funds come from to put the energy industry on a growth track?

To avoid an energy crisis without the infusion of enormous amounts of foreign capital is impossible. This situation is well understood by President Putin and the country's politicians, and to some degree not only determines the country's energy policy but also is shaping external relations with developed industrial countries, particularly within the European Union (EU).

In 2000, within the EU, much of the debate in the political circles has centered on the long-term strategic issue of how best to justify the constantly growing demand for energy and how to ensure a secure supply, given the union's significant and growing dependence on energy imports. The European Commission's green paper, "Toward a European Strategy of Energy Supply," clearly expresses renewed attention to the importance and inevitability of Russia as a supplier of oil and, in the greatest extent, gas to West European markets. By 2020, almost 70 percent of the European Union's gas will have to be imported. Up to 40 percent will come from the world's larger producer and largest reserve keeper—Russia.[4]

Therefore, the EU governments clearly have an interest in maintaining close relations with Russian authorities on energy policy matters. In fact, both sides decided to create the Strategic Energy Partnership, which was formally signed at a summit between Presidents Jacques Chirac, Romano Prodi, and Putin in Paris on October 30, 2000. The aim of the partnership is to build a long-term program based on the convergence of interests between the European Union and Russia in the area of energy cooperation. On one hand, the European Union has a growing demand for energy imports, which will become significantly greater after the East European countries join. On the other hand, Russia needs a substantial injection of foreign capital in order to increase oil and gas production, to modernize its power sector, and to secure an overall strategy for economic growth.[5] The Strategic Energy Partnership's aims and objectives are fully in line with the new Concept of Russian Foreign Policy adopted by President Putin in July 2000. The concept emphasizes the importance of attracting foreign investments into the key sectors of the Russian economy and a readiness to create the needed legal basis for economic cooperation and the security of foreign investments. The European Union's role in the energy partnership is that of a facilitator to improve investment opportunities for European companies, to upgrade the infrastructure, and to introduce efficient and environmentally friendly technologies. But the necessary preliminary step to investment is Russia's ratification of the Energy Charter Treaty, currently being stalled by Gazprom lobbies in the Duma.

The Strategic Energy Partnership Agreement calls for natural gas exports from Russia to Europe to rise to 200 billion cubic meters by 2008. As part of the agreement, Gazprom will form a consortium with leading gas companies from Germany, France, and Italy to build a U.S.$2 billion gas pipeline to carry an additional 60 billion cubic meters of gas to the European Union each year via Belarus, Poland, and Slovakia.[6]

Gazprom has recently begun focusing on another export project to carry gas from northern Russia to Germany and perhaps to Scandinavian countries via the Baltic Sea. The consortium agreement for a feasibility study was signed in spring 2001 between Gazprom, Fortum (Finland), and German companies.[7] With the changing political climate in Europe, it is realistic to analyze cheaper paths for crossing some Baltic countries.

Geographical proximity, economic necessity, and long-term strategic interests strongly stimulate both Russia and the European Union to move toward increased coordination of future energy policies. Such a coincidence of critically important strategic interests strongly favors political stability and fruitful economic cooperation in the region.

A perfect demonstration of that new climate and Russia's seriousness in improving relations with the West is the government's reaction to the tragic events of September 11, 2001. Russia's cooperation with the United States in antiterrorist actions and its clearly expressed intention of providing western Europe with additional deliveries in case of supply disruptions from the Middle East (as noted, for example, in President Putin's speech in Essen on September 26) opens a new era of political and economic relations. Both sides must take advantage of this favorable climate without delay.

However, it is unrealistic to expect that Russian oil will be able to replace shipments from the Middle East in the event of a serious political crisis. To be competitive in the international oil sector, Russia first must fundamentally improve its domestic energy sector. That will take a long time and huge investments. Russia's recent and speedy economic recovery has been coupled with growing domestic demand for oil and gas. Most of the growing oil production should go to the domestic market, which will not leave very much export expansion.

## RELATIONS WITH FORMER SATELLITES

The situation is very different for independent countries that were part of the former Soviet Union, and somewhat different for the east European countries. For Russia, it is difficult to rid itself of the imperial habits, traditions, and mentality that have lasted several centuries. Many of the newly independent states are experiencing a rise in nationalism and Russophobia, and they are ignorant of some very important realities. Moreover, the extremely painful economic transition in all of these countries means that mutually helpful economic relations continue to be unfavorable. However, the factors interact differently in different regions. For example, the processes in the Baltic countries are developing differently from those in the Caspian Sea region or in Ukraine or Moldova. Moscow itself is experiencing difficulties in the transition from the Soviet unilateral command style to relationships based on democratic, economic, and political cooperation between countries that are truly independent and sovereign but very young and inexperienced in self-governance. All of those countries, excluding the Caspian Sea region, completely depend upon energy supplies from Russia and do not have any alternative source in the near future. For Russia it is difficult to avoid temptation and not exploit this superior position. A variety of methods have been used over the past ten years. Just after 1990, Russia tried bullying, blackmailing, and direct cuts of supply. After 1991, when it became evident that restoration of the Soviet Union was impossible, Russia deployed an intelligence strategy to maintain significant influence or even control in one region or another, using oil, gas, and to a lesser extent electricity supplies.

The recent history of oil and gas supplies in the Baltic countries, particularly Lithuania, provides a good example of how Russia has developed methodologies to restore political influence in the post-Soviet area. Already the first attempts to cut oil and gas supplies in 1991 demonstrated that such actions are inefficient and generate adverse and undesirable effects for the initiator. Supply cuts are only effective and justifiable when caused by accumulated and sizable nonpayment.

As early as 1992, in almost every post-Soviet and East European country, Russia started to create joint ventures with local, newly established private enterprises trading oil and gas or penetrating industries whose products were based on imports from Russian raw materials. Some of these enterprises were managed by former local Communist Party bosses. Gradually, those companies began to dominate the gas supply and significantly influenced the oil trade with oil (particularly heavy oil). For example, in 2000 only 25 percent of the natural gas consumed in Lithuania was directly supplied by Gazprom to the Lithuanian grid operator and distributor Lietuvos Dujos. The remaining amount was supplied by the intermediate companies Stella Vitae, Itera Lietuva, and Itera Lit, jointly owned by Lithuanian private investors and Gazprom or Itera. The gas supplied directly to Lietuvos Dujos by Gazprom was always more expensive than that supplied by intermediates, yet the original owner was the same. Intermediates get a significant discount from Russian suppliers, which allows them a substantial profit. In 2000, Stella Vitae supplied 693 million cubic meters and earned a clear profit of U.S.$1.5 million. Itera Lietuva supplied 1.5 billion cubic meters and earned U.S.$8 million.

It is possible to conclude that such a scheme will gradually enable Russian energy companies to create financially strong, local, private companies, the further success of which completely depends upon the Russian "mother" companies. This means that the local companies must be loyal and obedient to the mother company.

In fact, newly developing Russian capitalists are using focused trade arrangements to develop strong economic and political lobbies everywhere. A similar plan has been put into effect in Poland, Slovakia, Hungary, and Bulgaria. In Poland, the owner of the large private company Bartimpex is tightly connected with Gazprom. In Hungary, the chemicals firm BorsodChem—the country's largest chemicals company—is controlled by companies representing Gazprom interests. In September 2000, Gazprom bought almost 25 percent of BorsodChem through its Ireland-based, offshore affiliate Milford Holding. But BorsodChem owns nearly 30 percent of TVK (Tiszai Vegyikombinát, a company providing intermediate petroleum products to BorsodChem), which stirred up fear in Hungary that Gazprom was using BorsodChem as a springboard for taking over TVK.[8] Meanwhile, Panrusgaz, a 50:50 joint venture of MOL (Hungarian Oil) and AEB Bank, the wholly owned Hungarian banking arm of Gazprom, posted a U.S.$8 million net profit in 2000. The company imported 8 billion cubic meters of Russian gas last year, around 60 percent of Hungary's supply. Finally, in Bulgaria, Lukoil owns 58 percent of the country's largest refinery, with a capacity of 7.5 million tons per year, and in 2000 made a net profit of U.S.$51 million. It is planning to invest this profit in the country. Lukoil wants to increase the number of its filling stations from 13 to 130 and to gain a 25 percent share in the retail fuel market by 2005. Similar examples can be found in other East European countries.

In general, Russia's giant, vertically integrated energy companies have gradually become strong and efficient instruments for Russian foreign policy, even in those countries that have succeeded in their economic transition and have avoided big debts to Russia. Future restructuring of the Russian energy sector involves the strengthening of new competitors for Gazprom and Lukoil (or even their possible fragmentation) and penetration of Western companies into upstream business. Thus, much stronger competition may make the aforementioned plan less efficient. But in any case it cannot be reduced to zero, as Russia will be the dominant, primary energy supplier for a few decades to come. Creating a balance for Russia's strong presence will be a challenging task both for local and Western political and economic strategists.

Danger to sovereignty is much greater for those countries that were not able to avoid huge debts for energy supplies from Russia. Ukraine owes Russia more than U.S.$2 billion for gas, Moldova owes close to U.S.$1 billion, and Georgia owes nearly U.S.$200 million. Despite the fact that gas and electricity are supplied to Belarus at very low prices, this country is also wallowing in debt. Widespread corruption, inefficient management, and an enormously negative trade balance with Russia caused by primary energy imports is pushing these countries to economic stagnation, and is igniting social discontent and political instability. Almost everywhere Russia is proposing or planning to exchange debt for shares of strategically important infrastructure installations: electricity and gas networks, refineries, the petrochemical industry, etc. The lack of proper radical reforms is preventing the expansion of Western economic assistance. It goes without saying that Russia's presence is expanding. Belarus has come closer to political unification with Russia; a similar trend is gaining more and more supporters in eastern Ukraine; and huge Moldavian debts are blocking possibilities for reunification with Romania.

Ultimately, very weak economies and the growing flow of Russia's energy to the West are preventing any chance for reducing the dependency of European and former Soviet countries on Russia's energy supply for the foreseeable future. It is difficult for them to believe that oil or gas imported from the West is competitive with Russian supplies. The significant presence of Western capital in the energy sector, as well as political influence in the West, may be strengthened and broadened only in cooperation with Russian companies. One good example is the sequence of events related to the Lithuanian government's deal with the U.S. company Williams International. In 1999, Williams International bought a 33 percent stake of the Lithuanian refinery Mazeikiu Nafta, together with an oil import-export terminal on the Baltic Sea coast in Butinge. But the refinery could not operate efficiently without long-term agreements with such Russian companies as Lukoil or Yukos, which were supplying oil via the existing pipeline. Imports through the Butinge terminal from the North Sea would not have been competitive. Negotiations for long-term supplies were not fruitful until an agreement was reached to sell a separate 27 percent stake of Mazeikiu Nafta to Russia's second-largest private company, Yukos, on June 25, 2001. The requisite legislative changes to implement this agreement were enacted by the Lithuanian parliament on August 2, 2001. The agreement opens a new period of positive economic cooperation in energy business between Western and Russian companies in the Baltic states and could be a catalyst for future cooperation in other regions.

The Williams International deal also marks the appearance of real competition between Russian companies. For many years Lukoil dictated the terms for supplying oil to the Mazeikiu Nafta refinery by refusing to sign a long-term supply contract and by significantly influencing its performance. Yukos' move broke Lukoil's dominance in the region. Another private Russian oil company, TNK, also wants to acquire shares in exchange for a long-term supply contract. Real competition is beginning to work even in this region.

## CASPIAN PIPELINES

Recent discoveries in and around the Caspian Sea have made the region one of the most exciting oil and gas provinces in the world. The climate is not too harsh, and the region is reasonably close to the principal consumers. But the development of a transportation system and ports system faces a long list of technical, political, legal, and other obstacles. It will require agreements between local governments, energy companies, and main potential consumers. There are also geopolitical interests involved.

The legal status of the Caspian Sea has been in dispute since the Soviet Union collapsed. Up until that point, the land around it was divided by just one boundary between the Soviet Union and Iran. However, now Russia, Kazakhstan, Turkmenistan, and Azerbaijan each have a claim to control some part of the Caspian region. During the 1990s, Russia blocked any decision about the legal status of the sea. But when President Putin came to power, Russia proposed to divide the seabed by medial lines providing each country with control over its own resources. The exact location of those lines has not yet been decided. Russia has also proposed to divide resources 50/50 between any two countries involved if oil or gas fields are found to overlap offshore boundaries, regardless of the volume of reserves lying in individual territories. Except for Iran, almost all of the countries have accepted the proposal. Iran is insisting that the Caspian Sea be divided into five equal portions providing each state with a 20 percent share. The medial line approach would give Iran around 13 percent.[9] Reaching a common agreement may take many years of difficult negotiations.

The presence of Western oil companies on Russia's southern border and the high political profile Washington has assigned to Central Asia raises fears that the U.S. military will not be far behind.[10] Russia has attempted to retain influence over Caspian oil and gas developments in a number of different ways, trying to ensure a partnership role for Russian companies by using the political influence stemming from the former Soviet infrastructure and its advantageous geographical position. It has also come to understand that it is impossible to prevent the construction of new pipelines that bypass Russia. Now the question is only one of time. Under President Putin, Russia is turning to economic competition and a partnership attitude. In fact, Russia increased Kazakhstan's quota of shipments into the Russian pipeline system and invited its Caspian neighbors to use the new pipeline to Makhachkala on the western Caspian shore in Dagestan (the Russian province bordering Chechnya). The Caspian Pipeline Consortium (CPC), which includes U.S., Kazakh, and Russian oil companies, has built a pipeline that can transport 28 million tons of oil per year from the Tengiz oil field to Novorossiysk on the Black Sea. It was scheduled to start operations by the end of 2001.

Recent new discoveries of oil and gas in all of the Caspian countries have resulted in the active return of Western companies. The inevitable large-scale energy exports through newly planned pipelines (i.e., Baku-Ceyhan, a Trans-Caspian gas pipeline, and connections with China) are more generally seen as a threat to Russia's strategic plans to dominate European energy markets and restore Central Asian supplies to Russia. Growing export demand, as well as increasing domestic demand, cannot be satisfied by domestic production alone. Now Russia is boosting imports from Kazakhstan and Turkmenistan,[11] because participation in the development of fields in this area may prove more economically worthwhile than exploring the remote and environmentally hostile Siberia and the Arctic.

The current nominal capacity of the system linking Turkmenistan with Russia is 65 billion cubic meters per year. Yet the pipes are crossing Kazakhstan. Why was Gazprom negotiating to replace Belgium's Tractebel as operator of the Kazakh gas pipeline network? Tractebel left Kazakhstan discouraged by low domestic prices and corruption scandals.[12]

Another area of competition is Turkey's gas market. Gas demand in Turkey is expected to rise rapidly from 13 billion cubic meters per year in 1999, to 55 billion in 2010, and 82 billion in 2020. At this moment Russia has gained a strong lead in the race to capture the Turkish gas market and already supplies 70 percent of the country's imports through the pipelines crossing Ukraine, Romania, and Bulgaria. Russia will maintain or even raise this figure after the Blue Stream pipeline across the Black Sea to northern Turkey up to Ankara is finished.[13]

If Turkey's demand growth proceeds as expected, then there will be room for several supply paths, including a Trans-Caspian pipeline. Transit via Turkey to southern Europe, where the expected growth rate is high, supports even the most optimistic projects. There is room for many actors and much competition, which is confirmed by the latest moves by such Western companies as Eni, Total Fina Elf, and BG, as well as Gazprom, and local Kazakh and Azeri companies (see Figure 4.1). A Caspian pipeline systems is not a dream, but an imminent reality: a reality in which pipelines cross almost all participating countries without any dominance or monopoly by any particular country. Thus, there is a good chance that economics and common sense will prevail.

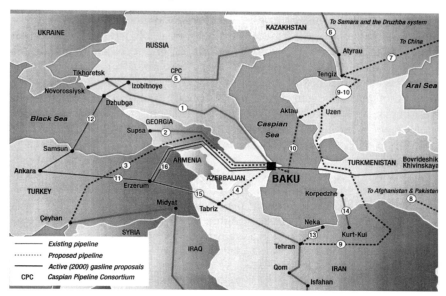

**Figure 4.1. Caspian Oil and Gas Pipelines**

1. Novorossiysk; used by AIOC.
2. Baku-Supsa; "early oil" line for AIOC fully operational March 1999.
3. Baku-Ceyhan; designated by the governments of Azerbaijan, Georgia, Turkey, and the United States as MEP route.
4. Baku-Iran (possibly Tabriz).
5. Atyrau-Novorossiysk; project now completed, operation scheduled for the end of 2001.
6. Atyrau-Samara-Druzhba system.
7. Tengiz-China; under study by China National Petroleum Corporation.
8. Chardzhou-Pakistan; with possible tie-in from Turkmen and Kazakh fields on/near the Caspian.
9. Tengiz/Uzen-Kharg.
10. TransCaspian Oil.
11. TransCaspian Gas.
12. Blue Stream Russia-Turkey gas line.
13. Neka-Tehran; financing being sought for line which could constitute major element in swaps/pipeline export system from Caspian to Persian Gulf.
14. The KKK gas line; opened in 1997, Turkmenistan's only current export line that does not transit Russia.
15. Tabriz-Erzerum gas connector; Iranian section completed by end of 1999.
16. Baku-Turkey gas pipeline; new 16 bcm\y line involving the linkage of existing lines in Azerbaijan and Georgia with a new line in eastern Turkey.

## CONCLUSIONS AND RECOMMENDATIONS

The significance of Russia's vast natural resources, particularly its energy resources, to the country's energy and foreign policy is hard to overemphasize. Russia controls a vast territory with huge oil, gas, coal, and uranium deposits. It has a comparatively well-developed technical infrastructure for exploration and development of those resources, backed by a cheap and experienced labor force. Now, in its post-Soviet period, Russia is using its treasures not only with regard to its domestic economic and energy policies, but more and more as a powerful instrument of foreign policy. This strategy pervades Russia's relations with all of its neighbors, but especially with the ex-Soviet and East European countries.

The energy sector can be a source of conflict, but it also offers much opportunity for cooperation between Russia and not only all of its neighbors, but all of Europe and Asia. But in any case, energy as a Russian policy instrument has been underestimated in the West.

Oil and gas exports generate roughly 50 percent of Russia's hard currency revenues. However, to maintain the existing energy sectors' export capacities, investments in each sector must be increased on manifold levels. Without being able to attract enormous amounts of foreign capital, growth will be impossible. The European Union looks ready to assist Russia in securing the needed investments for its energy sector. Moreover, the EU governments are clearly interested in maintaining close relations with Russia on energy policy matters.

Geographical proximity, economic necessity, and long-term strategic interests provide a strong stimulus for both Russia and the European Union to coordinate future energy policies. The overlap of very important strategic interests favors political stability and fruitful economic cooperation in the region.

The situation is very different for the independent countries of the former Soviet Union and somewhat different for the East European ones. Russia is encountering great difficulties ridding itself of the habits, traditions, and mentality from its imperial past. Many of the newly independent states are experiencing a rise in nationalism and Russophobia, and are ignorant of some important realities. Moreover, the extremely painful economic transition in all of these countries means that mutually helpful economic relations continue to be unfavorable. However, the interaction of these factors is different in each region. Processes in the Baltic countries are developing differently from those in the Caspian Sea region, Ukraine, or Moldova. Moscow itself is experiencing difficulties in its transition from the Soviet unilateral command style to relationships based on democratic, economic, and political cooperation between countries that are truly independent and sovereign, but very young and inexperienced in self-governance.

Russia's giant, vertically integrated energy companies gradually have become strong and efficient instruments of Russian foreign policy, even in those countries that have succeeded in the economic transition and have avoided big debts to Russia. Creating a balance for Russia's strength will be a challenging task both for local and Western political and economic strategists.

For the near future, weak economies and the growing flow of Russia's energy to the West have stifled any chance of the European and former Soviet bloc countries reducing dependency on Russia as a primary source of energy. The significant presence of Western capital in the energy sector and political influence in those countries may be strengthened and broadened only in cooperation with Russian companies. Ignorance of this reality will cause great economic and political losses.

## NOTES

1. "Energy Strategy of the Russian Federation" (Moscow: Ministry of Fuel and Energy of the Russian Federation, June 2001).

2. "Gazprom demands investment petroleum," *Economist*, January 2001, pp. 36–37.

3. "Strategy for Development of Atomic Energy in Russia for the First Half of the Twenty-first Century" (Moscow: Ministry of Russian Federation for Atomic Energy, 2000, in Russian).

4. European Commission, *Toward a European Strategy for the Security of Energy Supply* (Brussels: European Commission, 2001).

5. Ria Kemper, "EU Looks to Secure Russian Supply Future," *Petroleum Economist*, December 2000, pp. 28–29.

6. "Poland fights its corner: Gas connections," *Petroleum Argus*, vol. 5 (March 8, 2001), p. 10.

7. Kemper, *op. cit.; Petroleum Argus*, ibid.

8. *Petroleum Economist*, June 2001, p. 47.

9. *Petroleum Economist*, May 2001, p. 38.

10. A.M. Jaffe and R. Manning, "Russia, Energy, and the West," *Survival*, vol. 42, no. 2, pp. 133–152.

11. Financial Times, *East European Energy Report*, Issue 104, May 2000.

12. *Petroleum Economist*, September 2000, p. 20.

13. *Petroleum Economist*, January 2001, p. 40.

# 5

# Russia's Security Policy

*Marcin A. Piotrowski*

The orientation and strategic course of Russia's security policy is without doubt the most important issue in interactions between the Russian Federation and all its potential friends, neutral partners and even rivals. With the necessity of a military response to the terrorist attacks against the United States on September 11, 2001, questions arise once again regarding Russia's intentions toward the United States and the wider Euro-Atlantic community (i.e., the North Atlantic Treaty Organization; or NATO). This chapter does not present a full description of President Vladimir Putin's security policy for Russia, but rather offers a general framework of under-standing based on Russian perceptions and approaches. The first part of the chapter discusses the foundations of Russia's security policy in the context of political culture and the vision of priorities as outlined in basic official documents approved by Putin. It also touches upon such problems as geostrategic orientation, definitions of security threats and strategic goals, and tensions within the Russian military due to clashing priorities and the National Missile Defense (NMD) "Great Game." It is clear that Russia's expectations about its membership in the antiterrorist coalition are affecting the long-term strategic interests of the United States and many other coun-tries.

The second part of the chapter covers why and how Russia is not able to realize the majority of its traditional geostrategic and security interests through such instruments as military power. Consequently, Moscow is determined to use nontraditional, indirect means and tactics connected with economic strategies. In addition, the chapter assesses the future role of the Kaliningrad district.

In general, the conclusions are not very optimistic. Ten years after the fall of the Soviet Union, we are used to there being a thin margin of influence over Moscow's future policy. However, this does not and should not exclude the West's ability to modify Russia's geostrategic and security orientation. The West's lack of understanding regarding Russian policymakers' superpower mentality has hampered previous relations with Moscow. Thus, it is a mistake to work from a policy of double standards and agreement with Russian definitions of terrorist threats and proliferation challenges without clarification of their meaning and, where applicable, of the clashing interests behind them.

## FOUNDATIONS OF RUSSIAN SECURITY POLICY

The keys to understanding Moscow's present security policy lie in Russia's historical context and political culture. Psychological factors are also useful.[1] For Russians, the basic problem following the disintegration of the Soviet Union has been the issue of identity; and their identity is tied to decisions about the geopolitical orientation of post-Soviet state policy. During the last ten years, we have seen different answers to the question of the desired identity of the Russian state, nation, and society. However, it is wrong to analyze such questions only within the framework of a pro- or anti-Western orientation. Under both former President Boris Yeltsin and current President Vladimir Putin, the Kremlin has tried to construct a coherent and effective security policy. Results have been more or less in line with the expectations of different factions in the Russian elite.

Among the options for geostrategic orientation, we can observe three propositions rooted in three historical schools of thought about Russia and Russians themselves:[2]

- *Zapadniki* ("Westernizers") adhere to Russian ideology rooted in the nineteenth century that gives priority to Russia's modernization and its cordial relations with Europe. These ideas were prevalent in the policy of Andrei Kozyryev, the first Russian Federation foreign minister, as well as in later programs of the Center for Strategic Studies (headed by German Gref) and liberal-democratic factions in the Duma (the Union of Right Forces and Yabloko). According to this school of thought, Russia's history differentiates it from European nation-states, though the possibility of a similar path of development is not ruled out. Proponents of this viewpoint think that enlightened elites, or even one person, could Westernize the country, as was the case with Peter the Great. Contemporary *Zapadniki* argue that if the West does not support them, a vengeful "Weimar Russia" could be the result. The best solution, they feel, would be a form of strategic partnership that includes such elements as informal parity with other U.N. Security Council permanent members, *droit de regard* in relation to NATO or

G-7 decisions, and deep ties with the European Union—as motivated by the slogan "Common European Space." Such a partnership would also involve cooperation against the Islamic world and China. The present *Zapadniki* are sure that the West (especially the United States, Germany, and France) will see an inherent and natural connection in an alliance with Moscow and its now-independent neighbors.[3]

- *Vielikorossy* ("Great Russians") base their philosophy on arguments of the nineteenth-century Russophiles, as well as pan-Slavic ideology. They believe the main goal of the state is to lay the foundations for the "Rebirth of the Great Russia." Modern proponents of this school of thought include such diverse personalities as famous dissident Alexandr Solzhenitsyn, foreign affairs experts Sergei Baburin and Konstantin Zatulin, and the grotesque Vladimir Zhirinovsky (now vice speaker of the Duma) and his aide Alexei Mitrofanov. They are nationalists, stressing Byzantine traditions, the Orthodox Church, and other idealizations of the imperial past. To them, all ties between Russians, Ukrainians, and Belarusians pave the way for creation of a common eastern-Slavic state. They emphasize ethnic issues and the rights of Russian speakers in other Commonwealth of Independent States (CIS) countries. In other geopolitical matters, they support special ties with Orthodox countries: Armenia, Georgia, Greece, Serbia, and Bulgaria. There is a strong realpolitik component to this school of thought: spheres of influence, alliance with Germany, and balance of power.[4]
- *Yevraziytsy* ("Eurasianists") base their philosophy on the post-revolutionary emigrant movement developed in the Soviet Union by Lev Gumilev. They argue that Russia is a separate spatial subject, a real and mystical Eurasia or a true Heartland. Moscow's geostrategic interests are even wider than those of the whole area of the CIS. To them, the United States is the most expansionistic and hostile power vis-à-vis Russia. *Yevraziytsy* believe that there is no real conflict of interest with Asian powers, so Russia should create a bloc of countries in Eurasia dissatisfied with American dominance and globalization. They even argue there are no conflicts between Russia and the Islamic world, and that there is a possibility of uniting such different partners as the European Union, Iran, India, and China under strong Russian influence.[5]

Interestingly enough, experts from all schools almost uncritically support Putin's security and foreign policy. This support resurfaced after the terrorist attacks on the United States in September 2001. Russian politicians and experts fully supported the Kremlin's position toward the global antiterrorist coalition, even when they had expectations of different benefits from cooperation with the United States. On the one hand, we can interpret this phenomenon as a sign of strong consensus on national security issues among the elites. It suggests compromise among different schools of thought. It means that Putin's previous and current propositions are coherent and are heading in the right direction, at least for Russia and the Russians. On the other hand, it means that there is still no clear Kremlin answer to the issue of geopolitical identity. To put it simply, the Kremlin has not decided where it belongs in the new international system, nor has it reconciled former superpower ambitions with long-term domestic structural problems. Indeed, official documents contain many statements espousing a traditional Russian "besieged fortress" mentality and ambitions that are inconsistent with existing possibilities.

Another plausible explanation arises if we compare Putin's documents with actions undertaken during the last years of Boris Yeltsin's presidency. What has changed is a new and clear message: Russia is hardly determined to carry out its interests and is unsatisfied with Washington's hegemony. NATO's enlargement, alliance action in Yugoslavia, and the U.S. presence in the southern peripheries of Russia exemplify such hegemony. The National Security Concept approved by Putin stated two general tendencies in international relations: 1) a positive tendency toward regionalism and multidimensional integration, and 2) a negative tendency toward the new system based on Western domination with U.S. leadership. The section summing up definitions of an external threat declared: "Threats to the national security of the Russian Federation in the international sphere are showing through the attempts to hinder the strengthening of Russia as a center of influence in the multipolar world, and prevent the implementation of its national interests and weaken its position in Europe, the Middle East, the trans-Caucasus, Central Asia, and the Asia-Pacific region."[6]

Such a perception of the world is far from the previous written version of the concept, which stressed "widening the partnership and possibilities of multiplex integration of Russia within the international community."[7] These two statements not only suggest a more assertive and active approach, but also Putin's rejection of a limited role for Russia in world affairs.

Putin's approach becomes even more visible through comparison of the old and new texts of the Military Doctrine. A document from 1993 stated that Russia did not recognize any country as its foe, whereas the text from 2000 suggests that many actions will pose not only potential challenges but also actual threats to Moscow's security.[8] The interpretation of these and other statements within the framework of the Kremlin's actions suggests that this approach is strongly influenced by propositions offered by Yevgeni Primakov. They may be separated into two groups of strategic directives, focused on two dimensions of Russian security policy.

In the first group, directives are focused mostly on the global level of policy. They are subordinated to the promotion of the multipolar world. As one scholar put it, because Moscow is unable to restore Soviet potential and positions, its weakness has an essentially long-term character. Thus, Russia should play on the differences and contradictions among the interests of the emerging poles of world power. This type of strategy would not allow for a unipolar domination, and Russia would have no formal security alliances.[9] As we know, this is not only a theoretical recommendation, but also a practical course for Russia's actions toward the United States, European Union, Association of South-East Asian Nations (ASEAN) countries, China, and India.[10] In a multipolar world, Moscow's interests would be represented in almost all political, diplomatic, and military relations with the European Union, China, India, and Iran, to say nothing of the representation of this goal in contacts with smaller and weaker partners (even "states of concern").[11] Moscow is trying to describe some of these relations as a "strategic partnership"; however, it is clear that not all of the partners prefer this designation. Sometimes it is even a burden for Russia. A good example of the last case are relations with Iran: the Russians stopped describing them in terms of a strategic partnership, but they have continued extensive cooperation in the spheres of security and ballistic and nuclear issues. What is more, Moscow's security relations with Tehran, Beijing, and New Delhi are useful for securing Russian interests in Central Asia. A similar approach may be observed in Moscow's relations with the European Union. An alliance with the European Union is important from the multipolar point of view, but is also desirable as additional support for Russian interests in Ukraine and even EU candidate countries.

The second group of directives is aimed toward the promotion of the Russian equivalent of the Monroe Doctrine in the so-called "near abroad"— i.e., securing an exclusive zone of influence over the whole area of the CIS.[12] Putin has continued Primakov's recommendations for preserving Russia's strategic, security, and economic interests in the CIS countries. In this sense, Russia should use the guise of "integration at a different speed." This approach is focused on differentiation of bilateral relations in each case and selective engagement in military and/or economic dimensions. They may be summarized by three general goals. First, the Russian military's goals presuppose a military presence in client countries, like Belarus, Armenia, and Tajikistan. All of them guarantee possibilities for a Russian military extension into eastern Europe, the trans-Caucasus, Central Asia, and other nearby areas. Second, there is the goal of defending security interests in countries critical toward Russian policy. These countries are trying to create an alternative axis in GUUAM (Georgia, Ukraine, Uzbekistan, Azerbaijan, and Moldova). All members of the GUUAM group rejected the CIS Treaty of Collective Defense, and before Putin became president they had strongly favored cooperation with NATO and the European Union. A third goal is the creation of a common position for the CIS states toward armed Islamic extremists in the Russian northern Caucasus and Central Asian countries. Officially, the Islamic extremist movements are presented as a kind of common threat to authoritarian regimes. Moscow is publicly stressing those movements' external and international roots (Wahhabis, Taliban, and Osama bin Laden connections) and is silent on their deep internal and structural background. None of these goals can be analyzed outside the context of other Russian interests, such as political and economic influences in eastern Europe and the whole region around the Caspian Sea. In the case of security interests in Georgia and Azerbaijan, there is also a connection with Russia's acute internal problems in Chechnya, Dagestan, and other territories of the unstable northern Caucasus.

The formulation of equally important strategic interests at the global and regional levels has a negative impact on military policy. Even the text of the new Military Doctrine does not explain what kind of a threat is more serious for Russia, the hierarchy of threats, and their probability.[13] According to Alexei Arbatov, Moscow now has two separate and parallel military doctrines: the first focusing on strategic nuclear deterrence toward NATO, particularly the United States, and the second on conventional and local threats in Russia's more immediate environs.[14] Those two doctrines would have been congruent with each other in Soviet times, but current economic constraints make them unsuitable for a contemporary Russian army. If the Kremlin does not choose between them, there is sure to be conflict with Russia's military establishment. Tensions between the two military priorities have been evident in a now-famous conflict between then minister of defense Marshal Igor Sergeyev and the chief of the general staff, General Anatoliy Kvashnin. Conflict erupted in the summer of 2000, but it was no secret that they had been antagonists since 1997. Their disagreement was exactly about the interpretation of the doctrine's statements, its priorities, and interpretation of the secret document entitled "Concept of Development of the Armed Forces in Period till 2005":

- Sergeyev argued that the rebuilding of conventional forces is a long-term process and that Russia must be confident that it is protected by a powerful strategic and tactical nuclear umbrella. He and his supporters gave priority to the deterrence of other powers—i.e., the United States, NATO, and China;
- Kvashnin and younger generals with experience in Chechnya argued that nuclear deterrence is still important, but there is an urgent need to rebuild conventional forces. For them, the huge strategic forces from the Cold War are too expensive and irrational vis-à-vis the Russian military budget and interests in the CIS's territory.[15]

It is interesting that Putin was rather silent about the conflict at the highest level of military command and did not decide to remove Sergeyev and Kvashnin from their posts or clearly support one or the other. The situation may improve significantly after the nomination of KGB General Sergei Ivanov to the post of defense minister. But even now, it is still unclear how Putin and Ivanov will cope with tensions among strategic ambitions, real threats, lack of funds, and the dysfunctional structure of the army. For instance, Putin did not take radical steps toward rationalizing the military budget. He simply increased the budget without presentation of wider economic analyses and introduction of strict supervision of financial decisions within the Ministry of Defense.[16] The essential question here is whether Putin and Ivanov have an idea of the real changes that will be needed in overall military policy and structural reform of the army if they embrace an American-centered policy. Ivanov's announcements suggest that the Kremlin is determined to carry out the military reform plan. The new document is entitled "Plan for Building and Developing the Armed Forces until 2005," but its thesis is not very different from those in the previous plans. However, Ivanov agreed that the army must be prepared to face the new challenges and tasks. He and Putin have still thought about strong strategic and naval forces.[17] It simply seems impossible for Russia to reform its army when its military planning still remains within the Cold War paradigm.

Such a situation, including the evident weakness of the army, has implications for Russia's position toward the U.S. National Missile Defense plans. Last year, Kvashnin openly spoke about possible reductions in the strategic arsenal to the level of 1,500 warheads. He presented his opinion at the Security Council meeting at the end of July 2000. It received a sharply negative response from commanders of the Strategic Ballistic Missile Forces (RVSN).[18] When we compare Kvashnin's proposition with the evolution of Moscow's viewpoint concerning problems with the Anti-Ballistic Missile (ABM) Treaty and NMD, it seems that Russia had preferred compromise from the outset. In other words, all bargaining turns on the price offered by Washington. In the NMD debate, Moscow wanted to: at the most, according to rules of the ABM Treaty, preserve quantitative nuclear parity with Washington; and at the least, not to suffer evident and serious damage with regard to the rest of its former nuclear superpower image.[19]

Between these two poles, as will be addressed in the second part of this chapter, Russia has been using all the available diplomatic and propaganda tools. All of them are based on the best solution for Moscow—i.e., guarantees of de facto irreversible reductions and de jure parity with the reduced American arsenal. Here, scenarios of the future Russian strategic triad structure (offense-defense mix) are not important. What is important is the impossibility of keeping its level within the limit of 3,000–3,500 warheads set by the Strategic Arms Reduction Treaty II (START II). As mentioned before, Russian experts expect formal agreement and concessions on the basis of a treaty like START, supported by other elements: ceilings for NMD interceptors, a new verification regime, warning data exchange, and other transparency measures.[20] The "Great Game" of ABM, NMD, and START III is now without a final solution, but the assumed goals enumerated above, the nature of tools used by Russia, and two meetings between President George W. Bush and Putin suggest that sooner or later Moscow will reach a compromise with Washington.

For some time now, there have been interesting debates among U.S. experts about possible strategic compromises with Russia. These discussions were parallel to the accompanying inter-American controversies on the unresolved issue of the future of the Missile Defense architecture. Only a few frank opinions indicated Russia's geopolitical demands (i.e., the expected American concessions) in the agenda of strategic armaments.[21] However, Russia's demands seemed not to be limited to strategic arsenals. In fact, Russia was openly talking about NMD-ABM-START issues. Moscow clearly wanted to strike a deal that would secure its geopolitical and commercial interests.

With new aspects added to the international situation after the terrorist attacks on September 11, the Kremlin realized it had new chances to implement previous strategic goals, both at the global and the CIS level. American and Western public opinion in general underwent a change of attitude toward "Islamic threat theory." Putin and his diplomacy have renewed similar slogans of the terrorism (read "Islamic") threat from the Balkans, through the Caucasus to Central Asia, Kashmir, and Xinjiang.[22] By the end of September, previous strategic goals—even those verging on wishful thinking—turned out to be much more realistic, both in the American-Russian agenda and in Russia's relations with the European Union. We are not capable of reconstructing all long-term motives behind the Kremlin's position on the global coalition created by Washington. We also cannot reconstruct in full detail the reasons behind Russia's acceptance of Washington-Tashkent cooperation against the Taliban in Afghanistan. During his diplomatic offensive in September and October, Putin presented many arguments appropriate for his audiences in the Bundestag, NATO's headquarters, and the European Commission. He stressed Moscow's "European choice," the need to abandon anachronistic policy, and the need for extensive cooperation within all possible spheres. Putin also proposed ideas that were important from the American point of view, such as cooperation in providing military support for the Afghan Northern Alliance, intelligence sharing, and exerting pressure on other CIS regimes.[23]

At this moment—and in the near future—many questions arise: Will Russia be a credible partner in combating the so-called rogue states? Will Putin transform himself into a *Zapadnik?* Are we seeing the beginning of more cooperative behavior on Russia's part? What will the American side offer? At the moment answers to these questions seem simple, but they are not so clear when we take them within the framework of Russian strategic

lion and gas exports amounted to more than U.S.$16 billion.[36] Russia uses these products as policy instrument vis-à-vis the European Union, Central Europe, and CIS countries. It is made easier by the new relations between the Kremlin and the energy oligarchs, who are no longer independent as they were under Yeltsin. Companies like Gazprom or Lukoil are now almost obliged to support state interests, a change that is especially visible in policy toward Ukraine and the Caspian-area CIS countries. Among the numerous examples of this change in tactics are:

- Putin's declarations during the last EU-Russian summit concerning "chances for marriage of great economic potentials" (in practice the Russian Ministry of Energy expects western European investments of U.S.$50 billion in the gas sector by 2010);[37]
- Gazprom's lobbying for a new gas pipeline through central to western Europe, which would bypass Ukraine, thus guaranteeing Russia's position in the expanded EU gas market and weakening Kyiv's transportation position;
- Gazprom's long-term contracts with Turkmenistan, which oppose American plans for a trans-Caspian gas pipeline. They would guarantee a Russian transportation monopoly;
- Itera's pressing Georgia on energy debt payments (parallel to pressures on the issue of Chechen diaspora activity and the future of Russian military bases in this country); and
- Lukoil's and TNK's expansion in Ukrainian Black Sea oil terminals (directed against Kyiv and Warsaw's plan for an Odessa-Brody-Gdansk oil pipeline).[38]

Here, it must be stressed that during the last two years we have seen effective coordination of Russian tactics, tools, and modes of action in the CIS area. An examination of several of Putin's initiatives yields interesting insights into his administration's success at extending and consolidating Moscow's control over policy concerning the CIS. Putin's administration, disappointed with the CIS's political and economic structure, has preferred to develop a new framework like the Eurasian Economic Union (with Belarus, Kazakhstan, Kyrgyzstan, and Tajikistan) as a "core of multi-speed reintegration." Also, Moscow signed a series of bilateral economic agreements with Turkmenistan and every country of the GUUAM group, especially on their vulnerabilities, such as energy and military industry. Russia is still capable of maintaining some kind of control over unresolved conflicts in many post-Soviet "hot spots" as an instrument of pressure on Moldova, Georgia, Azerbaijan, and the Central Asian states. Putin sped up the development of cooperation between special services and armies within the multilateral framework by creating the CIS Counter-Terrorist Center and CIS Rapid Reaction Forces (with Belarus, Armenia, Kazakhstan,

Kyrgyzstan, and Tajikistan). Moscow has been using the issue of visas as leverage against the trans-Caucasus countries whose many citizens have been working legally or illegally in Russian territory. The threat of introducing a new, strict visa regime would threaten many Georgians and Azeris who work in Russia and send their earnings to families back at home. Russia also uses its media, which are very popular in many CIS countries, to influence local public opinion. For example, in Belarus during the summer of 2001, critical programs on pro-Kremlin TV zchannels pressured Alexandr Lukashenka to give in to Moscow's economic expectations. Lukashenka would not have been able to win the subsequent election with continued media criticism or media presentation of Belarusian opposition candidates.[39]

So far, thanks to these actions, Russia has been able to regain much of its lost influence in the CIS, as well as rebuilding its dominant position. Many decision-makers in Moscow are also sure that this trend will be only strengthened by new commitments with the United States and the European Union. The overall result is that Russia is convinced it has gained improved standing on the regional and global scene, despite a lack of resources to account for that feeling.

## KALININGRAD AS A LABORATORY FOR CONFLICT AND COOPERATION WITH THE WEST

Kaliningrad is a critical asset in terms of Russian military planning. It is valued as the strongest military base, with the potential for extending its power over the entire Baltic Sea region. It has undergone intensive change since 1989–91, when many former Soviet units were transferred to this area from eastern Germany, Poland, and then from the Baltic states themselves. During the last decade, manpower potential was reduced by approximately 90 percent. Ground forces in Kaliningrad (13,000 soldiers) should be analyzed within the context of the Russian-Belarusian military alliance, considering that for many years all exercises show full integration of command between Kaliningrad/Moscow and Minsk's staff.[40] Founded at the end of 1997, the Kaliningrad Defense Region (*Kaliningradtsky Oboronnyi Rayon,* or KOR) was the first reorganized and restructured autonomous base put directly under the high command in Moscow. In the middle of the last decade, the chief of the Main Operational Directorate in the General Staff (Anatolyi Kvashnin) and the chief of the Baltic Fleet Staff (Admiral Vladimir Kuroyedov, now head of the Russian navy) prepared plans for an autonomous KOR. Reductions and structural and doctrinal changes are also visible in Kaliningrad's naval organization. Its current naval role seems to be mainly defensive, restricted to the Baltic Sea. The reduced Baltic Fleet does not operate in the Atlantic, as it did during the Soviet period. Apart from some Russian declarations about the strategic importance of this fleet, what seems to be most important here is the prestige.[41]

In January 2001, an article in the *Washington Post*, containing Defense Intelligence Agency (DIA) information about nuclear weapons transfers to Kaliningrad, put many politicians in Poland and the Baltic states on alert. This brought to light the unclear situation in the triangle formed by the United States, Russia, and Kaliningrad, keeping in mind previous Russian declarations about full de-nuclearization of the Baltic region. Moscow denied the transfers to Kaliningrad, but we may also take into account the possibility that tactical nuclear warheads were never transferred from Kaliningrad to the core of Russia.[42] Regardless, it is a pity that after noisy statements from the different sides, nobody could say for certain what was going on in some installations of the KOR.

Ultimately, Kaliningrad is much more important politically than militarily. If certain EU and NATO expansions under discussion take place, Kaliningrad would not only be geographically separated from Russia, but would also become an "alien cell" within the homogeneous NATO and EU territory. As Russia seems militarily fully prepared for NATO's expansion, it is unclear how it will cope with the EU economic challenge. The economic and civilization gap between Kaliningrad and Poland or Lithuania is deep and is deepening. One of the last Kremlin Security Council meetings was exclusively focused on the implications of EU expansion for the district. Putin even criticized the economic and social situation of the district's population.[43] Many of Moscow's problems in Kaliningrad indicate an urgent need for cooperation on social, economic, and border and law enforcement issues between Russia, the entire European Union, Poland, and Lithuania. Real cooperation would improve matters within Kaliningrad and neutralize the region's nonmilitary challenges (organized crime, unemployment, health hazards, etc.).

However, such cooperation between the expanded European Union and Russia should not be viewed as a comparable price or a surrogate for NATO's Baltic enlargement. If the Baltic states joined NATO, the Russians would then see that there are no "red lines" on the territory of the former empire. It may prove that the West could not subordinate its political will to Russian imperial ambitions. It will help Russians to understand the superiority of long-term economic benefits over short-term costs in prestige. The overall result will be a rather swift adaptation on the part of Russia to new strategic realities and a focus on problems other than military ones. Poland's and Lithuania's membership in the European Union will create mutual benefits in regional and local economic cooperation. Unfortunately, Poland and the Baltic countries are not currently perceived in Moscow as potential valuable partners within NATO and/or the European Union. Thus, Russia may prefer to gain some kind of leverage over EU and NATO expansion, above all by playing on different priorities held by the United

States and leading western European countries, as well as emphasizing more important security issues.


## CONCLUSIONS AND RECOMMENDATIONS

Russia's security policy is based on the traditional concept of a hostile international environment and compromise among different schools of political thought. Thus far, Putin's decisions have not resolved issues about Russia's long-term geostrategic orientation. Putin's vision of Russia is not coherent and clear, though it seems so at first glance. Contrary to the satisfaction of many Russian experts, continuation of Putin's approach may damage Russia in the future. Putin wants to achieve strategic goals that are not compatible with the country's current potential or with opportunities for cooperation with the West and the developed countries (G-7). In essence, Russia is still trying to promote a multipolar world and to subordinate all the CIS countries.

In the sphere of traditional military policy, it is hard to expect speedy reform of the armed forces. Their buildup is impossible with present Russian priorities and possibilities, and with a prolonged second war in Chechnya. Only economic constraints can provide some changes, but the example of many previous plans and programs does not give much cause for optimism. U.S. plans for NMD will force the Russians to restructure their strategic arsenal, which means they will help in the general rationalization of its security policy against Moscow's will. Unfortunately, most of the Russian elite is still characterized by the Soviet mentality and security perceptions, with a hostile approach toward the United States and NATO. Renewed cooperation with NATO is directed at softening and weakening its cohesion by transforming it into a political organization like the OSCE or the United Nations.

Even Russia's position toward the European Union seems to be based on the balance of power, not on declared partnership and shared values. These relations will eventually involve the commercial interests of Russia's oil and gas companies to a greater extent (maybe one of the few effective policy instruments for the future). The issue of Kaliningrad will prove to be a serious test for the next round of NATO enlargement and Russian aspirations toward a real partnership with the European Union.

The newly formed global antiterrorist coalition is a good opportunity for testing Putin's long-term intentions, to see whether his policy is really based on the *Zapadniki* concept. The new international context may help in repeating to the Kremlin that the West is interested in a stable and prosperous—but not imperial—Russia. Such a dialogue would be based on strategic interests, which naturally may collide at some point. As a leading power in the Euro-Atlantic community, the United States may compromise on the issues of the ABM-NMD-START agenda. But those moves are mis-interpreted in Russia as not being connected with certain conditions. For example, they should not create an impression of double standards on issues of human rights, democratic values, and freedom of the press.

There is also a need to show counter-productivity in efforts to weaken NATO. Similarly, there is an urgent need to explain what is thought to be a common threat of transnational terrorism. It may be a tragic mistake to accept Russia's interpretation of what is and is not considered "terrorism." (See Moscow's tough policy toward the Chechen minority and Moscow's deep military cooperation with "states of concern" or rogue states.) Exactly this same clarification is needed in defining Russia's share in counter-proliferation efforts. In many critical ways the Kremlin's understanding of its share of the burden is contrary to U.S. understanding, as we can see in Moscow's unfinished transfers of weapons of mass destruction to irre-sponsible regimes. The United States may also indicate its long-term inter-ests in post-Soviet countries, which are afraid of aggressive Russian policy toward them. Many Russian experts think that the new global coalition is equally committed to transforming the CIS region into an "area of antiter-rorist responsibility," which implies acceptance by the West of lower polit-ical standards vis-à-vis pro-Moscow authoritarian rulers.

Washington now risks losing some of its influence in many countries and movements that had previously supported the United States, because of geopolitics as well as economic interests and political values. Historically Moscow has extended its power over its weaker neighbors, rather than focusing its efforts on internal modernization. Russians now need not only internal political and economic modernization after communism, but also adaptation to a new era of political and economic globalization. Apart from that, there is a need for a common Western policy toward Russia, oriented much more toward the problems of the Russian economy and society, rather than ambitions of the former Soviet "security community" elite. With this kind of clear policy, Putin and his advisers (or their successors) may recognize that American and Western investments and economic assistance will be contingent on deep internal reforms.

## NOTES

1. There are interesting conclusions about this in Alexander Kennaway, *The Mental and Psychological Inheritance of Contemporary Russia* (Sandhurst: Conflict Studies Research Center M20, 2000).

2. A similar distinction is made in Zbigniew Brzezinski, *Bolshaya shakhmat-naya doska* (Moscow: Myezdunarodnye Otnoshenya, 1999), pp. 120–35; and Dmitri Zamyatin, "Vlast' prostranstva i prostranstvo vlasti," *NG-Stsenari*, no. 6 (2001). For a discussion of differences between Great Russian "Nation-Builders" (Russophiles) and "Empire-Savers" (Eurasians), see Roman Szporluk, "Dilemmas of Russian Nationalism," *Problems of Communism*, no. 4 (1990), p. 118.

3. See works of modern *Zapadniki*: Dmitri Trenin, *The End of Eurasia: Russia on the Border Between Geopolitics and Globalization* (Moscow: Carnegie Endowment for International Peace, 2001); and Vadim Makarenko, *Kto soyuzniki Rossii?* (Moscow: Stradiz, 2000). See also Yuriy Davidov, *Should Russia Join NATO?* (Brussels: NATO Office of Information, 2000).

4. See S. Baburin, "Slavanskiye gosudarstva SNG piyered nashzestviem Atlanticheskikh Chennostey," *Nezavysimaya Gazyeta*, January 20, 2001, and A. Solzhenitsyn, *Rossiya v obvale* (Moscow: Russkaya Mysl, 1998).

5. From the long list of publications of contemporary Eurasianists see especially: Aleksandr Dugin, *Osnovy geopolitiki*, 3rd ed. (Moscow: Arctogeya, 1999); Aleksandr Dugin, "Evraziystvo: ot filosofii k polityke," *Nezavysimaya Gazyeta*, May 30, 2001; and Abdul-Vahed Nyazov, "Yevraziyskiy kontrglobalism—budushche Rossiyi," *Nezavysimaya Gazyeta*, February 3, 2001.

6. Citation from original Russian publication, version approved January 10, 2000: "Kontseptsya natsyonalnoy bezopasnosti Rossiyskoy Federatsii," *Diplomaticzeskiy Vestnik*, no. 1 (2000), pp. 3–13.

7. Citation from original version approved December 17, 1997: "Kontseptsya natsyonalnoy bezopasnosti Rossiyskoy Federatsii," *Rossyiskaya Gazyeta*, December 26, 1997. For further studies, see Jakub M. Godzimirski, "Russian National Security Concepts 1997 and 2000: A Comparative Analysis," *European Security*, vol. 9, no. 4, pp. 73–91; Mark Galeotti, "Russia's National Security Concept," *Jane's Intelligence Review*, no. 5 (1998).

8. Both documents are available in English translations under: http://www.fas.org.

9. The first person who proposed the multipolar model was Konstantin Sorokin of the Russian Academy of Science in 1993.

10. Such a strategy is explained in the Concept of Foreign Policy of the Russian Federation, approved on June 28, 2000. See relevant passages in document available on the Russian Ministry of Foreign Affairs (MFA) website: http://www.mid.ru.

11. See Putin's visits map in: Leonid Gankin, "Koniec russkogo otdiela," *Kommiersant-Vlast*, March 27, 2001.

12. It was declared especially in Primakov's report about the CIS published by the Foreign Intelligence Service (Moscow, 1993) and a document entitled "Strategic Course of Russian Federation Policy toward CIS States" (1995).

13. Maybe the reason for this is that only a small team (Security Council and General Staff) has prepared the doctrine without longer and serious consultations with the MFA and Duma, and with no influence from critical opinions. Based on author's interviews with persons from Russian diplomatic and academic circles, March 2000.

14. Alexei Arbatov, "Dillemy voyennoy politiki Rossyi," *Nezavysimaya Gazyeta*, November 16, 2000. Other *Zapadniki* experts (Pavel Felgenghauer, Alexandr Golts, Andrei Piontkovsky, and Dmitri Trenin) frequently use this kind of critical observation about military policy.

15. Details about the essence of their conflict were widely presented in Russian sources: Evgenii Bertlib, "Plan Kvasnina ili plen?" *Novaya Gazyeta*, August 21, 2000; and "Siergiyev i Kvashnin porugalis' iż-za d'yeneg," APN, July 28, 2000, at http://www.apn.ru/inside/2000/07/28/20000728154830.htm.

16. Under Putin there has been a stronger commitment than under Yeltsin to financial strengthening of the army. According to estimates by the Stockholm

International Peace Research Institute, Russian expenditures for national defense increased from 2.6 percent of gross domestic product (GDP) in 1999 to a provisional 2.75 percent of GDP in 2000, and further increases are budgeted for 2001. Increases have also been observed in military production: "Military Expenditures and Arms Production" found online at: http://editors.sipri.se/pubs/yb01/ch4.html.

17. Compare Sergei Ivanov, "Stroytielstvo Vooruzhennykh Sil budyet' otvyechat' vyzovam vremeny," *Krasnaya Zvezda,* August 10, 2000.

18. On the basis of sources in Note 15 and Oleg Odnokolenko, "Nye vynosi yadernyi musor iż izby," *Segodnya,* July 27, 2000.

19. This viewpoint is presented in almost all serious opinions about a new NMD-ABM-START architecture: Alexei Arbatov, "Eshcho raz o PRO," *Nezavysimaya Gazyeta,* July 4, 2001; Konstantin Cherevkov, "Stabilnost na novoi osnovie," *NVO,* no. 4 (2001); Vitaliy Tsygipko, "S Amerikoy—vmyestie ili porozn," *Nezavysimaya Gazyeta,* June 9, 2001; Sergei Rogov, "Slova groznye. A kakove budut dela?" *NVO,* no. 9 (2000); and Nikolai Sokov, *Vopros ne o zhelatelnosti, a o vozmozhnosti dialoga* (Moscow: MFTI, May 22, 2001).

20. Andrei Dyakov, *Rossiysko-amerikanskyie otnoshenya v oblasti sokrashchenya yadernykh vooruzhenyi: sovremennoye sostoyanye i perspektivy* (Moscow: MFTI, 2001). For detailed possibilities, organization, and potential of the Russian strategic triad, see *Nuclear Weapons, Fissile Materials, and Export Controls in the Former Soviet Union* (Washington, D.C.: CEIP-MIIS, 2001).

21. Those motives were rather underestimated in many reports, but realistic analyses were presented in Robert E. Hunter, "Nothing's Free in Dealing With Putin," *Los Angeles Times,* August 1, 2001; and Henry Kissinger, "What to Do With the New Russia," *Washington Post,* August 14, 2001.

22. "Teleobrashcheniye prezidenta Rossiyi Vladimira Putina," *Kommiersant Daily,* September 25, 2001.

23. Eduard Batalov and Viktor Kremenyuk, "Rossiya y SShA: druzya, sopernky, partnyory?" *Nezavysimaya Gazyeta,* October 6, 2001; and Sławomir Popowski, "Droga do Europy wiedzie przez Berlin," *Rzeczpospolita,* September 27, 2001.

24. For example, Russian forces in Central Asia are now reduced to garrisons in Tajikistan. But these forces have a semicolonial nature (the majority of soldiers are Tajiks) and officers are engaged in the narcotics trade (based on author's research in Tajikistan, August 2001).

25. About the approach to the role of nuclear weapons, see articles representative of internal discussions in the Russian Security Council and General Staff: Siyergei Kreydin, "O problemakh globalnogo i regyonalnogo yadernogo sdierzhyvaniya krupnomasshtabnoy agresii," *Voyennaya Mysl,* no. 5 (1998), pp. 49–53; Viktor Levshin, Andriey Nedelin, and Michail Sosnovskiy, "O primienienii yadernogo oruzhiya dla deskalacyi voyennykh diyeystviy," *Voyennaya Mysl,* no. 3 (1999), pp. 34–37; Andriey Nedelin, "O teoreticzeskich osnovakh yadernoy strategii," *Voyennaya Mysl,* no. 2 (1999), pp. 37–41; and Siergiei Voronin and Siergiei Brezkun, "Strategiczeskij vygodnaya assimetria," *NVO,* no. 36 (1999).

26. There is a good reconstruction of this meeting in Pavel Felgengauer, "Ogranichennaya yadernaya woyna? A pochiyemu by niyet!" *Segodnya,* May 6, 1999.

27. See sources in Note 25.

28. See documentation in the monthly journal of the Russian Federation's MFA, *Diplomaticheskiy Vestnik,* 1999–2001.

29. Compare Dmitri Rogozin, "Sammit sostoyalsia, glavnaya problema niye reshena," *NVO,* no. 20 (2000); and Oleg Odnokolenko, "Zvyezdne voyny: Epizod 2001," *Itogi,* April 24, 2001.

30. Vadim Solovev, "Washington cheliyesustremliyeno dvizhetsia k razvierty-vaniyu NPRO," *NVO,* no. 26 (2000).

31. See Table in *SIPRI Yearbook 2000* (Stockholm: Stockholm International Peace Research Institute, 2000), p. 357.

32. Compare data from: "Transfers of Major Conventional Weapons," http://www.editors.sipri.se/pubs/yb01/ch5.html.

33. This subject was raised again during a meeting of the Russian and German Ministries of Defense (according to Interfax, August 3, 2001).

34. Gazeta.Ru Service, September 26, 2001, at: http://www.gazeta.ru.

35. Amy Myers Jaffe and Robert A. Manning, "Russia, Energy, and the West," *Survival,* no. 2 (2001), pp. 133–52.

36. According to author's data collected from various Russian sources.

37. Slawomir Popowski, "Putin jedzie na spotkanie z NATO," *Rzeczpospolita,* October 2, 2001.

38. Based on studies of Ukrainian and Caspian cases during Putin's presidency. For details on the Russification of the Ukrainian energy sector see Marcin A. Piotrowski, "Ukraine: In Search for the Lost Time," *Rocznik Strategiczny 2000/01* (Warsaw: Foundation of International Relations, 2001), pp. 208–11 and 215–20.

39. For more information, see Marcin A. Piotrowski, "CIS: Second Chechen War....First Caspian?!" *Rocznik Strategiczny 1999/00* (Warsaw: Foundation of International Relations, 2000), pp. 179–98; and Marcin A.Piotrowski, "CIS: Security Above All," *Rocznik Strategiczny 2000/01* (Warsaw: Foundation of International Relations, 2001), pp. 220–39.

40. This had been implemented previously in Moscow's and Minsk's planning, but since the 1999 exercises Zapad (West) presented a high level of integration between separate units. The scenario is always based on NATO aggression, and this also presented the last large exercises of the Baltic Fleet (Interfax, August 16, 2001).

41. The KOR currently has 25,000 soldiers from all the armed forces. The ground forces have 850 tanks and 369 artillery systems. Most of the Baltic Fleet ships are stationed in the KOR, and most of them are quite modern (with fifteen years or fewer in service). In addition, Kaliningrad District has 5,000 soldiers from the Border Troops of the Federal Border Service and 1,000 soldiers from the Internal Troops of the Ministry of Internal Affairs. For detailed information, see Pavel Gazkun, *Rossiyskaya armiya na porogie XXI wieka* (Moscow: IEG Panorama, 2000), pp. 59–61, and Marcin Shiele, "Niebezpieczny sąsiad: Flota Baltycka i jej zaplecze," *Raport: Wojsko-Technika-Obronnosc,* no. 2 (2001), pp. 23–32.

42. "Tactical Nuclear Weapon in Kaliningrad," *CES Materials,* available at: http://www.osw.waw.pl.

43. Putin nominated its special representative, also responsible for monitoring relations between Kaliningrad District and the European Union. See notes from the council meeting: "Direktor Kaliningrada," *Vedomosti,* July 27, 2001; and "Kaliningradtskaya arifmetika," *Krasnaya Zvyezda,* July 28, 2001.

# 6

## Military Reforms in Russia

*Leonid Polyakov*

The Russian military, with its nuclear capability, is probably Russia's last holdover from its former superpower status. The success or failure of Russian military reform could very much influence Russia's place in the regional and global security equation—whether Russia becomes an asset, a liability, or something else.

After many unsuccessful attempts at military reform in the last decade, the latest started at the end of 2000, making prospects for military reform in Russia somewhat more promising. Strong political support from President Vladimir Putin has engendered many factors—at least as pertain to the military dimension of national security—which prompt a favorable view of the current efforts at reform in Russia. These include new military doctrine, vast intellectual and high-technology potential for the defense industry, and rich military traditions and experience.

However, a number of factors on the national level could blunt the success of military reform in Russia considerably, or simply make it irrelevant. These factors include the significant influence of the Soviet heritage (i.e., a "superpower" mentality, ethnic divisions, anti-Western politics), the acceleration of negative trends stemming from years of Mikhail Gorbachev's and Boris Yeltsin's attempts at reforms (i.e., weak economy, poor infrastructure, severe demographic crisis, etc.), and general deficiencies inherent in Russia's post-imperial (some would argue still imperial) structure.

Tension continues at the heart of military reform in Russia. On the one hand, since 1991 there has been a tendency toward a much more open and cooperative security relationship with the West, a change which could lead to a thoroughly transformed military, as well as Western assistance in transforming it. On the other hand, military policy continues to reflect apprehension of the United States and the North Atlantic Treaty Organization

(NATO) and gives priority to reviving Russia's military-industrial potential and its self-reliance. This apprehension limits the scope of military reform. At the same time, continuing economic weakness thwarts Russia's ability to achieve the goals for reform.

Russia's economic weakness, aggravated by its inability to end the policy of opposing the United States and NATO rather than cooperating with them, is at the heart of this chapter's largely negative answers to such questions as: Is Russia capable of ending its conscript system and establishing a professional army? Can Russia balance a strong nuclear capability with a robust conventional force structure? Moreover, the evident weakness of Russia's system of democratic civilian control over the military does not allow a definite answer to the question, "Can Sergei Ivanov make a difference as defense minister?"

This chapter discusses the prospects for military reform in Russia, and in this context it also touches upon the issue of Chechnya, inasmuch as this conflict has profoundly dangerous implications for Russia's military future and even for the future of Russia's statehood. Chechnya's aftermath could be much more dangerous for modern Russia than Vietnam was for the United States in the 1970s.

## PROSPECTS FOR MILITARY REFORM

During the last ten years Russia repeatedly attempted to expedite the reform of its military. All of the attempts were misguided, mismanaged, and unsupported by resources. Each time the result was basically the same—a reduction in numbers and the failure to change the deficient legacy inherited from the Soviet era. So, at the end of 2000, President Putin had to admit, "The current state of the troops and their leadership—morale, discipline, and military-technical state—still do not match the goals or the scope of the tasks facing them. We continue to talk and have meetings while the flywheel of reform runs mostly idle."[1]

In January 2001, President Putin adopted the Plan for the Development of the Armed Forces, to be in effect until 2005. The above-mentioned plan is secret and only excerpts were published. The State Program of Armaments Development, 2001–10, which logically has to be an integral part of the military reform plan, is still awaiting presidential approval.

From the information made public, the basic outline of the current military reform effort in Russia is as follows: 1) the army and the state power structure should be optimized, and parallel ineffective structures should be liquidated;[2] 2) the number of active servicemen should be reduced with simultaneous improvement of troop quality; the reduction of about 600,000 personnel from all military formations already has been approved, including 365,000 servicemen and 120,000 civilian personnel from the Defense

Ministry (currently employing 1.2 million military personnel) over the next three years; and 3) the defense budget is to be balanced from the current 70 percent (personnel) versus 30 percent on research and development (R&D), acquisition, and operations and management (O&M), in favor of a 60 percent to 40 percent ratio by 2006, and 50 percent to 50 percent by 2011, etc.[3]

The reform looks ambitious, and has the potential to become at least a qualitative success. However, the fact that the plan is secret provokes suspicion that the substantiation of the basic figures may not be strong enough and that the plan's developers were mostly concerned with avoiding criticism, rather than soliciting much-needed parliamentary and public support for the reform. In this case, if in the course of implementation the plan appears to lack proper resources and to not be well-coordinated with national priorities, Russia will ultimately have just one more reduction and restructuring of the military—meaning, another failed attempt at military reform.

To assess the prospects of military reform in Russia as they look now, the issue must be viewed through the prism of key factors on both national and military levels, which could influence the final outcome of the reform:

1) *Leadership*—political and military leadership;
2) *Strategy*—national security strategy (concept) and military doctrine;
3) *Resources*—economic and technological base for military reform; and
4) *People*—the country's demography and staffing of the military.

The combination of these factors will ultimately shape the prospects for military reform in Russia.

## LEADERSHIP

In terms of the post–Cold War role of civilian political leadership, Russia could be defined as a country traveling down the same road of transformation as the countries of central Europe. In fact, President Putin is determined to move Russia in the same direction. In addition, many indicators demonstrate that civilian leadership is now deeply involved in the process of military reform. For example, the wording of the new Military Doctrine of the Russian Federation unequivocally and specifically puts responsibility for providing "leadership of the construction, preparation, and use of military organization" on the president, who is the supreme commander in chief of the armed forces. Such clarity was not typical in previous documents.

After almost two years at the top of the Russian hierarchy, Putin continues to enjoy the unparalleled support of the Russian public, which is an important asset for any leader initiating reform. According to recent polls, more than 70 percent of Russians approve of Putin's work. Even more compelling proof that Putin intends to be an effective supreme commander in chief is his decision to appoint Sergei Ivanov, one of his most trusted men and his national security adviser, as minister of defense. There were numerous speculations about the hidden agenda behind this appointment, with the primary reason being Putin's realization that his vision of a strong, consolidated future for Russia will never come true without the restoration of Russia's military power. Therefore, this mission was entrusted to the best executive available.

Can Sergei Ivanov make a difference as defense minister? The short answer is probably yes. He is forty-eight years old and is a retired general of foreign intelligence. He prefers clear and concise reports. He is not superstitious and never forgives treason. He has never made friends with any of Russia's "oligarchs." He believes in a strong regulatory role for the state in the economy. As secretary of Russia's National Security Council, Ivanov proved to be preserving too much of the Soviet confrontational mentality. He has the reputation of being a conceptual designer respected by Putin—he was the key figure behind the preparation of the new Plan of the Development of the Armed Forces. It remains to be seen whether he will also be a persuasive and steady manager, capable of bringing about change in an environment as conservative as that of the armed forces. Therefore, the long answer to the above question will depend significantly upon how he manages his relations with the military brass, which represent a specific caste.

Many Russian generals reached their current rank based less on meritorious service than by having an aptitude for appeasing their senior civilian and military masters. They produced good shows during military exercises or provided good entertainment and lavish gifts for the inspectors and members of higher "commissions." These men may or may not have been criminal or dishonest at heart; they simply knew how the system worked and became masters at working it to their advantage. The result of applying that kind of "military leadership and management" led to difficulties in Afghanistan, and continued into the "new era" where it brought about the debacle in the first Chechen war and will apparently not bring much better results in the second. No wonder that during the 1990s numerous Russian generals were facing criminal charges for theft and abuse of power (though few were actually sentenced). So why should Russia's military leadership be expected to embrace civilian control, and (worse yet) modern methods of accountability in military training, operations, and management?

Andrei Nicolaev, retired general of the army and current head of the Duma's Committee on Defense, says that 90 percent of Russian generals are decent people, but somehow "it is not they who are holding the wheel of the main military structures…. On the surface always appear some mediocre figures."[4] Outside observers immediately predicted: "Ivanov is certain to run into conflict with the General Staff, which will resist any attempt to reduce its role to 'technicalities.' In this new bureaucratic clash, Kvashnin's General Staff could seek to mobilize support from the cohort of 'Chechen generals' and emerge as the center of opposition to any political solution in Chechnya. … The Chechen generals … are essentially demanding rebuilding the Soviet military machine, only slightly reduced in scale, and Putin might find it as difficult to explain to them the new economic realities, as it is to 'pacify' Chechnya."[5]

It did not take long for evidence of resistance to show in the open. In June, *Nesavisimaya gazeta* (Independent gazette) insisted that "Anatoliy Kvashnin (chief of the General Staff) is attempting to subdue all meaningful structures of the Ministry of Defense in order to leave Sergei Ivanov without real levers of power, to make him totally dependant on the chief of the General Staff. "According to General Kvashnin," the article continues, "the minister of defense should be the head of the support apparatus of the armed forces. The rest—military policy, military construction, financial issues—must be left to the General Staff."[6]

Kvashnin's position has two main roots. The first involves his resistance and ambitions to be the exclusive defense (not just military) adviser to the president for at least two major areas (Chechnya's military strategy and military reform priorities). He has received clear support from President Putin. The second is simply the traditional military bias against an inexperienced "civilian" outsider, who presumably cannot understand the true nature of the military.

However, an open conflict between Ivanov and Kvashnin (similar to that between former Minister Marshall Igor Sergeev and Kvashnin) is unlikely—both have the respect of the president. Relations between Ivanov and Kvashnin could be termed as "peaceful coexistence." Ivanov's political position vis-à-vis Kvashnin is much stronger, but the military brass, especially from the land forces, supports Kvashnin. Despite regular hints in the media about the pending ouster of Kvashnin, his dismissal is not certain. Until the country's political leadership decides that it is time to proceed to a political solution in Chechnya, or until Putin can find a replacement trusted by the ranks, as well as by himself, Kvashnin is likely to remain in his post.

The main problem here is not just the tension between a civilian minister and the top military officer, but the fact that civilian control over the military in Russia is severely handicapped now. After the Soviet Communist Party lost control of the military, Russia did not substitute viable democratic civilian control. Rather, control is limited mainly to the president and his top civilian officials, with no meaningful influence from the Russian parliament or society in general. This makes the top military personnel too influential in Russia compared to Western democratic society. Moreover, there is practically no system of civilian supervision within the military structure. In essence, the military basically controls itself and, where not directly threatening civilian power, it often holds modern Russian civilian leadership "hostage" due to lack of proper oversight. Important examples include Chechnya, the Slatina airfield takeover in Kosovo in 1999 after the end of NATO's air campaign, Russia's military-driven policy toward the Caucasus and Central Asia, etc.

The great strategist Karl von Clausewitz (1780–1831) pointed to a trinity in military affairs between ways, means, and political ends. When the ways and means do not support the political ends, they need to be reformed. In this regard, if in modern Russia the process of threat assessment is not quite relevant, then consequently the future model (ways) and the reformed military itself (means) in Russia is very much at risk of becoming inadequate to the nature of any future threat, as it was many times in the distant and recent past. The first war in Chechnya is a vivid example.

Let us look at what the commander in chief of the Russian Armed Forces (President Putin), tells his generals about one possible direction of the threat: "In the West, unfortunately, there are still forces that live by the laws of the Cold War. They still see our country as the main geopolitical enemy. In our consciousness this is largely in the past, but unfortunately, it persists in some circles in the West.... [Chechnya] should never be a source of radicalization of our population, and *immersion of Russia in the bloody mire of regional ethnic conflicts, [is] something our geopolitical adversaries dream of.*"7 What Western actor(s) did Putin consider to be Russia's "geopolitical adversaries"? Read on.

Furthermore, Minister of Defense Ivanov has demonstrated marked cohesion with his president: "NATO likes to repeat that it doesn't view Russia as a threat, but its expansion eastward continues unchecked," he said. "This detail, and Washington's plans to build a missile defense system, are the stumbling blocks in Russia-NATO relations. It doesn't look like Russia will be content with the role of 'junior partner' in its relations with the alliance. *Russia can bare its teeth too, as the West knows very well.*"8

Russia's Concept of Foreign Policy, as well as Russia's National Security Concept (both adopted by Putin in 2000), plainly imply that the main threat to Russia is the global hegemony of a single superpower in a unipolar world. The only superpower is the United States, which is also the key NATO player; thus Russia, by implication, will be in opposition to NATO.

Evidently, in the absence of real—rather than hypothetical or perceived—issues of conflict between Russia and NATO, the main reason for Russia's continuing opposition to NATO is probably internal: remnants of post-imperial trauma, the wounded psyche of a former superpower, the difficulty of openly admitting weakness vis-à-vis the United States and NATO. One example of this policy is found in the attempts to drive a wedge between NATO and the European Union over security matters.

Russia strongly opposes NATO enlargement, but at the same time seems much friendlier toward the European Union and sees no danger in EU expansion. Russia appears to view the European Union's Common European Security and Defense Policy (CESDP) as an alternative to NATO and has expressed a desire to take an active part in CESDP. Indeed, hopes that CESDP will move away from NATO and away from the United States are rather common among top Russian military officials.[9]

Some experts believe that after the terrorist attacks against the United States on September 11, 2001, relations between Russia and the United States may change. But so far the traditional anti-American agenda is still alive in the Russian military. Evidence exists that Russia's military and security officials are very concerned about a possible U.S. presence in the former Soviet republics of Central Asia north of Afghanistan: Uzbekistan, Turkmenistan, and Tajikistan. Among their basic concerns were not so much terrorism and the Taliban but possible spying over Russian military facilities by American planes and possible weakening of Russia's position in those countries.[10] According to the *Moscow Times*, Russia's top military brass was lobbying very hard against U.S. use of air bases in Uzbekistan or Tajikistan. "The problem is Russian policy in the region is not conducted by politicians, but by military people," an associate professor of history at Moscow State University said. "And unfortunately they lack vision: They still see America as the main enemy and the repressive governments as their main allies."

Nevertheless, the new Military Doctrine adopted by President Putin in 2000 is also less confrontational to the West. It is based on the realistic appraisal of politics and economics, rather than on ideology. The new doctrine stresses its own "transitional character," drops the previous tradition of mentioning of "world war," and puts more emphasis on diplomatic efforts as an important tool for avoiding conflict escalation. This looks like sober recognition of Russia's relative weakness vis-à-vis the perceived adversaries in the West in terms of conventional weapons and more reliance on nuclear power. Indeed, while the Russian military's nuclear component could still be regarded as on a par with NATO's (Russia has 9,196 nuclear warheads versus the United States at 8,876, Great Britain at 185, and France at 348[11]), Russia's conventional forces after the recent round of NATO enlargement are roughly 1:6 compared to NATO's.

Can Russia balance a strong nuclear capability with a robust conventional force structure or must it choose one or the other? Minister of Defense Sergei Ivanov also speaks about the "vital necessity of the balanced development of strategic nuclear forces and conventional forces." He argues that "to counterpoise them is wrong in principle. Both components are necessary." Their development, according to Ivanov, certainly needs to be prioritized, with strategic nuclear forces maintained at the "minimum appropriate level required to guarantee the infliction of unac-

ceptable damage to any aggressor under any condition." The priority for
conventional forces is on strengthening the "forces of permanent readiness," capable of accomplishing any mission when engaged in "possible
armed conflicts and local wars."[12] However, it is common knowledge that
the current "strong nuclear capability" has very dire perspectives. "With a
modern ballistic missile program struggling to produce ten rockets a
year,"[13] financially strapped Russia will have to significantly cut its nuclear
arsenal soon. For example, in the year 2000, only four missiles were produced instead of the ten that had been planned.

Additionally, the new Military Doctrine envisions a new role for nuclear
weapons, which could be used "in response to large-scale aggression using
conventional weapons in situations critical to national security." It is open
to speculation about who, when, and how it will be decided that a situation is "critical." This ambiguity could be interpreted as an attempt to off-
set conventional weakness by using nuclear deterrence, but with an
ambiguous hint that the threshold of resorting to nuclear weapons could
be significantly lower.

The potential also remains for Russia to ignore real security threats
(Muslim radicalism, hotspots in the Caucasus, Central Asia, and Southeast
Asia, and economic and social problems) in favor of a focus on perceived
and proclaimed security threats (NATO "expansion," U.S. "hegemony,"
etc.). In this case even the bright prospects for military reform in Russia
could once again make the future Russian military unprepared for real
threats, and leave it without proper strategic allies.


## RESOURCES

What are the foundations for Russia's security policy in terms of its economy and high technology? Opinions about the prospects for Russia's economy range very wide. There are many doomsday predictions about Russia's
economy either defaulting in 2003, or an infrastructure catastrophe not later
than 2005, yet current statistics say that the country's economy is growing,
if not booming. In 2000, federal budget revenues as a share of gross
domestic product (GDP) rose to more than 16 percent, while GDP grew
more than 7 percent. Arms production and arms sales have grown too.

This might appear as an optimistic outlook for Russian security policy in
terms of its economy. But the previous years left a heavy burden on the
ability of Russia's economy to sustain the country's defense. It is difficult
to disagree with Defense Minister Ivanov: "We must be realists; besides, we
must keep in mind that the state's economic potentialities are not limit-
less."[14] Even after the second significant year of growth, Russian military
output in 2000 represented only 17.5 percent of the 1991 level.

Again, Putin's leadership plays a decisive and encouraging role: "We have to know," he says, "the prognosis of economic development, to know how much we will have in the state budget through the next ten years, how much we should spend on defense and where specifically."[15] However, Russians also have to keep in mind that implementation of ambitious plans in Russia could be easily influenced by many unexpected events. The most dangerous of the potential impediments is probably the evident and endless infrastructure crisis. Ten years of scarce investment into pipelines, railways, power supply lines, storage facilities, bridges, etc., and mismanagement—even adventurism—brought about continuous natural and technological disasters, such as Chechnya and the Kursk submarine, and power shortages in the Far East.[16]

At the same time, if Russia's economy achieves the development predicted by Putin's analysts, by the year 2010 GDP will have grown 70 percent. This figure suggests that the defense budget could more than double from its current U.S.$7 billion to U.S.$15 billion by 2010. In terms of Western purchasing power parities—taking into account the low cost of Russia's labor, intellect, and resources—this figure might be able to purchase U.S.$30 billion to $40 billion worth of military power. But even then, Russia's budget will be approximately at the level of France's or Britain's budgets. Will this allow it to achieve military parity with the United States, China, or a united Europe? Certainly not. Russia might be able to put pressure on its neighbors, but it can do that now, even without reform. It probably suggests that in terms of economic impact on military reform, Russia ultimately will have to either rely primarily on nuclear forces against perceived "geopolitical opponents" or rely on conventional forces for dealing with local conflicts only. This is exactly what is envisioned in the new Military Doctrine, but it could still be too costly. Or Russia will have to take sides (i.e., form an alliance with either the United States, China, or Europe).

Even during the Soviet period, the military-industrial complex (VPK) devoted only a limited part of its capacity to weapons production. This was a deliberate aspect of state mobilization policy, which placed a premium on having spare capacity that could be quickly reoriented to military production in the event of war. Today, because of economic collapse and unemployment, the Russian defense industry uses even a smaller portion of its overall capacity than it did in Soviet times. As a result, there is a vast network of facilities that can be brought into production if investments and orders arrive. Unfortunately, however, these facilities are often in a state of dilapidation bordering on entropy. Moreover, lack of investment has impaired testing equipment and stopped development of many prospective weapons systems in favor of upgrading existing ones. Therefore, it is not accidental that the State Program of Armaments Development has considered directing as much as 40 to 45 percent of the state defense orders to R&D through the first six to eight years of reform, to end in 2010. Under this plan, the emphasis until 2005 would be placed on the modernization of armaments only, and only after that would Russia start the first significant acquisitions of new equipment. According to the first Vice Prime Minister Ilia Klebanov, "to have the possibility to buy new arms requires [the] concentration of [the] defense economy and maximum improvement of its effectiveness. Still, new arms should not be overly expensive."[17]

Therefore, to revive the defense production needed for military reform, Russia's economy must continue to grow and Soviet-era production and research facilities must be brought online. After the collapse of the Soviet Union, Russia inherited 73 percent of the Soviet Union's 55,000 defense production and research facilities. The Russian share of finished products of R&D in the former Soviet Union comprised as much as 91 percent. Whether Russia will be able to make good out of this situation will depend upon its ability to conduct the planned consolidations and mergers, and most of all on the ability to implement effective management, which Russia (and the former Soviet Union) often lacked before. This is especially evident in high technology areas. While in separate areas Russia had and still has state of the art technologies and products (which could serve as major deterrents to a would-be aggressor), the overall system of management is flawed. The Soviet tradition not to pursue cost effectiveness and its disregard of personnel's needs in favor of higher state goals could negate the benefits of having infrastructure and design.

When the Soviet Union collapsed, Moscow lost approximately 40 percent of its conventional military potential. Not only did it lose a huge chunk of troops, military infrastructure, and defense industry, but it also lost a pool of highly reliable military personnel from Ukraine, Belarus, and Georgia, etc. This loss is further exacerbated by the current deep demographic crisis, leading to the significant weakening of Russia's internal cohesion and geopolitical weight. "Since 1994 the adult population of Russia has fallen by two million, its young population by six million. In the past ten years mortality rates grew 31.8 percent for the whole population and 38.5 percent for the able-bodied population. In the past fifteen years the number of teenagers diagnosed as addicted to drugs has risen fifteen times."[18] Consider also: "Once American boys reach the age of sixteen, 88 to 90 percent of them go on to reach the age of sixty. But in Russia, only 58 to 60 percent of sixteen-year-old boys reach the age of sixty. Last summer ... he [Putin] warned the country that it could lose another 22 million people by 2015 [currently the Central Intelligence Agency estimates Russia's population at 146 million]."[19] According to former Secretary of Russia's National Security Council Andrei Kokoshin, it is demography that prompts the transition to the professional army: "We can't avoid [the] transition to [a] professional army, at least because of demographic reasons. Compensation for the reduction of its strength is possible only by improving the quality of training."[20]

Yet today, as for the last 127 years, Russia's armed forces are supplied by a draft: since January 1, 1874, when recruitment was abolished and despite Yeltsin's decree No. 722 of May 16, 1996, ordering a changeover to a volunteer system for all soldiers' and sergeants' positions from spring 2000. The major purpose of that declaration was probably political—not military—to increase the public's rating of the incumbent Yeltsin in the presidential elections in 1996.

Today the political declarations have turned promising once again. President Putin stated that: "A professional army is the goal to which it is possible and necessary to strive. To a significant degree we already have a professional army today: the navy, air force, missile forces, some other arms and services are 80 to 90 percent equipped with professionals. But can we reduce the draft today? I think that we can gradually reduce [the] draft and bring it to the minimum ... supposedly by 2010."[21]

Minister of Defense Ivanov said he "would slowly phase out conscription and train a smaller professional force—albeit in an evolutionary manner."[22] However, comments from professional military sound less optimistic. The Russian Defense Ministry believes that in the next five years Russia will not be able to form a professional army with sufficient national defense capability. This declaration was made by Colonel General Igor Puzanov, a top figure at the Defense Ministry. Puzanov agreed that the Russian military backs President Putin's intention of creating a professional army, but said lack of financing makes it impossible. General Puzanov said that the sums now allocated for the army are enough "only for providing food for servicemen." But they are not enough for the training process that would permit perfecting the professional skills of soldiers and officers.[23] The problem is not the conservatism of bloodthirsty generals or corrupt officials from the local recruitment commissions. Rather, Puzanov has once again proved the obvious: the key questions are not the pure desires (or wishful thinking) of politicians or the public, and not the formal difference between the ways of recruitment (whether by draft or by signing the contract). The key issue is that real professional soldiers, to be truly professional, should be intelligent and physically fit, they should be given all the conditions to gain and maintain their professional levels, and last, but not least, they should be paid accordingly if the country wants the best to stay in service. If those conditions are not met, we will see a continuation of today's catastrophic trend, reflected in the fact that one-third of all officers who retired from the armed services in 2000 were under the age of thirty.[24] Thanks to this attrition, almost half of all platoons are without a platoon leader. In sum, the officer corps is melting away.

As another Russian general admits, "A conscript costs us 17,900 rubles a year, while a professional soldier costs 32,000 rubles. A professional army would require the corresponding infrastructure, which would also cost a lot."[25] Right now a Russian contract soldier (corporal) is paid 1,294 rubles

(U.S.$44) a month; a *praporschik* (warrant officer) 1,541 rubles (U.S.$52); a lieutenant (platoon leader) 1,626 rubles (U.S.$55); a lieutenant colonel (battalion commander) 2,562 rubles (U.S.$86).[26] But even if those sums are tripled, it will hardly be enough, because of many other requirements, competition from the commercial sector, etc. Russia will hardly be able to pay for everything needed for the military to become professional by the year 2010.

The question of whether Russia is capable of ending its conscript system and establishing a professional army will not be answered until 2010. However, in terms of the prospects for military reform, a totally professional military is not the major priority. For example, it could be effective for Russia's armed forces to have 70 percent as a professional cadre and another 30 percent rotating as conscripts and then going into the reserves with further periodic training. But Russia must first improve its obsolete military education system, increase social benefits for servicemen, and finally change its military ethics in order to get rid of such current problems as *dedovschina* (hazing of draftees by their senior comrades), corruption, and abuse of power. The last challenge is no less challenging than ending the conscript system, but requires less money, which means Russia may be able to afford it sooner rather than later.


## THE CHECHNYA FACTOR

Chechnya might be worse for Russia than Vietnam was for the United States. In fact, if Russia disintegrates, the inability of the country's leadership to find a peaceful solution to the Chechnya problem would likely be the most important factor.

If Russia's leadership finds no peaceful solution to the unsolved Chechnya problem, further problems could ignite. The conflict could spill over the borders of the breakaway republic and destabilize the entire northern Caucasus. The Russian population may lose faith in the political leadership of the country. Regions could start moving away from Moscow. Russia's Muslim republics (Tatarstan, Bashkortostan, and the others), which are growing in population as the population shrinks in non-Muslim areas, are becoming more influential and may reorient toward influences outside the country.

Continuing the war in Chechnya is fraught with another danger: it has a negative influence on how military and security forces should deal with the civilian population. This can potentially influence the hostile behavior of the military not only in Chechnya but in other places too. The Russian military feels a sense of desperation when it bears the losses on "native soil."

In the "first" Chechen war Russian troops officially lost 3,959 persons, with 1,196 missing in action. Unofficial statistics put the number of military losses as high as 25,000 and the number of civilian losses between 25,000 and 100,000.[27] To this day statistics on the "second" Chechen war suggest that Russian troops already have sustained nearly the amount of casualties of the "first" war—more than 3,400 have been killed and more than 10,000 wounded.

But the population, and even the political leadership, seemingly lack proper appreciation for the casualties. According to Putin, "Often these are losses caused by lack of professionalism and not infrequently lack of elementary discipline. Such losses today are unforgivable."[28] This sense of desperation, accumulated with other similar feelings, can possibly precipitate unpredictable behavior by the military.

Certainly, war in Chechnya also brings many "advantages" to the military. It offers combat experience, enables the testing of new military equipment, exposes weaknesses, and prompts speedy reforms. However, the overall effect of this campaign at the national level could be catastrophic. As Russian military expert Pavel Baev recently suggested, "The most difficult decision [for Putin] is about Chechnya and, paradoxical as it may seem, the best case for Moscow in this war would be to return to political solutions and compromises, accepting yet another military defeat."[29]

Russia has three major policy options for trying to solve the Chechnya problem: political, military/security, and evolutionary. The most widely known political solution is that of former Vice Prime Minister Boris Nemtsov. This plan has two parts. First, make Chechnya a special subject of the Russian Federation and try to solve the problem by economic and administrative means. If the first approach fails, then in several years separate the mountainous territory of Chechnya from Russia and call it a "rebellious territory" with maximum isolation, giving the Chechen people the right to choose whether they live in the "flat" Russian territory or the mountainous "rebellious" one.

Regarding a possible military/security solution, some Russian security experts are seriously discussing the possibility of Russia adopting a policy akin to "the only good Chechen is a dead Chechen." This policy would be based on the assumption that most of the active, able-bodied male Chechen population would be physically exterminated. The Russian liberal democrat and leader of the Yabloko Party, Grigoriy Yavlinsky, in his address at the Nobel Conference in Oslo, Norway, recently warned that the policy of fighting the entire Chechen nation rather than just criminal elements brings growing disillusionment with Moscow's policy in the northern Caucasus.[30]

An evolutionary solution would entail a continuation of the current situation in hopes of wearing down the opposing force and attempting to find collaborationist locals. Russia would seek to break the will of the fighters by military and economic means; block sources of human and materiel for the rebels; and finally persuade the Chechen population to become part of Russia.

These solutions, though different, bear at least one resemblance—they each involve the possibility of marginalizing either the political leadership of the country, the military establishment, or the security services, and are ultimately fraught with instability and possible disintegration of Russia in the end. A political solution may alienate the military and security services, a military solution could make the political leadership hostage to the military and security apparatus, and an evolutionary approach bears danger for all.

## CONCLUSIONS AND RECOMMENDATIONS

The pace of military reform under Putin has noticeably intensified, but many key factors within Russia's military organization suggest that success will only occur under favorable conditions. The general prospects for military reform in Russia are still at significant risk of being held hostage to the national-level problems.

**Table 6.1 Basic Prospects for Military Reform in Russia**

|                | Leadership | Strategy | Resources | People | Chechnya |
|----------------|------------|----------|-----------|--------|----------|
| National level | +?         | –        | +?        | –      | –        |
| Military level | –          | +        | +         | +?     | +?       |

This table shows that prospects for military reform in Russia on the strategic (national) level are not very optimistic and questionable at best. However, within the military establishment itself the prospects look somewhat better and could possibly become the basis for noticeable progress, especially if Russia succeeds in further development of civilian control over the military and builds an effective military leadership selection system based on true merit, rather than personal connections. Past and current complicated relations between the minister of defense and the chief of the General Staff are certain to be of the same conflictive nature without solution of the above-mentioned problems.

In general, such a picture probably means that, despite the best efforts of Russia's defense-related agencies, the final outcome remains at risk. It could be hampered either by an inaccurate threat assessment on the strategic level, or the debilitating influence of the demographic situation, or the likely negative political consequences of the war in Chechnya. And these negative factors and misjudgments exist despite the political leadership's priority interest in military reform and its determination to provide necessary resources for the armed services. In sum, prospects for success of military reform in Russia are shaky.

As far as policy recommendations for the United States are concerned, analysis of past and current patterns in the development of Russian security policy in relation to the United States and NATO indicates that this policy derives from two major characteristic trends. The first trend, which is still stronger and generally dominant, could be defined as "assertive" and is based on Russia's continuous efforts to restore "Russian greatness," in particular by restoring a strong military capable of countering the "plots" of Western "geopolitical enemies." This is a policy more attuned to the desire for superpower status rather than to the real needs of the Russian people and Russian military. It is characterized by the demand to have equal say with the United States and NATO in all "geopolitical" issues and by Russian attempts to establish a "Russian sphere of influence" recognized by the United States and NATO. Another trend that could be defined as [reluctantly] "pragmatic" is less evident and is characterized by Russia's realization of the need to cooperate with the United States and NATO, and by a realization of the real benefits of this cooperation.

The question is still open as to which of the two major tendencies will prevail—the desire to show an "arrogant" United States its "proper" place vis-à-vis Russia by spending scarce resources on nuclear armaments, or a sober understanding that an "imperial virus" and opposition to the United States are exhausting Russia and making her spend scarce resources inefficiently.

Consequently, the United States and NATO will have to counter those two trends by adopting a more or less symmetrical approach, which could basically consist of two major complementary components: 1) "Engagement" through the continuation and strengthening of attempts to engage Russia in more cooperative relations and to persuade it of the nonthreatening character of U.S. policy; and 2) "Restriction" of the benefits for Russia in cooperating with the United States and NATO, as well as development of impediments and lost opportunities for Russia in case it chooses to continue with its confrontational approach.[31]

For example, on one hand, it was not that impossible for NATO countries to adopt a more favorable approach on cooperation with Russia by making a positive decision on a Ukrainian-Russian bid for medium transport aircraft An-70 (An-7x), and it was not that impossible to implement former U.S. Secretary of State Madeleine Albright's 1998 proposal for a joint U.S.-Russian peacekeeping brigade. But the West's domestic agenda and NATO experts' skepticism prevailed, and another golden opportunity to bring Russia closer to the West vanished.

On the other hand, if Russia successfully vetoes the accession of the Baltic countries into NATO, it will mean that the United States and NATO are still prone to a "Russia first" policy when it concerns Russia's self-proclaimed "sphere of influence," but still favor a "Russia out" policy when it concerns more vital interests of Western countries, the United States included. Such an approach is a remnant of the Cold War and provokes a freezing of Russia's confrontational mentality, rather than healing it.

## NOTES

1. Remarks by President Vladimir Putin at the Meeting of Senior Officers of Russia's Armed Forces, Moscow, November 22, 2000, http://www.mid.ru.

2. Vladimir Putin, "We made a step on the road to consolidation of the society," *Izvestia*, March 22, 2001.

3. Interview with the Minister of Defense of the Russian Federation, Sergei Ivanov, "Military reform is the organic part of changes in Russia," *Krasnaya zvezda*, April 24, 2001.

4. A. Nicolayev, "The Wheels of the Army Hold Mediocre Figures," *Moskovskiye novosti*, March 7–13, 2000.

5. P. Baev, "Putin's Military Reform: Two Trajectories for the First Presidency," Norwegian Atlantic Committee, *Security Policy Library*, no. 6 (2001), p. 13.

6. I. Korotchenko, "The General Staff Is Waiting for Changes. Kremlin Is in Search for the Substitution to Anatoliy Kvashnin," *Nesavisimaya gazeta*, June 7, 2001.

7. Remarks by Putin at the Meeting of Senior Officers of Russia's Armed Forces.

8. V. Sokirko, "Russia Is Looking for a Rambo," *Moskovsky Komsomolets*, May 31, 2001. Cited from WPS Monitoring Agency, www.wps.ru/e_index.html, by CDI Russian Weekly, no. 156, May 31, 2001, www.cdi.org/russia/.

9. Some high-ranking military officials put it in a very straightforward way: "We are ready to cooperate with the CESDP, but not with the one that is emerging now. If the CESDP is built up as something within, linked with, or additional to NATO, we cannot accept it. In other words, the problem is whether and when the CESDP moves out from under NATO's umbrella." See: V. Baranovsky, "Common European Security and Defence Policy," *National Security & Defense*, no. 9 (2001), pp. 40–42.

10. Ana Uzelac, "Central Asia Is Crux of Dilemma," *Moscow Times*, September 21, 2001.

11. As of January 2001. Appendix 6A, "Tables of Nuclear Forces," *SIPRI Yearbook 2001* (Stockholm: Stockholm International Peace Research Institute, 2001).

12. Interview of the Minister of Defense of the Russian Federation Sergei Ivanov, "Construction of the Armed Forces Will Correspond to the Challenges of the Time," *Krasnaya zvezda*, August 20, 2001.

13. I. Traynor, "Bush and Putin: The End of the Affair? With his latest visit, the American defence secretary has quashed Russian hopes of US magnanimity over arms control," *The Guardian* (United Kingdom), August 16, 2001.

14. A. Gavrilenko, "Russia Is to Modernize Its Navy," *Krasnaya zvezda*, May 24, 2001.

15. Vladimir Putin, "Positive Tendencies Do Exist," *Nesavisimaya gazeta*, December 26, 2000.

16. P. Baev, "Putin's Military Reform," p. 12. "The ongoing severe energy crisis in the Far East shows how fragile the most basic infrastructure has become, but going from one *Kursk*-like disaster to another—pragmatic policy as that might appear—would amount to following a pattern of state collapse."

17. NewsLine: "Russia Plans to Increase the Financing of Defense Research," Kyiv, Center for Army, Conversion and Disarmament Studies, August 5, 2001, http://www.defence-ua.com/rus/news/?day=05&month=08&year=2001.

18. I. Rodionova, "Latest Data on the State of the Population's Health Are Shocking," *Obshchaya gazeta,* February 28, 2001.

19. J. Dillin, "The Incredible Shrinking Russia," *Christian Science Monitor,* February 22, 2001.

20. R. Zaripov, "Army Service Only Teachers Will Be Able to Avoid," *Moskovsky komsomolets,* March 3, 2001.

21. Vladimir Putin, "We made a step on the road to consolidation of the society," *Izvestia,* March 22, 2001.

22. V. Bennet, "Pity the Russian conscript, his mum is his best hope of escape …," *The Times,* March 30, 2001.

23. Gosudarstvo, "Russia Cannot Have Professional Army in 5 Years to Come," June 5, 2001, http://www.prabda.ru.

24. K. Matvev, "If Studied and Retired—Pay," *Nesavisimoye voennoye obozreniye,* May 25–30, 2001.

25. V. Komarov, "Russia's Army Still Mired in Conscript Crisis," *Russia Journal,* April 24–30, 2000.

26. "Size of Military Pay," *GRANI.RU,* January 18, 2001, http://www.grani.ru/mil_spending/articles/allowance.

27. A. Trubinsky, "How Much Does the War Cost," *Deloviye liudi,* no. 110 (May 2000), pp. 8–12.

28. Remarks by Putin at the Meeting of Senior Officers of Russia's Armed Forces.

29. P. Baev, "Putin's Military Reform," p. 13.

30. Grigory Yavlinsky, lecture at the Nobel Institute, Oslo, Norway, May 30, 2000, http://www.eng.yabloko.ru/Publ/2000/Speech/yavl-oslo.html. "I think that this war has a dead end, given the way in which the government is implementing its policy there…. Now many people see that this conflict has reached an impasse: lots of blood is being spilt, but no solution is being found."

31. D. Karns, "NATO Relations with Ukraine: Prospects for Progress," *National Security & Defence,* no. 8 (2000), p. 36. "The best way to solve the 'Russia problem' is to give it fewer and fewer alternatives to being a constructive member of a peaceful, globalized community, where the final wrong choice is to collapse under the weight of its own irrelevance."

# 7

# Russia's Policy toward Ukraine, Belarus, Moldova, and the Baltic States

*Marko Mihkelson*

Vladimir Putin's first year and a half as president of Russia, since his election in March 2000, has revealed trends and directions that will likely determine the Kremlin's foreign policy for the coming years. The continuing crisis of the system is borne out mainly by the government's controversial and often inadequate world outlook, which results from the fall of the Soviet empire. The crisis also makes Russia a very uncomfortable partner for its western neighbors.

What are Russia's goals in its own geographic area? Is Russia capable of significantly influencing the political and economic situation in neighboring countries? Answering these questions is crucial for understanding the possible scenarios that could influence the future of the entire region from the Baltic Sea to the Black Sea.

The terrorist attacks against the United States on September 11, 2001, have already changed—and probably will change even more—the configuration of international affairs. Russia will probably play a more substantial role than during the 1990s, after the disintegration of Soviet Union. It is in the West's interest to engage Russia as much as possible, since Moscow's support in the fight against terrorism is vital for the worldwide campaign led by the United States. At the same time, President Putin has made clear that it is in Russia's interest to create a new agenda for relations with the West. Yet he is also trying to use the current international situation in his own favor.

Russia's deeply rooted isolationism (the saying "righteous loneliness in a hostile world" is not unfamiliar even today) and the fundamentally different interpretation of the principles of international relations and the international system[1] are real challenges for a new Russian-Western alliance. The ongoing ideological battle between Westernizers and slavophiles (or Eurasianists) perennially keeps Russia at some distance from the Western world, even if Moscow has declared Europeanization to be a priority.

One of the most influential foreign policy scholars in Russia, Aleksandr Dugin (also known as one of the ideologues of the Russian General Staff), describes Russia's goals for its western neighbors in his book, *Osnovy geopolitiki* (Basis of geopolitics). New borders are unavoidable and some regions should be divided up again, he writes. In every case, the most important goal is to create friendly, neutral units with maximum freedom in cultural, economic, and social spheres, but strategically dependent upon Moscow. The ultimate goal is the "Finlandization" of the whole of Europe, but first the territories most closely linked to Russia should be reorganized.[2] However, even scholars who are known as Westernizers, such as Vyatcheslav Nikonov, have set forth a very demanding position vis-à-vis the West. For example, Nikonov has declared openly that the North Atlantic Treaty Organization (NATO) should either cooperate with Russia and leave the Baltic states out of the next round of enlargement or face the Taliban without Russia's help.[3] Both Dugin and Nikonov know that almost one-third, or 31 percent, of Russians believe that the goal of Russia's foreign policy over the next 10 to 15 years should be to recapture its status as a superpower, similar to that of the former Soviet Union.[4]

## THE SLAVIC TRIANGLE PLUS MOLDOVA

Relations with Belarus and Ukraine, as well as with Moldova, have been the main priorities in Russia's foreign policy, especially within the context of the Commonwealth of Independent States (CIS). This has been confirmed by the emphasis placed on Russia's Foreign Policy Concept approved by the Kremlin in 2000, and by the fact that the first foreign visit of Vladimir Putin as president was to Minsk on April 16, 2000.[5]

Russia has not been secretive about its belief that the territories of the former Soviet Union belong to the sphere of Russia's "vital" interests. This has been emphasized in the "near abroad policy" and repeatedly on different political levels. By 1994, the Russian Foreign Intelligence Service (SVR), in its public report "Russia-CIS: Does the Position of Western Countries Need to Be Changed?" had already declared that Russia must play an active and dominant role in the area that was once the Soviet Union.[6]

In September 1995 President Boris Yeltsin issued an official document on Russian policy toward the CIS that codified Russian goals. It stated that

Russia's policy toward the CIS was to create an economically and politically integrated association of states capable of claiming its proper place in the world community ... to consolidate Russia as the leading force in the formation of a new system of interstate political and economic relations in the territory of post–[Soviet] Union space.[7]

Later, in the spring of 1996, the influential Council of Foreign and Defense Policy, announced that the main objective of Russian foreign policy is to "prevent the military and political dominance of other countries in the territory of the former Soviet Union." It was also emphasized that in order to achieve this objective two principal formulas must be followed: 1) leading as opposed to controlling; and 2) economic domination instead of political responsibility.[8]

Various politicians and experts have repeatedly declared Russia's strong interests in the territories of the former Soviet Union. The leader of the Russian communists, Gennadi Zyuganov, in his book *Geography of Victory: Principles of Russian Geopolitics*, published in 1997, wrote very vividly:

> Russia is again facing the need to solve the same three geopolitical tasks that it faced four hundred years ago: access to the Baltic Sea and to the Black Sea, gathering Russian territories, and determining the exact borders in the south and southeast. But now we do not have in reserve the three hundred years to solve these tasks.[9]

Yuri Luzhkov, the mayor of Moscow and one of the leaders in unifying Yedinstvo-Otetshestvo, said on July 29, 2001, in Simferopol, Ukraine: "I think that Crimea is Russian territory. It always has been Russian and never belonged to Ukraine. It should be marked in history."[10]

These statements and declarations have remained slogans. Russia has tried actively throughout the 1990s to use its power of influence and leadership in the territories of the former empire. It has been more successful in some countries (for example, Belarus), less successful in others (for example, Turkmenistan), and has experienced almost no success in a third group of countries (the Baltic states). According to this division, different approaches and political-economic mechanisms of pressure and coercion have evolved, which are analyzed below.

As stated previously, relations with Belarus, Ukraine, and Moldova have been a principal target of Russian foreign policy in recent years. During and after the collapse of the Soviet Union, the leadership of these countries emphasized national independence. At present, however, all three have declared Russia to be their strategic partner.[11]

In fact, Belarus has concluded negotiations for a Russian-Belarusian union. Moscow still keeps Minsk at some distance, because at present Russia does not need the additional economic problems and political responsibility that could result from deeper integration with Belarus. But at the same time Russia keeps Belarus facing firmly to the East. Nobody in the West seems interested in dealing with Belarusian President Aleksandr Lukashenko, which makes it easy for Russia to control this territory.

Without a doubt the cornerstone of Russia's foreign policy toward its immediate neighbors to the west is Ukraine. It is well known that Ukraine always played a critically important geopolitical role in Russian history. Indeed, losing Ukraine in 1991 was probably the most painful wound sustained by Russia in the course of the Soviet Union's disintegration. On the one hand, Russia definitely wants to reintegrate Ukraine at least within the CIS. On the other hand, Moscow has realized that achieving this goal would be very time-consuming or even close to impossible.

Moldova is still far behind Belarus and Ukraine in the hierarchy of Russia's interests, and it does not play an influential role in the region. Moldova's political and economic dependence on Russia makes this area a much easier candidate for Moscow to control or reintegrate.

The Kremlin's tactics and strategy are obviously part of Russia's move to dominate its western neighbors. First, Russia is using the political immaturity and economic weakness of Ukraine, Belarus, and Moldova to its advantage. This allows the Kremlin to integrate those countries into Russia's sphere of influence. It also means keeping or supporting military bases and activities within these countries and playing heavily on feelings of Slavic kinship. All those aspects are discussed below.

Russia has skillfully exploited the vulnerability of the political systems in Belarus, Ukraine, and Moldova. The processes of transition in those countries have been difficult to the point of being negative, especially when considered vis-à-vis the norms of civil society. Even more, we cannot be sure that all three countries will be viable as independent and functionally effective entities.

*Belarus.* The drift of Belarus into Russia's sphere of influence started as early as 1994, when Aleksandr Lukashenko was elected president. The former director of a state-owned collective farm (sovkhoz) was quickly, and without difficulties, able to suppress the political opposition. The opposition politicians were either forced to leave the country (as in the case of Zenon Pozdnyak) or were eliminated by the secret service (as were Yuri Zakharenko, Viktor Gontchar, and others).[12]

On February 21, 1995, Moscow and Minsk concluded a treaty of friendship and cooperation, and two years later, on April 2, 1997, the Russia-Belarus Union Treaty was signed. These documents have been followed by many other agreements that establish the attributes of the union, including the agreement to introduce a joint currency—the ruble—in 2008.

President Lukashenko's personality and ambitions have unquestionably determined the foreign policy orientation of Belarus. By 1995, Lukashenko had told his aides that his dream was to become the president of the union and live in the Kremlin.[13] On September 9, 2001, Lukashenko easily won a second term.

*Ukraine.* Absorbing Belarus has been an easy task for Moscow; however, winning back Ukraine will require much more effort. For example, in June 2001, while visiting Slovakia, Ukrainian President Leonid Kuchma announced that Ukraine would remain an independent state forever and not join the Belarus-Russia Union under any circumstances. Yet Kyiv's recent policy has shown signs of a growing orientation toward Moscow.

The increasing orientation toward Moscow has coincided with deep crises in domestic politics that were generated and directed by local secret services. It started with the disappearance and murder of independent journalist Georgi Gongadze in September 2000, along with the release of tapes to the public that incriminated President Kuchma. The ensuing scandal—which lasted for months—has tarnished Ukraine's reputation to a considerable degree. In addition, Ukraine has acquired an international reputation as an extremely corrupt state, perhaps second only to Nigeria and war-torn Yugoslavia. In the eyes of the European Union, Ukraine has reached the critical point where every step can bring about a new split on the continent.[14]

Kyiv's foreign policy rhetoric began to change markedly in autumn 2000, when President Kuchma replaced the Western-oriented foreign minister Boris Tarasyuk with Anatoli Zlenko. The latter made his first foreign visit to Moscow, thus declaring the inevitability of relations between the two neighboring nations. Also, President Kuchma has not concealed his sympathies. In February 2001, during a meeting with President Vladimir Putin of Russia in Dnepropetrovsk, he heralded the beginning of a new era in relations between the two states.

The growing number of political consultations between Kyiv and Moscow clearly shows Ukraine's drift toward closer ties with Russia. For example, last year presidents Kuchma and Putin met eight times. In July 2001, they met four times, and during the same period Putin held talks in Moscow with a head of Kuchma's administration and with Ukraine's secretary of national security. Russian Foreign Minister Igor Ivanov also visited Kyiv in July.

Undoubtedly, Russia's most significant step in moving closer to Ukraine was the naming of former Prime Minister Viktor Chernomyrdin as ambassador. Chernomyrdin is also the full economic representative of the Russian president in Kyiv, which is an unusual position for a regular ambassador. When he sent Chernomyrdin to Kyiv, President Putin said, "the time has arrived when we have to seriously consider the development of relations with one of our partners—Ukraine."[15] Ukrainian opposition politician Yulia Timoshenko characterized Putin's move as naming Chernomyrdin the new prime minister for Ukraine.[16]

In interviews, Chernomyrdin has made clear that it is in Moscow's inter-

est to achieve a strategic alliance with Ukraine. In fact, he has compared
Kyiv's desire to be a neutral country to Poland's fate in the 1930s.[17]
"Ukraine is not a western country but belongs to Slavic civilization and
Orthodox culture. Hundreds of years living together makes Ukraine
Russia's natural partner," Chernomyrdin told *Nezavisimaya Gazeta,* adding
another remark that is very typical of Russia's attitude toward the current
state of world affairs: "Nobody awaits either Russia or Ukraine in the West.
They'll try to be friends with us, they'll promise a lot to us, but they'll never
declare us as their natural partners."[18]

Interestingly, Putin's decision to send former Prime Minister
Chernomyrdin to Kyiv coincides completely with a group of 1996 recommendations from the Russian Council of Foreign and Defense Policy concerning how to force the CIS states to join Moscow. Leading analysts in
Russia wrote that one method would be to appoint respected Russian
politicians to those states as ambassadors.[19]

*Moldova.* Moldova is an excellent example of how a change of direction
in domestic politics also determines foreign policy trends. The communists
who achieved an overwhelming victory in the early parliamentary elections
(71 seats out of 101) in February 2001 have already declared Russia to be
their strategic partner, even though Moldavian foreign policy stresses "continuous neutrality."

Moldova also offers proof of how Stalin's heritage influences current
international affairs. Though 90 percent of the population in Moldova is
Romanian, the capital city of Chisinau has stronger political links with
Moscow than with Bucharest. Moldova's president, Vladimir Voronin, is
Russian by nationality and thus naturally has more connections with Russia
that could hasten Moldova's drift back under Russia's strategic influence.

A very important issue with Moldova is the problem of the Transnistria
Republic. This conflict gives Russia a perfect reason to be an active and
decisive force in the region. Using the principle of divide and conquer,
Russia is still controlling the conflict to further its own interests. (It uses the
same tactics in Caucasia.) A good example of Russian tactics toward
Moldova is the difference in the price of Russian natural gas. If Chisinau
pays U.S.$80 per thousand cubic meters, then Tiraspol (the capital of the
Transnistria Republic) pays only U.S.$45 for the same amount.

As mentioned below there are strong positive feelings in Chisinau about
the possibility of Moldova joining the Belarus-Russia Union. The first step
in this direction could be the Treaty of Friendship, which is about to be
signed by the presidents of Moldova and Russia.

In addition to political immaturity, their economic dependence on Moscow
makes Belarus, Ukraine, and Moldova easy targets. All three states clearly ori-
ent their foreign trade toward Russia. For example, Russia's share of Belarusian
external trade is 58.7 percent, of Moldova 40 percent, and of Ukraine 38 per-

cent (see Table 7.1). But if one considers the energy requirements of these states, then Russia's strategic importance becomes even greater.

According to Russian Foreign Ministry data, Ukraine is able to cover, with its own resources, only 10 percent of its oil requirements and 15 percent of its natural gas requirements. Dependence on coal imports is 30 percent; in fact, 66 percent of Russia's total exports to Ukraine consist of energy-related goods, mainly natural gas.[20] Moldova is totally dependent (99 percent) on energy imports from Russia, as is Belarus. Since August 1, 2001, both Ukraine and Moldova reconnected to Russia's energy system, which makes those countries even more dependent on Russia and Russia's economy.

Also, Ukraine and Belarus are important foreign-trade partners for Russia. In 2000, Ukraine was Russia's top export purchaser and was third in imports, while Belarus was third and second, respectively.

**Table 7.1. Ukraine's Main Partners in Foreign Trade According to Their Share in 2000**

| Export | % | Import | % |
|---|---|---|---|
| Russia | 23.0 | Russia | 48.1 |
| China | 5.8 | Germany | 8.6 |
| Turkey | 5.5 | United States | 4.0 |
| Germany | 5.1 | Poland | 3.3 |
| Italy | 4.4 | Italy | 2.8 |
| Belarus | 4.3 | Belarus | 2.4 |

Source: The Economist, *Pocket World in Figures 2001.*

Foreign investments have not been able to balance the economies of these states. A drastic example is Belarus, where reforms have been the slowest and where the economy is still subject to very strict state regulations. This is why foreign direct investment accounts for only 0.5 percent of gross domestic product (GDP).

Russian investment activity has grown markedly in Ukraine. According to official data, Russian companies invested more than U.S.$200 million in 2000 by buying Ukraine's strategically important assets. Though the volume of Russian investments does not exceed one-tenth of all direct investments in Ukraine's economy, the trend in recent months indicates the increase of Russia's money and influence. Analyst Bogdan Gavrilishin describes this trend as carefully planned economic aggression against Ukraine.

Several large and powerful Russian companies already have very strong market positions and strategic assets in Ukraine. For instance, Russkii Alyuminii owns an aluminum factory in Nikolayev and one of the biggest banks in Ukraine—UkrSibbank. Alfa-Group owns the oil company TNK-Ukraine, which controls up to one-fourth of Ukraine's oil market. Alfa-bank in Kyiv is close to being one of the top five banks in Ukraine. Lukoil owns an oil refinery in Odessa and a chemical factory in Kalushk. Finally, Gazprom owns the chemical factory Rivneazot; is close to buying a pipe factory in Harzysk; and owns the bank NRB-Ukraine, which is linked to the National Reserve Bank of Russia, in which Ambassador Viktor Chernomyrdin has shown interest.[21]

During Russian Prime Minister Mikhail Kasyanov's visit to Chisinau on October 5, 2001, he was handed a list of sixty Moldavian enterprises that are for sale and desperately need Russian investments. In the year 2000, Moldova was the number-one country for Russian direct investment per capita, followed by Belarus and Ukraine.[22]

Without a doubt one of Russia's objectives in keeping Belarus, Ukraine, and Moldova off the Western path is to ensure an ongoing Russian military presence in these countries. Moreover, the westward-looking activities of military structures have significantly decreased following President Putin's rise to power.

Naturally, the most intense military cooperation enjoyed by Russia is with its direct ally Belarus. Though Belarus does not currently house any Russian military bases, Moscow and Minsk are moving toward the formation of joint armed forces. At a meeting of defense ministers in Minsk in April 2001, the union's military doctrine, the integration of legislation, and the joint use of military infrastructures were discussed. At present, Minsk and Moscow are each responsible for their own military forces in case of a military threat. In the future, there are plans to set up joint bases in Belarus, in the Moscow military district, and also in the Kaliningrad *oblast*.[23] Though the military doctrine of this union has not been made public yet, it has become known that the main geopolitical threat is considered to be NATO's strong military potential and its plans to extend into the Baltic states.[24]

In January 2001, Moscow and Kyiv concluded a cooperation treaty whose fifty-two clauses make very unlikely any further active participation by Ukraine in NATO's partnership programs as ratified in November 1998. According to this treaty, Russia will have unlimited rights to organize military exercises on Ukrainian territory, to form a joint naval unit with Kyiv, and to jointly produce weapons.

On July 22, 2001, the Joint Command Desk of Russia and Ukraine was launched in Sevastopol to monitor the Black Sea area. At the same time both sides are establishing a joint naval brigade agreed upon in January 2001. The joint brigade is inevitable, given that Russia already has a naval presence in Ukrainian ports, but it will a priori put a stop to large-scale cooperation by Ukraine with NATO, for example. In addition, the treaty covering division of the Black Sea fleet was finally concluded in 1997 after years of dispute. It is evident that military cooperation between Moscow and Kyiv has significantly intensified in the last few years.

A different situation is developing in Moldova. As mentioned above, the communists coming into power made it almost inevitable that Moldova would join the union of Belarus and Russia. Moldovan politicians also support Russia's keeping its Fourteenth Army in the Transnistria Republic. As we know, at the 1999 summit of the Organization for Security and Cooperation in Europe (OSCE), Russia agreed to remove all its military forces and equipment from Moldova by the end of 2001. Today only two military echelons have left Moldova while it would take at least 150 echelons to move out all of the equipment. At present, the arsenal of the former Fourteenth Army consists of 49,476 firearms, 805 artillery guns, 4,000 cars, and 655 units of various military equipment. This arsenal is enough to arm four rifle divisions.[25] Though Moscow has declared its readiness to withdraw the weaponry from Moldova, so far everything has been done to slow this process as much as possible. Russia has not concealed the fact that in the context of NATO enlargement, a Russian military presence in Moldova is clearly in Moscow's interests.

In spreading its dominance over Belarus, Ukraine, and Moldova, Russia has frequently brought up and emphasized their common national-religious background. An emphasis on Slavic identity and geographical proximity (see Table 7.2) was part of Moscow's politics throughout the 1990s. During the past few years, however, Moscow has become more methodical. In early June 2001, the first Conference of Russian, Belorussian, and Ukrainian nations took place in Moscow, where the leader of the Russian delegation was the chairman of the Duma, Gennadi Seleznyov. Seleznyov characterized the conference as a platform from which the extensive unification movement of these nations could begin, as could pressure on other countries neighboring Russia to voluntarily join this union.

### Table 7.2. Ukraine, Belarus, and Moldova: National-Religious Composition

| | Belarus | Ukraine | Moldova | Total |
|---|---|---|---|---|
| Territory | 207,600 km$^2$ | 603,700 km$^2$ | 33,700 km$^2$ | 845,000 km$^2$ |
| Inhabitants | 9.99 million | 49.28 million | 4.3 million | 63.57 million |
| Russian inhabitants | 1.1 million or 11% | 10.8 million or 21% | 0.56 million or 13% | 12.46 million or 19.7% |
| Orthodox | 80% | 80% | 99% | 86% |

Source: *The World Almanac and Book of Facts 2000.*

Moscow Patriarch Aleksius II pointed out that Russia, Belarus, and Ukraine were Christianized at the same time, that they share a common history, and are soul mates that cannot live without each other. Metropolitan of Smolensk and Kaliningrad Kirill (also the Russian Orthodox Church spokesman) announced that the church considered the dissolution of the Soviet Union to be a sin. Participants declared that the "creation of the political union is the pledge of our salvation."[26]

Emphasizing the so-called Slavic card is a clear example of how the post-imperial identity crisis influences present-day attitudes and approaches. Playing on a sense of national belonging to form a political movement, rather than basing it on political ideas, is a prime example of political immaturity. Yet, this is still one of the strongest positions from which Russia backs its aspiration to control and influence the territories of the former Soviet Union.

During the last year, we have seen a very strong drift in Ukraine and Moldova toward backing the idea of reunification with Russia. In July, the "Russian Bloc" political movement was formed in Ukraine. This group will participate in the parliamentary elections scheduled for March 2002, with the goal that the Russian people should be united again. On July 16, 2001, demonstrations were held in eighty-seven towns throughout Ukraine to support this very same idea.[27]

In the beginning of August a new political movement was established in Moldova that supports the idea of unifying Moldova with the Slavic triangle—Russia, Belarus, and Ukraine. One of the leaders of the new movement, Valery Klimenko, told news agencies that the organization plans to collect signatures for a referendum on joining the Union of Russia and Belarus.[28]

On July 25, 2001, the presidents of Ukraine, Belarus, and Russia met in Vitebsk at the Slavic festival to show their common aspiration to build closer ties on the level of national identity rather than shared values. It seems that the Slavic card and common background (Soviet mentality) of top politicians in each country makes it easier for Moscow to get Kyiv and Minsk to back its interests.

## THE BALTIC STATES

Though the Baltic side of Russia's foreign policy has been unfruitful and depleted of ideas, Moscow does not seem willing (or able) to abandon its intention of keeping this region in its sphere of influence as long as possible. In fact, one could argue that during the 1990s Russia did everything possible to push the Baltic states to join the Euro-Atlantic alliances.

Russia's attitude toward the Baltic states has been influenced by several factors:

(1) The Baltic states have belonged to Soviet and Russian empires;
(2) Different outlooks and understanding of history;
(3) Sizeable Russian populations reside in the Baltics, especially in Estonia and Latvia, including a large number of Russian citizens;
(4) The Kaliningrad enclave is a critical component of Russia's security startegy; and
(5) There is a conflict of interest between Russia and its western neighbors.

Russia's Baltic policy has developed from the objective of forcing the Baltic states into international isolation, thus making them more prone to Russian influence. By playing the "Russian minority card," the Kremlin hoped in particular to make Estonia's and Latvia's paths into European groupings that honor human rights at least very difficult if not impossible.

**Tables 7.3 Ethnic Composition of Latvia by January 1, 2001**

| | | |
|---|---|---|
| Latvians | 1,367,395 | 57.9% |
| Russians | 693,382 | 29.4% |
| Belorussians | 95,422 | 4% |
| Ukrainians | 62,545 | 2.6% |
| Poles | 59,003 | 2.5% |
| Lithuanians | 33,021 | 1.4% |
| Others | 49,563 | 6.2% |
| Total | 2,360,331 | 100 % |

Sources: Latvian Register of the Population.

**Table 7.4. Ethnic Composition of Estonia by January 1, 2001**

| | | |
|---|---|---|
| Estonians | 939,310 | 65.3% |
| Russians | 403,925 | 28.1% |
| Ukrainians | 36,467 | 2.5% |
| Belarussians | 21,125 | 1.5% |
| Finns | 12 762 | 0.8% |
| Tatars | 3,232 | 0.2% |
| Others | 22,376 | 1.6% |
| Total | 1,439,197 | 100 % |

Sources: *Statistical Yearbook of Estonia 2001*.

As shown by Tables 7.3 and 7.4, a remarkably high percentage of the Russian population in Estonia and Latvia is rooted in Soviet colonization (in Ukraine, by comparison, Russians make up 22 percent of the population). This has caused problems at the outset for the governments of Estonia and Latvia, as the integration process between different cultural groups is always a long-term proposition, especially in the Baltics.

In the 1990s, Estonia was able to rethink its eastern policy by exchanging reactive rhetoric for a pragmatic approach and taking active steps in the integration process. (From 1992 to 2000, for example, the number of noncitizens was reduced by nearly 60 percent—from 494,000 down to 175,000.) However, Russia has stubbornly stayed with its demands. Here we have to take into account that Russia's Baltic policy has always been closely related to the background system of domestic policy. This has decreased the flexibility and room to maneuver in its foreign policy. By making the humanitarian issue a prerequisite for solving all other questions, Russia has steered itself into a dead end. Thus, Russia has delayed the conclusion of many treaties (border treaty, economic treaties) with the Baltic states, hoping for better conditions in foreign policy. At the same time, Moscow is applying for membership in the World Trade Organization (WTO) and therefore must sooner or later, for example, remove the double customs duties imposed unconditionally on Estonia.

In all honesty, we can say that after Russia's armed forces departed from the region in August 1994, Moscow's relations—especially with Tallinn and Riga—have been in a deep shadow. Russian foreign policy toward Latvia and Estonia has primarily been centered on defending the rights of the Russian minorities. In Lithuania, where this card is useless, Moscow has implemented more balanced tactics.

Moscow has continuously used Lithuania as an example for the other Baltic states of how to behave with Russia. However, this example is useless, because Lithuania's problems are much different than those of its northern neighbors. The future of the Kaliningrad *oblast* is largely dependent on Lithuania and in this case Moscow must show more patience. At the same time Russia continues to use all available means to influence Lithuania. The Lithuanian-Russian Border Treaty still has not been ratified though the relations between the countries certainly support it. The strategically important Mazhieikai oil refinery has come under partial Russian control (28 percent belongs to Yukos), which provides Russia with the opportunity to present its demands to Vilnius concerning the Kaliningrad transit corridor.

Weak Baltic cooperation is in the interest of Russia. For Moscow it is important to influence problems between the states, as well as their domestic policy conflicts. In the case of Estonia, Moscow's attempts to influence domestic policy have been unsuccessful. In the cases of Latvia and Lithuania, it has been easier to find influence factors.

In spite of everything, Russia's policies toward the Baltic states have been a failure, as seen above, and need new ideas. The rapidly developing economies of the Baltic states, especially Estonia and Latvia, are already closely connected with the European Union's common market.

According to diplomatic sources, all of the Baltic states have made significant advances in negotiations with the North Atlantic alliance. It is evident that integration of the Baltic states into the Euro-Atlantic security and economic alliances forces Russia to reassess its policy in the region. To what extent and how this policy will change depends on the enlargement of the European Union and NATO.

At present, we can already see some changes in Russia's official rhetoric. However, after the terrorist attacks against the United States in September 2001, Russia has expressed a reasonable and more flexible attitude toward NATO enlargement. "If NATO takes on a different shade and is becoming a political organization, of course we would reconsider our position with regard to such expansion, if we are to feel involved in such processes," President Putin told the international press corps in Brussels on October 3, 2001, after meeting with NATO Secretary General Lord Robertson.[29]

Putin's words might mean that Russia will accept the enlargement of NATO only after the alliance changes its basic nature. At present, that seems to be a hopeless diplomatic dream. On the other hand, it might also mean that Russia is trying to find a less painful way to formally accept Baltic membership.

Another positive development is that Russia itself is starting to understand that there is no substitute for NATO in the Euro-Atlantic security field. After September 11, 2001, several top Russian Western-oriented analysts have suggested that Russia should become a member of NATO. As Sergei Karaganov, the chairman of the Council of Russian Foreign and Defense Policy, said in an interview with UPI on October 5, 2001:

> Unfortunately, the European Union's security dimension is going nowhere, or almost nowhere, and is no substitute for NATO membership.... Many educated Russians who are shaping the opinion of the country believe that Russia should belong to the West. Being in NATO will give us a future.[30]

The West's second attempt at engaging Russia since 1991 (the first attempt ended in 1992–93 due to strong influence on the Kremlin by Russian orthodox military officers) might yield an absolutely new configuration of power lines in the world. But it might end with nothing as well. We do not know yet what will be the result of the war against terrorism.

In the context of the Baltic states, NATO, and Russia, it is absolutely vital for everybody involved to go ahead with the enlargement of NATO. We have seen again how the security status of the Baltic states was questioned by the larger nations during the recent crisis. To avoid any future divisions, it is very important to strengthen the alliance with new members and with a more sophisticated partnership treaty with Russia at the same time.

Though Russia has reproached both Estonia and Latvia for the problems of the Russian-speaking minorities, Latvia became the main target of Russia's attacks as of March 1998. These developments offer a vivid example of how the Russian propaganda machinery is able, when necessary, to use the local Russian populations for its own interests.

The coincidence of several circumstances—Latvia was not invited in summer 1997 to the first round of European Union enlargement negotiations; confusion in Latvian domestic policy and an uncompromising position on the questions of integration; arrival in Riga of the new Russian ambassador, Aleksandr Udaltsov, who is very much at home with Baltic questions—in early spring of 1998 made Latvia a very attractive object for the attack by Russia.

On March 3, 1998, hundreds of Russian pensioners organized an unapproved demonstration in the center of Riga. To prevent the blockage of traffic, Latvian police used force against the picketers. The carefully and provocatively planned demonstration was broadcast the evening of the same day on all Russian TV channels to show how violent the attitude in Latvia was toward the Russian pensioners. Hardly two weeks later in Riga, on March 16, the traditional parade of World War II veterans who fought in Waffen-SS was held. Russia was able to turn this event against Latvia by creating significant international reaction. It must be admitted that the Latvian authorities themselves facilitated this (for example, the commander of the Latvian armed forces was present at the parade).

Since then diplomatic relations between Latvia and Russia have been frozen. Moscow has agreed to further talks only if Latvia fulfills Russia's demands in solving the so-called humanitarian questions. Nor has anything changed in the meetings at the highest levels, though President Vaira Vike-Freiberga of Latvia hoped to achieve a breakthrough in relations in a surprise meeting with President Putin in spring 2001. The meeting did not produce any tangible results, and Russia's demands persisted.

Putin brought up the Latvian theme again very vividly on June 16, 2001, in Slovenia during the joint press conference with U.S. President George W. Bush. Putin turned around the question concerning the Balkans to address the human rights situation in Latvia and how Russia is patiently solving the situation there.

The permanent and sometimes quite emotional official statements made by the Foreign Ministry of Russia on humanitarian issues toward Latvia and Estonia show that Russia's interest is to have as many troubles as possible for the local Russians rather than to seriously help improve the post-colonial situation, which was left after the Soviet Union broke up. The very latest, and by content very remarkable, Russian statement against Estonia came on August 1, 2001. It happened right after an incident in Paldiski, Estonia, where in a local bar, members of the Estonian peacekeepers training group were provoked and beat up a few Russians. An official from Moscow reacted to the incident using very tough language, even using the word "racism" in his statement.[31]

Presently, about 110,000 Russian citizens live in Estonia, while in Latvia there are up to 50,000 Russian citizens (8 and 2 percent of the population, respectively). The governments in both Tallinn and Riga will face serious problems for years, because by having such a large number of Russian citizens in the region, Moscow will always be able to use those citizens for its own interests. Up to now, Russia has not shown any change in its policy toward fellow compatriots in the Baltic states.

The political elite of Russia tend to believe that the economic success of the Baltic states is mainly based on reselling Russia's resources. Thus, the Baltic economies could be pushed over the edge simply by closing down or limiting these sources of income.

Indeed, Russia already has tried vigorously to close off the sources of profit (for example, imposing double customs on Estonia or the periodic ban on imports of food products from Latvia). However, all three Baltic states, especially Estonia and Latvia, have reacted by seeking out markets in the West.

During the first part of the 1990s, Estonia's economy was very sensitive to the curve of the Russian economy (i.e., comparison of GDP and stock exchange index). Since the late 1990s—especially after the 1998 ruble crash—there has been a significant change. Estonia's economy turned clearly toward the European Union market.

In fact, all three Baltic states appear to exhibit a clear tendency to shift foreign trade away from Russia and toward the European Union. In the first three months of 2001, for example, Estonian exports to the European Union totaled 73 percent, Latvian exports 65 percent, and Lithuanian exports 49 percent. Russia's share was 2.1 percent, 4.2 percent, and 8 percent, respectively.

**Table 7.5. Russia's Share in the Foreign Trade
of the Baltic States and Finland, January 2001**

|  | Export | | | Import | | |
|---|---|---|---|---|---|---|
|  | Million USD | Percentage | Rank | Million USD | Percentage | Rank |
| Estonia | 5.33 | 1.9 | 10 | 30.53 | 8.3 | 4 |
| Latvia | 5.87 | 3.9 | 7 | 25.54 | 11.1 | 2 |
| Lithuania | 19.96 | 5.8 | 4 | 131.21 | 30.8 | 1 |
| Finland | 129.51 | 3.8 | 7 | 279.44 | 11.4 | 2 |

Source: Statistics Offices of Estonia, Latvia, and Lithuania.

Unlike exports, the share of imports from Russia is somewhat bigger in Russian–Baltic states trade. The first place is clearly taken by the transit of goods. During the year 2000, Russia sent 56.5 million tons of goods through Baltic ports. A staggering 73.4 percent of Russia's northwest-directed liquid bulk trade cargo was transshipped via Baltic ports.[32]

Russia's growing attention toward a single transit policy, and through this toward the use of domestic resources, will undoubtedly influence the Baltic states in the near future.[33] It is no secret that businesses directly or indirectly related to transit produce up to one-fourth of Latvia's GDP and one-fifth of Estonia's GDP. Though the partial launch of port projects around St. Petersburg has already put the brakes on the flow of goods through the Baltic ports, it does not necessarily mean they have completely dried up. For example, the international consulting firm KPMG has said that in a worst case scenario, the flow of goods to and from Russia through the ports of Tallinn could decrease up to 38 percent.

At the same time it is clear that the use of its own transit corridors and the increase of competitiveness also improves Russia's potential for playing political games. The most vulnerable country is Latvia, because its transit volumes might decrease significantly when the Baltic Pipeline System is completed in several years. For example, if the port of Ventspils in Latvia can transship 14 million tons of oil per year, then the Baltic Pipeline System, once completed will be able to transship up to 30 million tons. However, the Baltic Pipeline System is already booked for 25 million tons, which pushes oil companies to find additional routes of transport whether they like it or not.[34] Throughout the 1990s Russia has had a very low image of the Baltic states. This has been facilitated both by official policy and also by the emotional background of what are known as the "Baltic problems."

Largely due to the Russian mass media, which has vigorously reflected official Russian policy, the Baltic states have been portrayed as troublesome midgets who despise Russia and Russians. In addition, the high emotions brought about by the dissolution of the Soviet Union have played a considerable role. Even today, 75 percent of Russians consider the fall of the Soviet Union to have been a great disaster. It is no surprise that many Russians continue to view one of the main agents of destruction—the Baltic states—as a political villain.

Thus, it is relatively easy to understand why so many Russians have an aggressive attitude toward the Baltic states. According to a poll conducted by the All-Russian Center for the Study of Public Opinion (VTsIOM) in May 2001, the Baltic states were ranked second after Afghanistan as potential enemies of Russia. Every fifth Russian sees the biggest threat to Russia as coming from Estonia, Latvia, and Lithuania. According to this indicator, the Baltic states draw more animosity than the United States of America.[35]

Moreover, analysts of Russian foreign and security policy believe the admission of the Baltic states into NATO to be one of the biggest threats to Russia's national security. A poll supported by the Moscow Ebert Fund showed that the possible entry of the Baltic states into the North Atlantic alliance was almost as threatening to Russia as the spread of international terrorism, the low competitiveness of the state economy, and the increasing scientific-technological backwardness compared to Western countries.[36]

The negative background of public opinion is undoubtedly very disturbing and dangerous. Russia knows it can rouse public support for taking "adequate steps." Another question is whether or not Russia will use it.

## CONCLUSIONS AND RECOMMENDATIONS

Russia's main foreign policy goal toward its closest neighbors is characterized by the attempts to keep the Euro-Atlantic security field away from its direct borders. Here we see Russia's activities in Ukraine, Belarus, and also Moldova as designed to keep those countries firmly in its sphere of influence.

In the short term, Moscow is probably not interested in uniting these territories under its direct political control. In 1996, influential experts and

politicians from Russia's Council of Foreign and Defense Policy emphasized that the "restoration of the Soviet Union in its previous form is a
utopian dream." At the same time it was believed that partial reunification
of the former union at the beginning of the new century as a confederacy
or even as a federation is quite realistic.

In 1996, the most probable candidates for the new union were consid-
ered to be Russia, Belarus, Kazakhstan, Kyrgyzstan, Tajikistan, and Armenia.
These countries were followed by states with a lesser probability—Ukraine,
Uzbekistan, Georgia, and Moldova. The inclusion of Azerbaijan and
Turkmenistan was even less probable. The admission of Latvia was not
probable, but neither was it considered to be zero. Inclusion of Estonia and
Lithuania was considered to be almost impossible.[37] Five years later, this
prediction may still come true. Since 1996, only the Baltic states have firm-
ly distanced themselves from Russia.

Russia's growing activity in Ukraine, Belarus, and Moldova show that
Moscow has been able to achieve a strategic advantage over its western
neighbors—at least during the past few years—by using mainly economic,
cultural, and political means of influence. The process could be modified
if these countries enact major changes in domestic policy, but that looks to
be almost impossible in the near future. Moldova is a communist country
with an ongoing territorial dispute; Ukraine's high level of corruption
makes it extremely vulnerable; and Belarus just cannot form any substantial opposition movement to Lukashenko. All of this makes the three countries easy prey for Russian diplomats and the secret services.

However, any union of the Baltic states with Russia without using force
is utterly unlikely at present. At the same time it is evident that during the
next year or two, since the Baltic states have not yet joined the European
Union or NATO, Russia will use all available means of influence to slow
down the process. This especially applies to NATO enlargement, toward
which Russia's rhetoric has been totally negative. At the same time, the
experiences of Poland, the Czech Republic, and Hungary have shown that
Russia's rhetoric is not backed up with tangible steps. Thus, the Baltic
states are unlikely to face a different scenario.

To alleviate Russia's fears, the best course of action would be for NATO
to invite all three Baltic states together to be new members during the 2002
summit in Prague. This would significantly decrease Russia's room to
maneuver, and it would create a more stable foreign policy situation in the
Baltic region. Otherwise, Russia will continue in its attempts to make the
Baltic states a sort of buffer zone like the one it has very nearly created in
Ukraine, Belarus, and Moldova.

# NOTES

1. The different interpretation of many principles underlying international relations is why negotiations with Russia have always been very difficult, as well as why the agreements concluded have frequently turned out to be null and void. Consider, for example, what the well-known theoretician Walter Lippman had to say about national security: "A nation has ensured its security if it does not have to sacrifice its legal interests to prevent war or if it is able in case of need to defend these interests by the means of war." Lippman's thesis is reasonable and understandable if proceeding from the common logic of Western civil society. But if proceeding from the nostalgia for great power that is rooted deeply in Russian society, then the term "legal interests" will have a very different meaning. In other words, Russia and the West define the "legal interests" of a state in very different ways. For Russia, legal interests are not limited to its own territory and national security, but also encompass the "historic territory" that is mainly the territory of the former Soviet Union.

2. Aleksandr Dugin, *Osnovy geopolitiki: Geopolititsheskaya budushtsheye Rossii* (Moscow: Arktogeya, 1997), p. 369.

3. NTV, October 2, 2001.

4. VTsIOM poll, June 2001, in Interfax, July 19, 2001.

5. Excerpt from Russia's Concept of Foreign Policy, approved by President Vladimir Putin on June 28, 2000: "The priority of Russian foreign policy is to ensure the bilateral and multilateral cooperation with the CIS states according to the objectives of national security of the state," available at: www.mid.ru.

6. Rossiya-SNG, "Nuzhdaetsa li v korrektirovke pozitsiya Zapada?" (Moscow: 1994).

7. Zbigniew Brzezinski, *The Grand Chessboard: American Primacy and Its Geostrategic Imperatives* (New York: Basic Books, 1997), p. 107.

8. *Vozroditsa li Soyuz? Budushtshee postsovetskogo prostranstva. Tezisy po vneshnei i oboronnoi politike* (1996), pp. 18, 24.

9. G. Zyuganov, *Geografiya pobedy. Osnovy rossiiskoi geopolitiki.* (Moscow: 1997), pp. 134–35.

10. Interfax, July 29, 2001. Vassili Shandybin, a well-known Russian Communist Party member in the Duma, said in an interview with the Estonian daily *Eesti Päevaleht* that Russia should expand back into its old territories. "The process with Belarus and Ukraine has already started. After them follows Armenia, and finally the time will come for the Baltics," he said (*Eesti Päevaleht,* May 18, 2001).

11. Belarus realigned itself with Russia in 1994 with the election of Aleksandr Lukashenko as president, though Ukraine has become more submissive to Russia only since 2000. Several factors have influenced this outcome, but certainly Russian President Vladimir Putin has played a very important role. Moldova turned toward Russia after the overriding Communist victory in the early Moldavian parliament elections in February 2001, in which the Communists won 71 seats out of 101.

12. *Kommersant,* June 15, 2001.

13. Semyon Sharetski, interview by author, May 26, 1997.

14. Göran Persson (prime minister of Sweden) and Romano Prodi (president of the European Commission), article in *International Herald Tribune,* May 22, 2001.

15. *Komsomolskaya Pravda,* May 12, 2001.

16. *Vremya Novostei,* May 28, 2001.

17. *Financial Times,* July 12, 2001.

18. *Nezavisimaya Gazeta,* July 11, 2001.

19. *Vozroditsya li Sojuz?,* p. 26.

20. Country paper by Russian Foreign Ministry, available at www.mid.ru.

21. www.nuvse.com, information posted on July 19, 2001.

22. www.strana.ru, information posted on October 5, 2001.

23. *Krasnaya Zvezda,* April 19, 2001.

24. *Nezavisimaya Gazeta,* April 18, 2001.

25. *Nezavisimaya Gazeta,* May 23, 2001.

26. Based on Russian mass media (Majak, KM-News, NTV.ru).

27. *RIA Novosti,* July 16, 2001.

28. *RIA Novosti,* July 16, 2001.

29. Interfax, October 3, 2001.

30. UPI, October 5, 2001.

31. Official statement of Foreign Ministry of Russia, dated August 1, 2001, available at www.mid.ru.

32. Baltic News Service, June 8, 2001.

33. PRAIM-TASS, May 17, 2001.

34. Igor Skoks, president of Ventspils Nafta, interview with www.rusenergy.com on June 29, 2001.

35. Polit.ru, June 6, 2001.

36. Baltic News Service, May 26, 2001.

37. *Vozroditsya li Soyuz?,* pp. 21, 26.

# 8

# Russian Policy in the Caucasus and Central Asia

*Krzysztof Strachota*

Russia is a Eurasian power with ambitions to be one of the most important powers on a global scale. The key to achieving this goal is its position in Asia, which is politically and economically the fastest-developing region in the world. However, though Asia offers Russia tremendous opportunity, it also presents the greatest threats. Russia is now trying to deal with both these questions.

A fundamental aspect of Russia's efforts to strengthen its superpower position is how it achieves or maintains the fullest possible political and economic control in the region of the former Union of Soviet Socialist Republics. This clearly applies to Central Asia and the Caucasus, both regions in which the power struggle is at its most severe. Russia still dominates in this region thanks to political and economic instruments, as well as the internal weakness of the new states during the transition period. However, it is not certain whether Russia will be able to maintain and fully exploit what appears to be the recent erosion of the region's net of political, economic, and cultural dependence. Above all, it remains uncertain whether Russia will be able—as it has thus far—to dictate security in the region. Russia's position and its strategic goals in the region have acquired special importance since September 11, 2001.

More than ten years have passed since the collapse of the Soviet Union. Since 1991, Moscow has systematically lost status as one of the world's two superpowers. For the first time in two hundred years, Russia—against the will of all political forces in the country—was absent from the first rank of countries that create the world order, a direct result of the disproportion of forces between the United States and other world powers. It now appears that Russian foreign policy aims mainly to combat the unipolar global system (focused on the United States), and to fulfill its desire to obtain a leading place in the world, even if this has to be divided into equal shares with other states within a multipolar global order.

Parallel with the loss of its superpower status, Russia's spheres of influence have clearly shrunk in the last decade. Since 1991 Russia has significantly limited its global policy; it has almost completely withdrawn from Africa and Latin America, lost control over central Europe, and was obliged to put the brakes on its expansion in Asia. Its most spectacular loss involved the Soviet republics that did not join the Russian Federation: the Baltic states, Ukraine, Belarus, Moldavia (now Moldova), the southern Caucasus, and Central Asia. For more than two hundred years, these areas had been subject to Russia, regardless of whatever shocks it experienced. Now, Russia's capacity for keeping and restoring the strongest possible control and a supraregional power monopoly on "Asiatic" areas (the Caucasus and Central Asia) has extreme importance for the future of Russia's position in global policy. Russia's control of this region is strong enough now, but it is getting weaker year by year.

The third factor that seems to be of ever greater significance for Russia and its position in the world is Asia's unprecedented growth in importance. This has been especially noticeable since the end of the Cold War, as the economic, technological, and demographic development of the Asian countries (or even of civilization itself, in political scientist Samuel Huntington's sense of the word) has begun to achieve international political significance. This is as true for China, India, and Japan as for Islamic civilization (from Pakistan via Indonesia to Iran, by way of such supranational movements as fundamentalism).

Russia, as a Eurasian power, needs to conduct very active policy in Asia. On the one hand, Russia finds full sympathy in Asia for its idea of a multipolar world order, and has political (and economic) partners with similar thoughts. But on the other hand, it must play an intensive game in order not to become an object of Asian expansion. Asia will decide the future of the Russian Empire. Without doubt, the changes that have come to the world since September 11, 2001, will strengthen the importance of each of these three factors even further, and will oblige Russia to cultivate them.

## RUSSIA AND CHINA

Russia has traditionally taken a predominant interest in India, Iran, and above all China. The weakness of Russia's economy does not allow for intensive trade exchange, or even an exchange of investments. Yet the above-mentioned countries do receive Russian strategic export goods, including weapons and military technologies.[1] For Russia, this is a way to provide more funds for government coffers and maintain its own military industry: it is one of the most important instruments for efforts to bring some balance to the global distribution of power.

China is obviously the most important of the aforementioned countries, because of the potential of its surroundings, and also it shares with Russia the philosophy of keeping its distance from the United States. One important stimulus that brought China and Russia closer together was the intervention by the North Atlantic Treaty Organization (NATO) in Yugoslavia in 1999. NATO's actions showed both countries that the alliance (specifically the United States) could use force to solve problems outside its sphere of influence without taking into consideration the attitudes of Moscow or Beijing. Russia and China announced that they placed strong emphasis on mutual friendship, a common vision for the distribution of global power, and the need to increase economic cooperation. This series of declarations was crowned by a friendship treaty between Russia and China, which was signed on July 16, 2001, during Jiang Zemin's visit to Moscow. Both countries aim "to support the world's strategic balance and security."

This cooperation between Russia and China was reflected in a burst of activity in the reconstitution of the Shanghai Cooperation Organization (SCO) at its summit meeting in June 2001. (Originally founded in 1996, the SCO—once known as the "Shanghai Five"—originally comprised Russia, China, Kazakhstan, Kyrgyzstan, and Tajikistan, and concentrated on solving border-related problems and instilling confidence in China and neighboring post-Soviet countries. Uzbekistan joined at the June 2001 summit.) It is becoming clear that the SCO's goal is to weaken the international position of the United States. Numerous events point to this conclusion: the meeting between Chinese President Jiang and Russian President Vladimir Putin received more emphasis than the Russian-American summit; the SCO expressed disapproval of the National Missile Defense (NMD) project; its position in the region (how Moscow and Beijing interpret Uzbekistan's accession to the organization); and the settlement of supraregional conflicts (China's attempts to include Pakistan in the organization are still being attacked by Russia).

One of the SCO's main goals is to fight separatism, Islamic fundamentalism, and extremism in the region. The organization is preparing formal conditions with China and Russia for a common regional security policy and military cooperation (that is, a practical local alliance). However, it appears that both Russia and China (especially China) are trying to strengthen their own positions in Central Asia at the expense of the other. For example, China directly interfered in Kazakhstan in the Uighur case and armed Uzbekistan during the Batken crisis (attacks by mujaheddin from the Islamic Movement of Uzbekistan [IMU] on Kyrgyzstan and Uzbekistan). This broke Russia's regional security monopoly, including its monopoly on arms. Furthermore, the common Russian-Chinese declarations against fundamentalism have nothing to do with their opinions of the Taliban. The Russian-Chinese alliance against fundamentalism is really a propaganda slogan, or even a form of competition, rather than a real basis for cooperation.

A number of other important discrepancies are concealed behind Russia and China's "alliance." Despite some emergency actions taken by President Putin, such as depriving Yevgeny Nazdratenko (who was strongly prejudiced against China) of the governorship of the Maritime Territory, and closing the Russian naval base in Cam Ranh Bay in Vietnam in June 2001, the scope for cooperation may become narrower.

Apart from long-term economic, military, and demographic perspectives, which are disadvantageous for Russia and in sharp contrast with Chinese indices and prospects, a number of current issues also remain unsettled. Although certain agreements have been concluded, and discussions of border issues between both countries have resumed, Beijing continued to express a cold attitude toward the border agreements signed by imperial Russia and China.[2]

The most serious conflicts may soon appear within the territories of Central Asia, which Russia treats as its own sphere of influence. China is much more concerned about its western territories. As a result, it is drawing up plans for huge investments to develop towns and industry in the western provinces.[3] Thus, the countries of Central Asia now have a strong economic and political center linked to transport routes, which deprives Russia of its monopolist position.[4] Moreover, a number of other major regional problems have resurfaced. These concern international borders (a very controversial border shift between China and Kyrgyzstan in spring 2001) and water resources (Chinese management projects for the Ili and Irtysh Rivers would be disastrous for east Kazakhstan and, to a lesser degree, for Russian territories located in the drainage area of the rivers).[5] Relations between China and Central Asia have been growing more strained due to disagreements over Uighur bases in Kazakhstan despite the efforts made by the government in Astana. The growing importance of China to the Central Asian countries may be an opportunity to analyze the wide discrepancies between Beijing and Moscow: Moscow does not want to lose its control over the economy, the transport routes, or the shape of the states of the former empire.

The relations between Russia and China bear more resemblance to a game than to a long-range alliance. They are focused predominantly on declarations, gestures, and prestige, and not on real cooperation, which could be transformed into a strategic partnership. Moreover, each country would prefer to become the dominant party in an agreement, which in turn remains unacceptable to the other party.

## THE CAUCASUS AND CENTRAL ASIA

Central Asia and the Caucasus have decisive importance for Russia's position in Asia and its imperial character. From a geopolitical viewpoint, there is a range of contacts and collisions between Russia's influence (which today is undoubtedly the strongest) and the leading political centers of Asia. The latter include China and (indirectly) India, as well as "Islamic civilization" in its political dimension (Iran, Turkey, Pakistan) and its ideological dimension (i.e., that the region is attractive to fundamentalist movements such as Afghanistan's Taliban). In this region, the game between superpowers, as they play the field for collaboration and for conflicts, is most apparent.

A number of the countries in the region have common interests in Afghanistan (e.g., supporting the Northern Alliance), which represent an opening for Russia's ever closer cooperation with Iran and India. As a result, Moscow has an indirect influence on Pakistan's position in its conflict with India. Russia's joint position with Tehran regarding the division of the Caspian Sea allows it to use Iran as a pawn to weaken Western influence. One example is the Iran-Azerbaijan crisis of August 2001, which forced BP AMOCO to withdraw from controversial strata on the sea bed, and notably weakened the interest of Western businesses in getting involved in such an unstable region.

The ongoing contest regarding the antiterrorist coalition and military operation in Afghanistan under U.S. command confirms and strengthens the region's importance. Russia's hostile attitude toward the coalition would definitely not have allowed the United States to use Uzbekistan for actions in Afghanistan. In fact, Russia's influence over the Northern Alliance in Afghanistan allows it to control the course of operations in Afghanistan. It also ensures that Russia will have a key voice in establishing the country's future status. Russia may play an especially important role vis-à-vis the ongoing controversies between the United States and Pakistan, and between Russia and Iran, about the participation of the Pashtun or so-called moderate Taliban in a government after the success of the military operation.

Finally, from Moscow's point of view, the importance of both the Caucasus and Central Asia is quite measurable and straightforward. This is the focus of Russia's most crucial economic interests and direct external threats. It is impossible to overestimate the role of energy resources in the Russian economy,[6] as energy exports are of the highest importance for the country.[7] One of the most important products is Caspian gas, set to become a key Russian export, as the domestic gas industry has a number of problems. Russia may apply higher prices when exporting gas to the western countries; furthermore, the payments and the political benefits Russia is supposed to receive are more secure than those obtained from domestic entities. Russia does not have sufficient financial means to exploit new deposits; but if it takes control of Caspian oil and gas deposits, it may increase its budget revenue (obtained from transit activity or from its share in such deposits) and strengthen its ability to influence the global prices of raw materials.

The southern part of the Commonwealth of Independent States (CIS) is still the "soft underbelly" of the Russian Federation. Setting aside Russia's role in the development of the regional situation, both the Caucasus and Central Asia have enormous potential for destabilizing the Russian Federation. Russia's withdrawal from the region resulted in the loss of a well-adjusted border area that in the past separated the Soviet Union from its southern neighbors (including Turkey, which is a NATO member). The existing border between Russia and Kazakhstan, as well as the border running through the Caucasus, do not offer any security, nor do they allow any control over the flow of people and goods. Taking into consideration such problems as the number of conflicts in the southern territories of the CIS, social delinquency, and the emergence of radical fundamentalist terrorist groups, this is not a purely theoretical problem. It is also impossible to overestimate the transit role of the southern parts of the CIS and Russia in global drug trafficking. This is a multilateral problem, as it includes a purely criminal aspect (particularly involving organized crime),[8] a social aspect (an increase in the number of drug addicts),[9] and political and economic aspects (the enormous amount of capital remaining outside state control).

There is relatively little time left for Russia to strengthen its position in Central Asia and the Caucasus, regardless of the post–September 11 events. Moreover, demographic trends in Russia are extremely disadvantageous (a negative birthrate in Russia, a population explosion in Central Asia, and Russians leaving the region).[10] The society currently emerging in Central Asia and—to a lesser extent—the Caucasus is only marginally connected with Russian culture (as was the case with the Soviet Union). Therefore its links with Russia, which today are of decisive importance, may well become less and less cohesive, and the resistance to Russia's presence in the region and the influence of its competitors will gain in strength. The most viable cultural alternative is the one offered by Islam, which will become even more dangerous as it starts adopting fundamentalist features (which tend to affect the whole spectrum of life—including its social, economic, and political aspects—for both individuals and groups of people).

Thus, for Russia, loss of influence in the region may imply not only that it has renounced its aspirations to become a world power (not a superpower), but also has lost its strategic prospects. For all these reasons, Moscow is making and will continue to make every effort to maintain its present position.

From the point of view of the Caucasus and Central Asian countries, Russia remains the most important reference point, despite the fact that almost ten years have passed since the eight Soviet republics in the region became independent states. The initial fascination with Western political, social, and economic patterns was quickly suppressed by local limitations and "the way to democracy based on specific cultural features," and/or the need to renounce the adoption of Western concepts of state, society, and economy. The discrepancy between the appetites of local elites and the careful policy of Western states has become glaring. The countries of the Caucasus and Central Asia are still unable to solve their strategic problems themselves without taking Moscow's opinion into account. This includes regional political problems, contacts between the region and other countries, and relations between individual states. Although the countries in the region have huge reserves of natural resources (such as oil and gas in Kazakhstan, Turkmenistan, and Azerbaijan),[11] as well as geographical locations that offer good transport potential, nobody has managed to come up with an alternative solution for Russian transport routes or how to get the countries' economies out of Moscow's control.

For Russia, the need to rebuild the country is an important obstacle in carrying out its own policy. The differences between the economies of Kazakhstan (definitely the best), Uzbekistan, and Turkmenistan, or between the efficiency of the democratic mechanisms of Kazakhstan or Armenia (undoubtedly the most efficient) and those of Turkmenistan or Tajikistan, are huge. Today, the democratic political and social institutions of those states, as well as their free markets, constitute a mere facade. All those countries are bound by numerous limitations, and are endangered by government systems based upon clans. The main problem is that power is concentrated in the immediate inner circle of the president and those related to him by consanguinity, common origin, political past, or place of birth. For these reasons it is much more difficult to adhere to an effective policy, as there are grounds for conflicts about prestige and people-related issues, not about programs. The limited economic possibilities, together with a population explosion in Central Asia, the marginal role of the opposition and regional elites, and hidden ethnic conflicts, all have enormous destabilizing power. The elites that wield power in each country constitute another anxiety factor vis-à-vis the ability to function independently of Moscow. The presidents of six of the eight countries are former members of the Central Committee of the Communist Party of the Soviet Union; with Russia's help, the presidents of Georgia and Azerbaijan "replaced" the democratically elected leaders, and two others (President Robert Kocharian of Armenia and President Emomali Rachmonov of Tajikistan) won their political positions thanks to Russian military support.

What seems most dangerous is the lack of clear-cut mechanisms for transferring power. In the southern Caucasus, the changes in government structure were brought about by civil wars (Georgia) or coups d'état (Azerbaijan and Armenia). The only change that occurred in Central Asia resulted from the civil war in Tajikistan. This kind of situation can threaten further implementation of current policy. The two most acute examples are Georgia and Azerbaijan. In the case of Azerbaijan, President Geydar Aliev's desire to assure succession for his son Ilham has led to a visible rapprochement of relations with Russia, which is inclined to support the move. In fact, President Putin expressly stated this during his visit to Azerbaijan in June 2001. Also important is the fact that most political-opposition activists from the Caucasus and Central Asia have found refuge in Moscow.

The main obstacles to Russia's exclusive dominance over the southern republics of the CIS are economic. At present, Russia is unable to bring either the southern Caucasus or Central Asia under its economic control. It lacks not only the resources to make investments, but also the capacity to use Caspian oil and gas deposits on its own. All Russia can afford to do is prevent its competitors from taking control of those areas: for example, to block all communication routes that do not pass through its territory or interfere with exploitation of deposits. Economic limitations have prompted Russia's strong criticism of the Atyrau-Baku-Ceyhan pipeline, of its own involvement in the Afghanistan war (which prevented activation of the gas pipeline from Turkmenistan to Pakistan), and its cooperation with Iran on the status of the Caspian Sea. The fact that the problem has not been resolved is an important obstacle to the exploitation of the areas in question and to any activities performed in the sea. Economically speaking, therefore, in the economic field, Russia presents a rather conservative approach to the existing distribution of power.

Another challenge is reflected in the development of the Collective Security Agreement (CSA). Initially aimed at establishing a common security area, the CSA seemed to offer a perfect legal basis for creating regional rapid reaction forces in Central Asia, the southern Caucasus, and Belarus. Regional rapid reaction forces were established at the CSA summit in Bishkek in 2000, in response to the Batken crisis. Surprisingly, progress in establishing these forces is quite advanced, as is work on creation of the antiterrorist center in Bishkek. Although the emergency forces (supposed to number between 1,500 and 1,700 soldiers) are not particularly strong—due to both the number of soldiers and to their organizational and logistical deficiencies—they constitute evidence that Kazakhstan, Kyrgyzstan, and Tajikistan looked to Russia for help and accepted Russian military units in the region because they felt endangered. The CSA itself only acts as a screen for bilateral military arrangements between its members and Russia. Nevertheless, the informational and legislative contributions of the CSA to Russia's increasing importance in that region cannot be underestimated. The proposed Eurasian Economic Community may have similar objectives, as it is aimed at consolidating the economic, customs, and legal policies of its member states. At present it is still in the planning stages, but in the future it may become a gateway for Russia to the markets of its member states.

## EXPLOITING INSECURITY

For ten years, Russia's most important tools for modifying the situation in the southern part of the CIS have invariably included both military influence and the ability to provoke or control conflicts. These conflicts seriously restrain the political independence of the countries involved, and create economic and social problems. Moreover, they destabilize the region by making it unattractive for Western investors (including projects involving transregional transportation routes) or Western political involvement. The conflicts always tend to affect countries looking for an alternative to Russia (Georgia and Azerbaijan in the Caucasus; at first Tajikistan in Central Asia, and currently Uzbekistan and Kyrgyzstan).

These conflicts are both provoked and resolved by the Russian military presence, as Russian bases were and remain important support for brewing Caucasus-area separatist movements (the Abkhaz and Ossetian movements) and for those about to boil over (Armenian separatism in Javakhetia and Adzhar separatism). The Russian military presence—and the conflicts strongly connected with it—are still important trump cards in the negotiations held between Moscow and Tbilisi. (For example, the problem of dismantling the base in Gudauta, Abkhazia, was raised at the end of June 2001.) Discussions regarding new Russian military bases in Central Asia raise similar issues. It is impossible to ignore the fact that Caucasus and Central Asian airspace is fully controlled by Russia.

Although military activity in the southern Caucasus had been suspended since 1994, the existence of independent "para-states" has made development and regional cooperation for both countries impossible. (The para-states were established with Russia's help and can only be maintained with Russian help. They comprise Nagorno-Karabakh in Azerbaijan, and South Ossetia and Abkhazia in Georgia.) Russia imposed visas on Georgians and not Abkhaz or Ossetians; this appeared to be clearly anti-Georgian, as work in Russia made it possible for hundreds of thousands of Georgians to earn a living while staying in the country. In addition, despite the enormous efforts made both by mediators (recently the United States and France) and the presidents of Azerbaijan (Geydar Aliyev) and Armenia (Robert Kocharian), there is little chance that the Karabakh conflict will be resolved, as it is very easy to raise social objections to the president's position. (Former Armenian President Levon Ter-Petrosian was pushed out of office because of his willingness to make concessions on the Karabakh issue.)

Russia's main problem in Central Asia is Islamic fundamentalism. At the beginning of the 1990s, Russia supported the government of Tajikistan in its struggle against the Islamic opposition. Russia took full control of the state, and by maintaining its own military bases there, managed to dominate Tajikistan much more thoroughly than the other CIS states. We should not forget, however, that the peace treaties signed under the patronage of Moscow ensured the opposition a strong influence in the country. The Russian army has been entrusted with the role of arbitrator in political events, a role accepted by both parties to the treaties.

The second upsurge of Islamic fundamentalism in Central Asia, which has focused on Uzbekistan, is a much more complex problem. A number of issues have coincided: political (the marginal position of the Fergana clan, or the suppression of political opposition in all its forms), cultural (Uzbekistan's strong Islamic background and the lack of ideology after the Soviet Union's collapse), and social and economic (a baby boom and increasing unemployment). All these events have established ideal conditions for the Uzbek opposition to become more Islamic and more radical. In addition, the Uzbeks have found friendly support in Tajikistan and Afghanistan. The activity of the Islamic Movement of Uzbekistan (currently, the Islamic Party of Turkestan), which has declared its intention to overthrow President Islam Karimov and to establish an Islamic state in the Fergana Valley, was reflected in the Batken crises, which shook the whole region. Due to Russia's inability to solve the problem on its own, and because of the breakdown in regional cooperation, Russia has become the sole state that can guarantee security in the region. This has resulted in closer political and military cooperation with Russia, a reformulation of the CSA, and the granting of almost unanimous permission—or even encouragement—for the Russian army to come back to the region. The return of the Russian army would be based upon the establishment of regional emergency forces, new military bases (as in Chkalovsk, Tajikistan), or the reinforcement of existing ones. Such a situation is a blow mostly against Uzbekistan, which has been attempting to become the region's leader and replace Russian influence with the cooperation of the United States, Turkey, and China.

Indeed, since it gained independence, Uzbekistan has tried to take advantage of its military and demographic potential (including Uzbek minorities in neighboring countries) to achieve political hegemony in Central Asia. The main area of Uzbekistan's expansion was in Tajikistan, where Tashkent supported post-communist forces during the civil war (1992–97), and still supports the Uzbek minority and the Khujand clan (including opposition politicians who escaped to Uzbekistan). The same situation exists with the Uzbek minority in Afghanistan, and the Uzbek forces of General Rashid Dostum, which it backs. Also, Kyrgyzstan and Kazakhstan are seriously troubled by Uzbekistan's arbitrarily changing borders between the countries. Moreover, Tashkent forces pricing conditions on them for using Kyrgyzstan water, as well as forcing them to buy Kazakhstan coal and sell gas for Kyrgyzstan. Uzbekistan's policy is to strengthen relations between the region and Russia.

For Uzbekistan, the most important goal is to find serious support among those countries that compete with Russia in the region, including China, but mainly the United States and Turkey. Any sign of a close relationship with the West (declarations, visits, military support, equipment, training, etc.) strengthens Uzbekistan's position toward Russia. It should be mentioned that President Karimov has tried to have his own (that is, neither Western- nor U.S.-oriented) regional policy. For example, he exhibited his independence very strongly when he criticized the Western concept of democracy and human rights during the 1999 Organization for Security and Cooperation in Europe (OSCE) summit in Istanbul. He also froze relations with Turkey in 1999, because Turkey granted asylum to his opponents. However, Uzbekistan is the most important and independent player in Central Asia, and could be the best partner for the West (specifically, the United States—as can be seen after September 11) for stopping Russian and/or Chinese influence in the region, and rebuilding security and the political system.

In Central Asia, Islamic fundamentalism—the Islamic Movement of Uzbekistan/Islamic Party of Turkestan (IMU/IPT), instead of the Hizb-ut-Tahrir party—which is mainly Uzbekstan's problem, plays a role similar to that played by the para-states and ethnic conflicts in the southern Caucasus. Fundamentalism also provides a very convenient justification of Russia's military presence and political supervision in that region, an argument that is presented in the Russian media and generally accepted in Central Asia. Paradoxically, Russia's implicit support for the IMU/IPT seems rather obvious; Russia tolerates the movement's bases in Tajikistan (although it has sufficient resources to suppress them), and it allows the Russia-dependent government of Tajikistan to support IMU/ITP activities (the government thus attempts to weaken Uzbekistan's position, and prevents the Uzbeks from taking any actions against the IMU/ITP bases). Also, Uzbekistan has many times threatened to bomb those camps, but Russia and Tajikistan have objected. Finally, it is impossible to overlook the fact that the country which is Russia's closest neighbor and still under Russian control has in fact been broken up into sovereign principalities governed by specific camp commanders (representing the government and the opposition). Therefore, it is not unlikely that Tajikistan will become an example of Russian order in Central Asia while having no power sources of its own. Tajikistan determines the limits of Russia's expectations from that region in regard to its military control, its position as super-arbitrator in a decentralized state, and as a blockade against the influence of other powerful states.

## AFGHANISTAN BEFORE AND AFTER SEPTEMBER 11

Another important political factor exploited in the relations with Central Asia is Afghanistan. Apart from fundamentalism, the menace created by the

Taliban is an equally important reason for Russia's presence in the region. For Russia, the war in Afghanistan is a guarantee that the region will be blocked off from the south, both politically (from the impact of Islamic countries, in particular Pakistan) and economically (from a possible blockade of pipelines). This may be an explanation for the resolute support Russia provided to the Northern Alliance after the Taliban's spectacular victories in the autumn of 2000. The effect could have become even stronger through direct military actions by Russia in Afghanistan. This was suggested both by the regular preparation of Russian society for unavoidable conflict with the Taliban, and by the obvious fact of the strengthening of Russian military forces in that region (the regional emergency units, reinforcement projects for military bases, and personnel changes in the Russian army). Such a scenario would obviously have been supported by the majority of soldiers and the war industry lobby. Afghanistan offers the opportunity to demonstrate Russian force and tighten the traditional cooperation with India and Iran, which is one of the most important issues for Moscow's power policy.

Together with the attacks on Washington and New York, Russia has been confronting new challenges since September 11. First of all, it has appeared that Islamic terrorism is a real threat of global character, which potentially threatens Russia itself. (Russia's Muslim population is estimated at 20 million, and in the whole area of the CIS at more than 70 million); in addition, the threat of Afghanistan as a base for fundamentalism has ceased to be merely apparent and has become a reality.

Second, the prestige of the United States as the only superpower was significantly impaired. This forced Washington to organize an act of retaliation, supported by a broad coalition, aimed at terrorist centers in Afghanistan—a borderland of Russia's vital interests. The necessity of preparing a political base for the military action in Afghanistan was naturally linked with a sudden animation of American diplomacy in the region of the future conflict (Pakistan, Iran, India, and the countries of Central Asia). Russia confronted a dilemma: to compete with the United States and the coalition, and thus weaken the world order constructed by the United States, or to join in with the action. In a similar situation in 1999 (the NATO intervention in Kosovo), Russia chose to boycott, a move that brought it no benefits and marginalized it in the Balkans. This time President Putin has joined in, albeit after hesitations and with many ambiguous signals. However, it would appear that not all his people, especially those in the so-called power departments, support his move. Russia is counting on a fundamental rebuilding of its relations with the West, and above all on achieving the status of a strategic, essential, and equal partner in the eyes of the United States. Putin spoke openly about approaching Western structures (NATO and the European Union) during his visit to Brussels. Russia could then increase its international authority, thus weakening NATO's potentially threatening (to Russia) structure.

It was unavoidable that Central Asia would find itself at the center of the antiterrorist coalition and the operation in Afghanistan. In the face of frozen American-Iranian relations (despite signs of both sides' desire to normalize) and the uncertain situation in Pakistan (owing to resistance from very influential Pakistani fundamentalist circles, as well as from Pakistan's links with the Taliban), the countries of Central Asia could become an alternative base for military operations. The first suggestions of cooperation from within the coalition demonstrated an awareness of the situation and a desire to take advantage of the coalescing factors: on September 15, Kazakhstan proposed "help by all available means," and two days later Uzbekistan made its bases available, assuming the United States would approach with such a request. At first, Moscow saw this as a threat to its own interests, and forced the presidents of the region to distance themselves from these offers. However, in the face of active efforts by the diplomatic services of America, Kazakhstan, and Uzbekistan, and also in connection with devising a position of its own that would be open to cooperation with the coalition—as seen in Putin and his representative's consultation with the "departments of force" in Sochi on September 22—Russia agreed to American involvement in the region. In effect, an American military base is currently operating in Uzbekistan (a minimum of 1,000 soldiers from the Tenth Mountain Division, intelligence agents, etc.), at the military airport in Khanabad; a de facto Uzbek-American alliance has also appeared, as revealed on October 12. Uzbekistan will allow the United States to use Uzbeki territory as a base for its military presence in the region, in return for which it offers limited guarantees for Uzbekistan's security, and creates mechanisms for cooperation in case of any threat to the Uzbekistan's stability and territorial integrity. This agreement forms a basis for building stability and security in the region in support of the United States.

At first glance, the events of September and October 2001 signify Russia's expulsion from Central Asia to the benefit of the United States, and the literal breaking of Russia's monopoly on creating regional security. At this moment it is the United States that has a military presence in the region, and it is they who are militarily liquidating the regional threats. The Uzbek-American agreements also indicate that Washington does not intend to withdraw from the region upon the conclusion (especially upon a quick conclusion) of the operation in Afghanistan.

Superficially, it may seem that all these developments are happening with Moscow's consent. It may appear that Moscow is collaborating with the United States, does not object to American soldiers in the region, and has declared its desire for a long-term rapprochement with West. However, a closer analysis of the situation reveals the range of Russia's bargaining chips. First of all, Russia is becoming a reliable partner of the West (especially Western Europe); it has declared the same values, cooperates, and actively engages in constructing a post–Cold War security system. Secondly, it is becoming an invaluable partner of the United States in the Afghanistan conflict; it has cooperated politically by sharing both intelligence and military facilities (by supporting anti-Taliban forces). Its role will presumably grow in tandem with the lengthening operation in Afghanistan. Such influence ensures Russian influence over the Northern Alliance, as well as a convergence of interests and cooperation with Iran regarding Afghanistan. Paradoxically, the U.S. victory over the Taliban will allow Russia to strengthen the positions of its clients (Northern Alliance) in Afghanistan. (True, it is difficult to imagine that in the face of Washington's consistent pro-Pashtun and pro-Pakistan policy, the United States could succeed in weakening Russia and Iran's influence among the Tajiks, Hazaras, and Uzbeks. However, the cooperation between the United States and Uzbekistan allows some certain room for maneuvering.) Thirdly, U.S. involvement in Uzbekistan will inevitably entangle Washington in a range of this country's internal structural problems, ranging from its economic problems to the fundamentalism in the Fergana Valley. A solution to these problems would require enormous political and financial investment from the United States before Uzbekistan became a reliable partner and ally.

Finally, Russia seems still to have control over the "entry" of the Caspian region into the wider world: Afghanistan, pervaded as it is by war, will not be suitable for this for a long time yet. Iran still does not seem ready for close cooperation with United States, while the Caucasus is still experiencing successive tremors (Georgia, the unresolved Chechen question— after September 11, suggestions appeared in the Russian press to "liquidate the bases of Chechen terrorists" that Georgia supposedly harbors, also commenting that the U.S. operation in Afghanistan may serve as a precedent—and the currently growing Abkhaz problem). At the beginning of October 2001, Georgian-Abkhaz relations worsened following the appearance of a Chechen division that had fought its way through from the Pankissi Ravine (in the east of the country) to the Kodori Ravine in Abkhazia. Air bombardment of Georgian border villages by (most likely) the Russian air force also began opportunely. This conflict will significantly worsen, and such bad Russian-Georgian relations call the withdrawal of the Russian base in Abkhazia into question (especially as Abkhazia has renewed its request to join the Russian Federation). This also speaks very badly of Georgia's internal stability: giving the Chechens passage through the country is undoubtedly an element of the contest between President Eduard Shevardnadze and the opposition (presumably focused around the leader of parliament, Zurab Zhvania, and the minister of internal affairs, Kakha Targamadze). The crisis in Georgia, and the evident Russian instruments of influence on the situation in this country, guarantee Moscow that Georgia would be ruled out as a political partner for anyone, and also as a transit region for Caspian raw materials.

In October 2001, once Caspian oil began flowing onto the European market via a Russian pipeline to Novorossiysk, the plan for an Atyrau-Baku-Ceyhan pipeline supported by United States underwent another crisis because of the conflicts between Azerbaijan and Turkmenistan, and between Iran and Kazakhstan. In September 2001, Azerbaijan significantly distanced itself from the proposed trans-Caspian oil pipeline from Kazakhstan.

## CONCLUSIONS AND RECOMMENDATIONS

As the antiterrorist coalition has expanded, the new era of U.S. involvement in the south of the CIS has become fact. Never before has the United States had a direct military presence here. This creates both enormous opportunities and enormous dangers.

The presence of the United States in the region seems inevitable: a state that wants to play the role of a superpower cannot allow itself to be absent from a place where the influences of the greatest powers of Asia (at once partners and rivals of the United States) clash, four of which have nuclear weapons (Russia, China, Pakistan, and India). This is especially true as Pakistan, hitherto the linchpin of U.S. support, is undoubtedly experiencing immense internal tensions that threaten destabilization with far-reaching results beyond the region's borders. Thus, it becomes key to provide enormous and constant support—both political and economic—for building independent and efficient states in the region.

U.S. involvement also seems beyond debate in a region where the Islamic fundamentalism that has given birth to terrorism plainly has perfect conditions for development (both in Afghanistan and Tajikistan, the entire Fergana Valley, and the northern Caucasus, Chechnya, and Dagestan). The problems that accompany (and frequently precede) fundamentalism include uncontrolled trade in drugs and arms, as well as problems both social and humanitarian (such as refugees). Despite its rhetoric, Russia is not able to solve these problems, and even seems to generate them (considering the example of Chechnya, and indirectly Tajikistan). The current Russia-centered defense system therefore requires fundamental revision; otherwise problems will snowball out of control.

Nor does it seem debatable that stocks of Caspian energy raw materials must be controlled, as they may serve as reserves in case American-Arab relations become inflamed. The danger of conflicts of interests with Russia exerts a very strong influence on the elites, counter-elites, and societies of the Caspian region. Another hurdle is the multi-level political, economic, social, and cultural crisis in the countries of the region, which is called "transformation." To overcome its causes and results—which is necessary to stabilize the region and join it to international political and economic currents—will require many years, even generations. This will entail pressures and efforts, as well as peace at a considerable price. Unfortunately, the costs of such efforts may appear too high for the United States: among other things, it would require a revision of Washington's hitherto inflexible policy of promoting American democratic and civil standards. (The other extreme—supporting local despots, as was done with the Pahlavi family in Iran—is also unsafe, of course.) American society also seems excessively disinclined to sacrifice the lives of American soldiers for this goal.

In the end, the United States has proved very weak at recognizing the terrain and the local problems. Russia, as do Iran, Pakistan, and Turkey, has an overwhelming amount of knowledge of the local realities, and also a network of links with local elites. Stabilization of the region is impossible without their cooperation. In other words, without considering the interests of Russia and Iran, and indirectly of the Northern Alliance, the success of the operation in Afghanistan seems impossible, despite its obvious goal of creating a stable order, liquidating conditions for the development of terrorism, and the possible opening of Afghanistan to the transit of Caspian raw materials. In the long term, therefore, the best guarantee of stability in the region (and beyond it)—and of the protection of American interests—would be creation of a zone of regional cooperation with Russia, and especially with Iran. Nevertheless, while it is true that all three countries would undoubtedly have to make a colossal effort to revise their previous strategic assumptions, hope is raised by the fact that the first signals of readiness for such changes are evident in all three countries.

Without a doubt the Asian countries will contest Russia's future position in the world order, although the United States will also play a fundamental part in this process. Russia's position toward China, India, Pakistan, and the Islamic world will to a considerable degree depend not only on the imperial character of Russia, but also on its internal situation and economic development. The scale of challenges that Asia presents Russia is demonstrated as much by the challenging cooperation and rivalry with China as by the problem embodied by Afghanistan.

The process of reconstructing Russia's influence in Asia gained in intensity after September 11, 2001, because of Russia's importance in the antiterrorist coalition and strong political factions in Afghanistan (especially after the defeat of the Taliban) and the surrounding region. Russia's most important entry point for the future is its position in the south of the CIS, in Central Asia and the southern Caucasus. This is the region that will decide Russia's superpower potential. So far, as a result of traditions and weak economic tools, Russia had been building its influence in this region by playing on weaknesses and local conflicts. This destabilizes the region and hinders its development, but this policy seems to be successful in the short term. In the longer term it may have catastrophic results beyond the region. The great threat for this policy after September 11, 2001, is strong military, political, and economic engagement on the part of the United States (and the European Union in the economic sphere) in Central Asia and the Caucasus. This calls into question Russia's monopoly, gives a geopolitical alternative for the region, strengthens the independence of the new states, and encourages growth in terms of regional stability.

These opposing tendencies—U.S. involvement in Russia's sphere of influence and the growing role of Russia in the coalition, Russia's particular influence in Central Asia and Afghanistan together with Russian flexibility in Moscow-Washington relations—create a completely new style of policy for Russia in the south of the CIS. Thanks to its position in the region, Russia has become an important player in global (Asiatic) policy and a kind of partner and ally for the United States. Though thus far it is symbolic, the breaking of Russia's monopoly in Central Asia by the United States seems to be a good price to pay for the change in Russia's position, particularly as Moscow has been keeping fairly tight control of political processes in the region. Russia's biggest problem will be keeping these political instruments and finding solutions for the region's social, economic, and cultural problems.

## NOTES

1. The value of weapons and technologies to be exported by Russia in 2001 is estimated at U.S.$4.4 billion (with 70 percent falling to China and India): M. Galeotti, "Russia's Arms Bazaar," *Jane's Intelligence* (April 2001). The export of arms to China planned for the next five years is supposed to reach U.S.$15 billion: S. Blank, "Russia Seeks to Profit from Iranian Rearmament," *Jane's Intelligence* (April 2001).

2. See, for example, J. Urbanowicz, "Wejście smoka," *Wprost*, no. 34 (August 23, 2001).

3. G.B. Bessarabov and A.D. Soyanin, *Novyj zapadnyj pohod* (Report of the Transcaspian Project, February 22, 2001).

4. For example, the agreements on the construction of railways from Uzbekistan to Kashgar signed in Shanghai in 2001.

5. D. Biliouri, "Keeping the Lid on Central Asia's Water Dispute," *Jane's Intelligence* (April 2001); I. Amanzolov, "Konfliktnyje istoki transgranichnyh rek 2001," http://www.caapr.kz/show.php?kza0502-02.htm.

6. Katarzyna Pełczyńska-Nałęcz, Russian Gas Industry—Current Condition and Prospects (Warsaw: CES Studies, April 2001).

7. Together with other raw materials: 42 percent of the value of exports sold outside the CIS; 57 percent of the value of exports to the CIS member states.

8. In 1999, there were 216,364 drug-related crimes recorded within the Russian Federation: *Human Development Report 2000*.

9. It is estimated that about two million to five million people in the Russian Federation are drug addicts.

10. According to the average estimates of the State Office for Statistics (Goskomstat), the number of inhabitants of the Russian Federation will decrease from 145.6 million (2000) to 138.7 (2010): www.undp.ru/NHDR/summary_2000_eng.htm. At the same time, the birthrate in Central Asian countries is on the increase. For example, in Uzbekistan, 37 percent of the population is under 14, and in Tajikistan 42 percent are under 14. See Central Intelligence Agency, *The World Factbook 2000* (Washington, D.C.: U.S. Government Printing Office, 2000).

11. A. Wolowska, *Caspian Oil and Gas: The Facts at the End of the Year 2000* (Warsaw: CES Studies, April 2001).

# 9

## Putin's European Policy

*László Póti*

More or less a decade after the change of regimes, with the dissolution-disintegration-divorce of states in Eastern and Central Europe and the end of the Cold War, Europe has expanded eastward via the North Atlantic Treaty Organization (NATO) and has also decided on further expansion and its serious internal reform via the European Union (EU). Yet the biggest entity in Eastern Europe—Russia—has consolidated itself internally, reached a broad consensus on foreign policy, and is keen on ensuring itself an appropriate role both in world and European politics.

At this point, it is appropriate to make a balance sheet of how relations between these two parts of Europe have evolved, with the emphasis on where Russian policy toward Europe stands now. This chapter is aimed at the analysis of the following questions: How do Russia's policies toward Western Europe differ from its policies toward Eastern and Central Europe? Is there a basis for a future Russian partnership with the European Union, and is President Vladimir Putin seeking a real partnership, or is his policy mere propaganda? Does Russia view relations with the European Union in economic terms alone? Does Moscow seek to drive a wedge between Europe—most notably France and Germany—and the United States? What are the consequences for Russia of EU enlargement to Central Europe? Does Russia have a strategy to counterbalance possible negative consequences? Will Moscow propose a deal accepting EU enlargement in lieu of NATO expansion?

First, President Putin has brought about a marked shift in Russian foreign policy toward Europe, but it is not a return to the pro-Western course of the early nineties. Second, although Russian policy toward Eastern and Central Europe (primarily the ex–Warsaw Pact countries) has undergone a process of standardization during the last decade, there are still a number of specific features that color Russia's European policy. Third, Russia-EU relations are characterized by a double asymmetry: while Russia's basic interest is in the economic domain, the European Union is mainly interested in political and soft security matters. Moreover, within the area of economics, Russia is clearly dependent on the European Union, while the reverse is not the case. Fourth, it is of little analytical value to use the so-called "wedge-driving scheme" to study Russia-Europe-U.S. relations—that is, to view any growing closeness in Russia-Europe relations as a way for Russia to drive a wedge between Europe and the United States. Fifth, the perceived negative consequences of EU enlargement by Moscow are partially real, but to a great extent intentionally exaggerated to achieve extra benefits. Sixth, there have been some nicely formulated Russian ideas to "counterbalance" the perceived negative consequences of EU enlargement, but they have not been transformed into a strategy. Finally, Putin's policy toward the European Union is definitely not mere propaganda, but it may not be considered as a policy aimed at full-fledged partnership either.

## BACKGROUND OF RUSSIA'S EUROPEAN POLICY

In order to provide adequate answers to the questions posed in the introduction, a brief discussion of the theoretical and conceptual evolution of Russia's new foreign and security policy is in order. First, how does Russia's foreign and security policy relate to international relations theory? Second, what has been the outcome of the grand debates about Russia's international orientation? And third, what is the end result of the official establishment of concepts and doctrine during the 1990s?

At the level of international relations theory, the formation of Russia's new foreign and security policy is a story of gradual movement from the idealist/liberal paradigm to the realist one.[1] The roots of the policy lie in Mikhail Gorbachev's "new political thinking," which promoted creation of a new global community in a more interdependent world, on the basis of common universal values.[2] It attached great importance to international organizations and regimes, and regarded cooperation as the main characteristic of international interaction. By contrast, Russia's new policy relies increasingly on realism, has put national interest at center stage, and has emphasized different types of state interests in a multipolar world. As one analyst put it, "Russian decision-makers appear more prone to perceive the outside world in terms of conflict, clashes of interest, and a zero-sum game than through the lenses of mutual interest and common approaches ... thinking in terms of spheres of influence, windows of opportunity, and power vacuums has gained an astonishing degree of respectability."[3]

With regard to Russia's international orientation, during the early years, the main dividing line was between two schools of thought, whose debate

relatively soon resulted in a kind of synthesis that has become the mainstream school of thought determining the official course as well. The first
approach can be labeled as Atlantist, Westernizer, or liberal international-
ist. According to this school, Russia is an organic part of European civilization; its interests are close to or identical with the West; the quickest
possible integration into the European and world communities is desired;
relations with the West should be accorded the highest priority; Russia
does not have any enemies; and it does not want to be a global power.
The second school of thought—usually labeled as Eurasianist—claims that
Russia is neither part of European nor Asian civilization, but is a special
mixture of the two; its interests differ from the West; and Russia should not
be integrated into Europe, but rather it should be the center of integration
itself for the region surrounding it. Relations with the Commonwealth of
Independent States (CIS) countries should be its top priority; Russia should
stick to its great power status; and it does have enemies. The debate
between these schools of thought has brought about a synthesis of the two
philosophies called "geopolitical realism," which by 1993–94 had begun to
dominate political discourse.[4]

The representatives of this approach do not identify themselves with
either the Atlantists or with the Eurasianists. Rather, they take in elements
of both. The representatives of this somewhat amorphous approach start
from the proposition that the basis for Russia's new foreign policy should
not be any mythic or abstract concepts but should derive from pragmatism
and rationality. They rely on the "geopolitical realities," since their theory
is based on securing Russia's interests, first of all, in a certain geopolitical
space. Some of the "realists" even call for a kind of "reductionism" in
Russia's desired foreign policy behavior, calling for a "continental strategy"
for Russia because the basis for Russia's influence in the world has significantly decreased.[5]

The representatives of this school[6]—adopting a kind of Russian Monroe
Doctrine—regard the post-Soviet space as a sphere of vital Russian interest. They argue that Russia has its own interests that run counter to the
interests of the West. These interests can—but do not necessarily—lead to
conflicts. The geopolitical realists try to achieve balance between Europe
and Asia, want to avoid isolating Russia, and strive to reach great power
status only in the long term.

President Putin does not seem to fit into any of these three main schools
of thought, but he comes close to the last, synthesizing one, with an added
pragmatic tone.

Since the formation of the Russian Federation there have been three
waves of official foreign and security policy doctrines. In addition, a number of semi-official policies have been promulgated in which Russian policy toward Europe has been formed as well: the foreign policy concept and
military doctrine in 1993; the national security concept in 1997; and the

national security concept, the military doctrine, and foreign policy concept in 2000.

As to Europe, three more or less constant features of the Russian approach can be observed. First is the priority given to relations with multilateral institutions, as opposed to bilateral relations, in channeling Russian interests into the continent. Second, at the institutional level, there is an obvious preference for the all-European organizations as opposed to the western European institutions. Third is the intentional, or unintentional, identification of NATO with the West, while the European Union has remained more or less neglected. To the extent that the European Union receives any attention, it has been perceived positively.[7] From its original "neglected" position, the European Union gradually gained more importance from the Russian perspective. The organization first began to be regarded as one of the centers of the multipolar world, and then as a desired "equal and constructive" partner for Russia. Current foreign policy directives, however, do not contain any conceptual elaboration or any kind of distinctive place for the European Union in Russia's foreign policy hierarchy. The most relevant document, the foreign policy concept, limits itself by stating that "relations with the European Union have key importance," it is an "important political and economic partner" of Russia. The few paragraphs dealing with the European Union are descriptive and not at all innovative or ambitious. Moreover, they are quite defensive in making repeated references to Russia's expectation for "taking its interests into account in the process of enlargement." With regard to the European Union's establishment of a common security and defense policy, the document presents a wait-and-see position.

However, it would be misleading to end the discussion of mainstream Russian perceptions of Europe at this point. The last one and a half years have witnessed further important changes both in Russia's perceptions of Europe and the recommended policies. At a minimum, new proposals arose for building relations with the European Union that would lead to "permanent association,"[8] or even "setting the long-term goal—two to three decades—of the accession of Russia to [the] European Union."[9]

Even if these propositions have not yet become a full part of official discourse, important shifts have been observed recently. Foreign Minister Igor Ivanov, evaluating ten years of Russian foreign policy in April 2001, reaffirmed the second place of Europe in the foreign policy hierarchy, and called the European Union a "natural and very perspective partner ... [Russia's relations with which] have been given [a] new quality in recent months."[10] On another occasion he revived the notion of building a "strategic partnership"[11] with the European Union. The language of Russian-EU joint statements has systematically used this latter notion since the sixth summit in October 2000.[12] In April, in his annual address, President Putin stated, "the importance of further efforts to form [a] partnership with the

European Union is growing. The course of integration with Europe is becoming one of the key directions of our foreign policy."[13]

The Russian interpretation of the notion of integration differs significantly from the Western and Central European interpretations of this term. In Western and Central Europe, integration means—in its classical sense—formation of a community of states in which national sovereignty is relative, in order to reach a new quality of relations among the members. The Russian interpretation is much looser, meaning not to be left out of international (European) organizations; that is, to avoid isolation. (It should be noted here that in public international discourse, the term "integration" is often used improperly—e.g., it is used in connection with NATO, which, strictly speaking, is not integration.)

An analysis of the theoretical-conceptual background of Russian foreign policy reveals that attention to Europe decreased at the levels of international relations theory and grand debates of different foreign policy schools. At the level of official concepts and doctrines, there appears to be no place identified for Europe in Russia's foreign policy hierarchy. Finally, at the level semi-official inputs and recent policy discourse, there is a marked shift toward Europe.

## THE NATURE OF RUSSIAN-EUROPEAN RELATIONS

Formally and institutionally, Russia-Europe relations have been well-elaborated and structured. The Partnership and Cooperation Agreement (PCA) signed in 1994, which took effect in December 1997, not only substituted for the old Soviet–European Community agreement, but also went beyond simple trade regulation and increased and widened the scope of interaction between the two entities. In 1999, both Moscow and Brussels further concretized their respective policies by adopting the European Union's Common Strategy on the one hand, and the "Medium-term Strategy for the Development of Relations between the Russian Federation and the European Union (2000–10)" of the Russian government, on the other. Both sides have arrived at the mutually positive conclusion that Russian-EU relations have reached a "new quality." The PCA regulates trade relations on the basis of most-favored-nation (MFN) treatment. The gradual elimination of quantitative restrictions enhances economic cooperation in the field of energy, transport, environment, etc., and promotes justice and home affairs cooperation in the areas of drug trafficking, money laundering, and organized crime. Finally, it introduces increased and institutionalized political dialogue at all levels.[14] As for trade, the European Union represents Russia's largest partner, accounting for 36.7 percent of Russia's imports and 33.2 percent of its exports. Russia is the European Union's sixth-largest partner, with 3.3 percent of its imports and 1.9 percent of its exports.

Indeed, judging by the basic documents regulating Russian-EU relations, other high-level declarations, and the ongoing practices, it can be concluded that the basis for a future partnership exists, and this basis consists of profound interests on both sides. However, there is a striking asymmetry between each side's focus. While Russia wants the partnership predominantly for economic reasons, the European Union's main interest lies elsewhere, in the fields of security, stability, democracy building, and ecology.[15]

It is important to note that, although the increased Russian interests in the European Union have coincided with the latter's move in the direction of the Common European Security and Defense Policy (CESDP), it would be misleading to interpret it as a main driving force for increased Russian interest in the European Union. The first attempt to frame some kind of cooperation in the security field came from the European Union, in its Common Strategy. It laid down very ambitious plans including the creation of "a permanent EU/Russia mechanism for political and security dialogue," and even the development of "joint foreign policy initiatives."[16] During the Paris summit in October 2000 the two sides issued a joint declaration on "strengthening the dialogue and cooperation on political and security matters in Europe." Both mainstream Russian analysts and politicians have attached great attention to the evolving CESDP, and during the last summits the Russian side tried even to institutionalize the cooperation, but the move was rejected by the EU "troika."

Russia's first and foremost goal of partnership with the European Union is to adopt a modernization model that will help Russia become an integral part of the "European economic and social space." However, it must be noted that there is a strong asymmetry vis-à-vis economic relations, which is quite obvious from the above-mentioned trade statistics: the asymmetry of dependence. Russia badly needs the EU market, but Russia is marginal for the European Union. Yet we must not overlook that in the field of energy, where the European Union is highly dependent on Russia.

There are two economic issues in which the European Union is directly interested in further developing relations with Russia: the energy sector and the euro. In 2000, the European Union launched a "strategic energy partnership" with Russia, in which the European Union intends to double its energy import from Russia within twenty years. As of today, Russia covers 20 percent of the European Union's gas and 16 percent of the European Union's oil consumption.[17] According to Russian estimates, gas consumption in Europe could increase by 40 to 70 percent by 2010, and Russia will try to preserve 25 percent of that market in the forthcoming decades.[18] In connection with the other issue, the EU troika put forward a proposal during the last Moscow summit in May 2001 to introduce the euro instead of the dollar in EU-Russian trade.

The Russian approach to NATO enlargement has gone through different phases since the issue was placed on the agenda. Moscow's approach has not always been a priori negative. It started with a short period of hinting at the idea of potential membership; continued by going to the other extreme (vehement rejection of the enlargement); and in 1997, ended up reaching a compromise in the form of the NATO-Russia Founding Act, and NATO's self-obligation on nondeployment of troops and nuclear weapons in the new member states. Up until now, the Russian approach that reached this kind of compromise avoided the repetition of both pro-Western illusions and Soviet-type arrogance, and remained within the realm of typical behavior between countries.

NATO's 1999 air campaign against Yugoslavia resulted in a considerable cooling down of relations with Russia, but by a year later Moscow had returned to business as usual. However, the second wave of enlargement, to be announced in 2002, will seriously test Russia's approach.

The terrorist attacks on New York and Washington had two types of positive effects on Russian policy toward Europe. First, they reaffirmed the trend of further strengthening of Russia-EU relations; second, they brought about the possibility of a breakthrough in Russia-NATO relations. As to the first, the EU-Russia summit—scheduled prior to the September events—held in October resulted in establishment of a permanent body that further institutionalized bilateral relations and has become a kind of parallel to the already existing NATO-Russian Joint Permanent Council. In addition, Moscow seemed to soften its tough approach toward Chechnya by hinting at a possible nonmilitary solution to the problem. This move may prove Moscow's desire to deal with this delicate issue in a more European-like manner. As to NATO-Russian relations, the most obvious elements of Russia's new attitude are: 1) within weeks Moscow changed from being a rival of the United States to becoming a key ally; 2) the possibility of Russia's accession to NATO has ceased to be perceived as something unrealistic and only a kind of political rhetoric; and 3) the importance of NATO enlargement has been relativized from Moscow's perspective. All in all, paradoxically the terrorist attacks brought about a number of positive developments in key areas of European and international politics.

## MOSCOW'S POLICIES TOWARD CENTRAL EUROPE

Terminologically it is interesting to note that the region of eastern and central Europe (ECE) has been called in Russian political discourse the "far abroad" (*daln`eye zarubez`ye*), "middle abroad" (*sredn`eye zarubez`ye*), and "near West" (*bliz`niy zapad*). All three terms are rooted in the well-known expression "near abroad" (covering post-Soviet space) and refer to some kind of special status of the region. Russian foreign policy divides

ECE into three subregions: the central European (ex–Warsaw Pact countries), the Baltic, and the Balkans, with each having a specific image and role for Russia. As regards the first region, the evolution of Russia–eastern/central Europe relations in the 1990s has been a process of "standardization."[19] This has included the following elements that characterize the present state of affairs as well. First, Russia's policy toward ECE is no longer a special part of Russian domestic policy but a normal part of Russian foreign policy. Second, ECE has fallen greatly in prestige and has found its naturally low place in the system of priorities of Russian foreign policy.[20] This means that, as opposed to Soviet times when the ECE region represented an artificially high priority in the priority system for Soviet foreign and security policy, Russia's new leadership has gradually distanced itself from such an evaluation. From Moscow's perspective, the region has lost its direct value. As a matter of fact, Moscow typically approaches the ECE region—i.e., within the context of Russia-Europe policy.

The term "direct value" is used here to point out how differently the ex–Warsaw Pact countries were viewed in Soviet times than by Russia now. While in those times this region did have an autonomous, direct value for Soviet foreign and security policy, that is not the case with Russia. For Moscow the ECE countries represent a certain value primarily in the wider context of its European policy. By contrast, the countries of the former Soviet Union, such as the Baltic states or Ukraine, still represent direct value for Moscow, as was the case during Soviet times with the Warsaw Pact countries.

The third change is that instead of the previous bloc approach, Russian policy handles these countries individually or regionally; that is, differentiation has come to the fore. Fourth is that relations with these countries have been demilitarized and de-ideologized, as well. Finally, all major problems that had to do with the Soviet past (the Warsaw Treaty, Soviet interventions, the consequences of troop withdrawal, and the inherited debts) have been settled.

Thus, one might conclude that the already standard relations with ECE do not make Russian policy toward this region different from Russian policy toward western Europe. Yet there are some factors that set apart Russian policy toward ECE. First, although the "bridge concept" of the ECE region vis-à-vis western Europe and Russia is gone, there still remains a role for this region as an entity that unites Russia with the rest of the continent. This is seen mostly in economic terms, with ECE serving primarily as a transit route for delivery of Russian goods—especially energy—to western Europe. Second, in a wider security context, the ECE countries are of special importance to Russia from the point of view of their ongoing accession to the Western institutions that Russia is not part of, because Moscow fears being isolated from the continent.

The importance of the central European countries—most of which will gain entry to the European Union in a few years—has considerably grown in Russian eyes. This is embodied, first of all, in the growing amount of Russian economic activity in these countries. Therefore it is proper to label the current Russian policy toward ECE as "economized."[21] With the disappearance of the traditional political and military means for asserting will, and the forthcoming perspective of the ECE countries' accession to the European Union, Russia gradually switched to developing economic ties with these countries. The main fields of this new "economized" Russian policy are, foremost, the energy and finance sectors. The existing Yamal pipeline in Poland, another planned gas pipeline through Poland and Slovakia, and increased Russian share in Hungary's chemical industry offer good examples.[22] According to press reports from all over the region, Russia's secret services have stepped up activities in the ECE in recent years. The aim of these actions would be to slow down or to stop the rapprochment of the countries in the region with western European institutions. Obviously we know quite little of these actions—due to the non-transparent character of secret-services activities—but if we judge by the results of these operations, they do not seem to be very effective.

The Baltic region still plays a special role due to the common past, its geopolitical position, and the Russian minority living there. The Balkans have preserved their traditional role as a region of special Russian interest, primarily in security terms. Furthermore, with the ongoing Balkan crises, this region's importance has even increased, which is well-illustrated by Russia's active involvement in the peacekeeping efforts of the international community, and by Russia's own numerous acts and initiatives to solve the conflicts.

## RUSSIA, THE EUROPEAN UNION, AND THE UNITED STATES

When analyzing Russia-Europe-U.S. relations, it is quite common to apply the "wedge thesis," that is to describe Russia's strategy as wanting to drive a wedge between Europe and the United States, in order to loosen their strong alliance and, thus, to decrease U.S. influence in Europe. It is easy to support the idea that Russia wants to drive a wedge between the United States and Europe (the European Union, France, or Germany). An analysis with an emphasis on the elements of continuity of Soviet/Russian power behavior, the conflicts in Russian-U.S. relations, converging positions of some European powers with the Russian stance on certain topical issues (National Missile Defense, Iraq), as opposed to the American stance would support the case. Though it is undeniable that Russia will always point out and make use of the differences between U.S. and EU positions, the "wedge thesis" is not convincing enough.

First of all, it is not correct that transatlantic relations are a system of links in which each side has identical interests. Such a perception would very much resemble the first period of Russia's foreign policy, characterized by a misperception of interests between Russia and the West. As a matter of fact, it is often the western European countries that initiate interactions that give the impression that Russia–Western Europe rapprochment is being achieved to the detriment of Europe-U.S. relations. The best examples have been provided by the French, who from time to time come up with proposals aiming at defense industry cooperation. Second, the Russian foreign policy worldview has gone through a rather substantial evolution, and by now it has reached a stage that can be regarded as relatively stable and consensual. Russian foreign policy has gradually shifted from the original U.S. orientation toward Europe/EU, due to the recognition of Russia's decreased international status, its economic needs, and the rise of the European Union in world politics via deeper integration and readiness for enlargement. In this sense Russia's increased interest in Europe should not be perceived in anti-American terms but rather as a more balanced approach to both of them. Third, in general, the wedge thesis seems to be of little analytical use in the post–bipolar world order, because it made the most sense in the conditions of a two-bloc system, where gains and losses were interpreted as zero-sum games. Finally, if there can be any analytical use of the wedge scheme, then it should be applicable to all actors of international relations; it should not be limited to the description of Russian behavior and motivations vis-à-vis the United States, because that would mean a biased approach.

Official Russian declarations try to avoid giving the impression that increased Russian interest in Europe would hamper Russian-U.S. relations.[23] Indeed, the spectacular evolution of Russian-European relations in recent years can be interpreted not as part of Russian strategy against the United States, but rather as a reflection of both sides' recognition that there is an elementary need for establishing and maintaining business-like relations that would help solve inherited problems (debts), and develop existing or evolving projects (e.g., energy).

The relations within the Russia-EU-U.S. triangle differ qualitatively. The Russia-U.S. dimension is characterized by "quarrelsome" dialogue, the EU-U.S. by alliance, and the Russia-EU by "strategic" partnership. Obviously, dialogue and partnership are very different categories. The first refers to a state of affairs between states where there is more dissimilarity than similarity of interests, while partnership refers to more common elements in the interests of the two sides.

There are two more points that do not support the wedge thesis. First, the erosion of the United Nations' position in world affairs and the strengthening of the European Union's position have led to a situation where the roles of European institutions have increased from the Russian perspective. If we add to this the recent diversification of Russia's ties with individual western European states (in addition to the traditional orientation toward Germany and France), such as Great Britain, Spain, and Italy, the importance of bilateral relations with the states of traditional importance seem to have decreased in relative terms. Second, Russia has been in favor of some kind of "triangularization" of U.S.-EU-Russia relations.[24] Both Russia and the European Union have expressed their intentions of continuing this format and possibly giving it a permanent character.[25]

Although the different Russian foreign policy concepts and other guiding documents do not refer to any special role of Germany and France, these two countries stand out as distinguished partners for Russia. At the risk of some simplification, it can be argued that the Moscow-Berlin "axis" is based upon primarily economic interests, while the Moscow-Paris "axis" is on security calculations. Germany has more or less been Russia's number one trading partner (with 10–12 percent of Russian trade turnover), and Germany is also Russia's biggest creditor with some U.S.$30 billion out of U.S.$150 billion in overall Russian foreign debt. (Some suggestions have held that part of the debt could be repaid by offering shares of Russian companies to Germany. Among others, Ruhrgaz is keen on increasing its share in Gazprom to 5–10 percent.) In terms of energy, Germany is much more dependent on Russia than the European Union's average. In 2000, Russia provided 35 percent of Germany's gas and 33 percent of its oil. For 2002 Germany plans to increase Russian oil deliveries by 13.4 percent.[26] In comparison to the Helmut Kohl–Boris Yeltsin era, a certain shift has been observed from both Chancellor Gerhard Schröeder and President Putin, from a kind of emotional policymaking toward more pragmatic attitudes.

During the French presidency of the European Union, a spectacular activation of Russian-French relations was witnessed. Putin attended the EU-Russia summit in Paris in November 2000, where the already mentioned "strategic energy partnership" policy was launched. However, the main domain in which Paris and Moscow can count on each other is traditional security policy. The sharp French criticism with regard to Chechnya does not prevent the two sides from occupying similar positions on some important issues of world politics, of which National Missile Defense and Iraq are the most obvious examples. Parallel to the closeness of positions on such issues, bilateral ties have also been activated, especially in the sphere of defense. During the visit of French defense minister Alain Richard, in the beginning of this year, an agreement was reached on such matters as high level military visits, joint exercises, and exchange of students in military education facilities.[27] The recent visit to Moscow of President Jacques Chirac of France once again reaffirmed the close relationship between the two countries.

## CONSEQUENCES OF EU ENLARGEMENT

The original, neutral-positive Russian attitude toward EU enlargement remains basically unchanged, but it has been become more sophisticated. Moscow has identified both positive and negative consequences vis-à-vis its own interests. Positive consequences include the following:

- The widening of the zone of political and economic stability in Europe;
- Increased attractiveness of the European part of Russia for investors;
- The contribution that Russia's integration will make to the all-European economic space, especially to the united transport and communication systems; and
- Increased potential for trade due to simplified and unified customs procedures, and accounting.

Possible negative consequences can be divided into four groups:

- Trade and investment, i.e., the continued reorientation of the new members toward EU markets, further decrease of Russian–new EU member trade, especially in terms of Russian energy deliveries; and redirection of foreign investment to the new members at the expense of Russia;
- Movement of people, i.e., crossing borders will be more complicated due to the visa regime to be introduced;
- Kaliningrad, i.e., communication, supply, and transportation with and through Kaliningrad will be more problematic; and
- Political isolation, i.e., Russia will not only be pushed further to the edge of the continent, but the number of those opposing the European Union's closer cooperation with Russia will increase by the enlargement.

It is very clear that both the perceived negative and positive consequences of EU enlargement have to do, first of all, with economic considerations, and political or security policy fears have emerged only marginally or indirectly.

As a matter of fact, the problems put forward by Russia in the context of EU enlargement do not seem to be real ones. For example, concerning the first point, average industrial tariffs are currently higher in the acceding countries than in the European Union itself. In addition, the new members will have to apply the MFN regulations, while in the field of energy there is little room for maneuver for alternative sources of supply. As to the visa issue, although the prior Russia-ECE regime was formally visa-free, it was a de facto visa regime.[28] The issue of Kaliningrad seems to be the most real in terms of possible negative consequences, but even with its unique exclave/enclave status, it remains marginal when considered against the entirety of Russia-EU relations. The last concern is not convincing either, for the new members will have to apply the union's Common Strategy, which stimulates relations with Russia.

In the beginning, Russia's strategy (when the issue of enlargement became apparent) was defined as the "minimization" of negative consequences. Originally (as early as the beginning of 1997), Moscow was considering another trilateral format, namely Russia's direct involvement in the accession talks of the candidate countries and the European Union. When this turned out to be impossible, the Kremlin changed its tactics and began to follow a two-track policy. On the one hand, it began to take relatively active steps to establish economic and financial bridgeheads in the countries of the expected first wave of enlargement. On the other hand, it has tried, in the different fora of Russia-EU dialogue, to ensure that special Russian interests are taken into account during the accession talks.[29]

Russia's current strategy with regard to EU enlargement departs from the consideration that it has no means for changing the strategic choice of the ECE countries to join the EU, and that it is not useful to regard the European Union as a rival of Russia in the region. Instead (goes the Russian logic) Moscow should pursue a policy of trilateral engagement. The original "damage-limiting" course and the idea of trilateral accession talks have been substituted for a more realistic approach. Its core is, instead of a formal involvement in trilateral negotiation formats, the implementation of trilateral EU-ECE-Russia economic projects. The idea is to avoid presenting the EU and Russia as two opposing poles, but rather as "complementary parts of the European economic unity."

Not negligible is the question of the possible consequences of EU enlargement on Ukraine and Russia-Ukraine relations. It is important to note that the Ukrainian and Russian perceptions of the two enlargements have been very different since this issue came to the fore. After initial hesitation, NATO enlargement was accepted and supported by Kyiv, but EU enlargement was found to be more problematic (first of all, for fear of changing the visa regime). The Russians had an opposite reaction, because Moscow vehemently opposed the enlargement of NATO while it accepted that of the European Union. Kyiv's opinion of EU enlargement and negligence on behalf of the union, therefore, will probably result in a growing uncertainty regarding the proclaimed Ukrainian integration course into Europe, and correspondingly will lead to more intense and close ties with Russia. There have already been signs of such a shift recently.

Will Moscow propose a deal of accepting EU enlargement in lieu of NATO expansion? Generally speaking, Russia has always proposed all kinds of alternatives to the alliance's expansion, including EU enlargement, and there is no reason why it would not insist on this further. At the same time, Moscow has experienced the difficulties of making these ideas acceptable. However, the lesson learned from NATO enlargement is that deals can be concluded not with the involvement of another institution (e.g., the European Union) but within the given institution. In other words, based on previous experience, the probable Russian deal will be aimed at: 1) in the context of NATO enlargement, asking for further guarantees and additional institutional measures; and 2) in the context of EU enlargement, pushing for mechanisms or incentives for trilateral projects through which Russia can reach the desired level of involvement and influence.

## CONCLUSIONS AND RECOMMENDATIONS

Russia's basic interest in Europe is not just to avoid isolation from the continent, but also to maintain a considerable level of ability to assert its will in European politics. From this point of view, the last decade for Russia has meant a constantly deteriorating position. Interpreting this phenomenon in a wider context, we might say that Russia has faced a major dilemma in Europe, what might be called the dilemma of the "missing middle." This means that if we want to understand Russia's problems in Europe, it is worth putting it in a wider context, and to compare Russia's capabilities of asserting its will at three levels: global (permanent Russian membership in the U.N. Security Council), at the medium level (Europe), and at the regional level (post-Soviet space). While at the global level, through its veto right in the U.N. Security Council, and at the regional level, through the bi- and multilateral mechanisms in the post-Soviet space, Russia has managed to assert its basic interests; in Europe, at the medium level, it completely lacked the same kind of means. Russia has lost what the Soviet Union used to possess in Europe: a bloc with its own institutions that used to have a say in European affairs. As a result of the developments in the second half of the nineties, the solution for Russia's European dilemma seems to have been brought about not by catching up in Europe to the universal or regional level of power assertion, but rather, by the erosion of Russia's position both in the U.N. Security Council and in the post-Soviet space. At the same time, Russia has indeed achieved certain improvements in its involvement in European affairs by signing the Founding Act with NATO. The perspective of developing something similar with the European Union would be an additional element of going beyond the dilemma of the "missing middle."

In theory, various patterns of Russia-EU relations could develop in the future. The list of the possible patterns of Russia-EU relations is long, ranging from being enemies of each other, through rivalry, neutral/low priority relations, partnership, distinguished partnership, permanent associate membership, to full-fledged membership. The current accent on Europe favored by President Putin is leaning in the direction of some kind of distinguished partnership with the European Union. It is much more than just mere propaganda, but it can hardly be qualified as a strategy aimed at full-fledged partnership either. Though it is based on pro-Western pragmatism, it is not a return to the original pro-Western course of the early years of Russian foreign policy. It can be regarded rather as a tactical element in a much wider and ambitious strategy; i.e., to rebuild Russia internally, and to re-create Russia as a great power. On the road to this aim enhanced relations with the European Union are very helpful.

## NOTES

1. In international relations theory the idealist/liberal and the realist paradigms are considered to be the two main competing schools of thought. As scientific terms, they should not be identified with the common meaning of "liberal" or "realist" policy courses. Furthermore, none of these paradigms characterizes the policy of a certain state, but rather they offer different perspectives about world politics. They differ substantially on such questions as who are the main actors of international politics, the role of conflicts and cooperation, the role of ideas versus capabilities, whether international relations are characterized by anarchy, etc.

2. Typical universal values include the rule of law, democracy, the primacy of international law, etc. Although Gorbachev has never abandoned his reform-communist views, at the end of his rule his policy followed converging socialist and capitalist systems of values.

3. Mette Skak, *From Empire to Anarchy: Postcommunist Foreign Policy and International Relations* (London: Hurst and Company, 1996), p. 174.

4. The term "geopolitical realism" was coined by Olga Alexandrova, a senior researcher of the then Cologne-based Institute for East European and International Studies (now in Berlin), and cited by O. Lazebn'ikova in her excellent analysis on early Russian foreign policy debates, *Zapad i borba v polit'icheskih i nauchnih krugah Rossiyi po voprosam eye vn'eshn'ey polit'iki v Evrope (1991–94)*, Dokladi Instituta Evropi, no. 16 (Moscow, 1995).

5. Lazebn'ikova, *op. cit.*

6. The main representatives of the "geopolitical realist" school centered around the Council on Foreign and Defense Policy led by Sergei Karaganov.

7. The European Union has typically been regarded by Russia's leadership as an entity that did not bring about any security threat to Russia, and the European enlargement process has been regarded as an international organization that could substitute for NATO enlargement.

8. "Rossiya i osnovniye inst`ituti bezopasnost`i Evropi" (Russia and the main security institutions of Europe), www.pubs.carnegie.ru/books/2000/06dt/toc.asp.

9. Council on Foreign and Defense Policy, "Strat`egiya dlya Rossiyi: Povestka dlya prezid`enta—2000" (Strategy for Russia: Agenda for the president—2000), www.svop.ru/book2000_chapter2.htm.

10. Lecture delivered at the meeting of the Russian Association of International Studies entitled "Foreign Policy of Russia Today," in Moscow, April 20, 2001, available at: www.ln.mid.ru.

11. See www.strana.ru/state/foreign/2001/05/11/989528534.html.

12. See www.europa.eu.int/comm/external_relations/russia/intro/index/htm.

13. See www.strana.ru/state/kremlin/2001/04/03/986299751.html.

14. This latter includes annually two summits of presidents, cooperation councils at the ministerial level, cooperation committees at senior official levels, and subcommittees on technical issues. The latest (the seventh) summit took place in Moscow on May 17 and 18, 2001.

15. The priority areas of the Action Plan for implementation of the EU Common Strategy are: foreign policy, economic dialogue, civil society, rule of law, democracy, and the "Northern Dimension;" www.eurunion.org/news/speeches/2000/001116/c.htm). Chris Patten, EU commissioner for external relations, in a recent speech summarized the areas of cooperation: trade and investment, health and environment, organized crime, and Russia's place in the world; www.europa.eu.int/comm/external_relations/ceeca/news/ip_01_72.htm. Finally, the European Union's proposed agenda for the latest summit lists the following topics: investment climate, WTO accession, trade issues, environmental protection, nuclear safety, organized crime, stability in Europe, disarmament, and nonproliferation; www.europa.eu.int/comm/external_relations/russia/intro/index.htm.

16. *Common Strategy of the European Union* (Official Journal of the European Communities), June 24, 1999.

17. *Alexander's Gas & Oil Connections,* vol. 5, no. 21 (November 16, 2000), www.gasandoil.com/goc/news.

18. "Rossiyskiy Institut Strat'egicheskih Issledivan'iy," *Rossiyskiy vektor—2000,* Informatsionno-Analit'icheskiy Bullet'en', no. 3.

19. The expression belongs to Gerhard Mangott (Austrian Institute of International Relations), "Russian Policies on Central and Eastern Europe: An Overview," unpublished, 1999.

20. For example, as opposed to the 1993 version of the foreign policy concept, the 2000 version does not refer to eastern and central Europe as a region of vital Russian interest. See *Diplomat`icheskiy Vestn`nik,* no. 3 (1993) and no. 8 (2000).

21. The recent statement of Foreign Minister Ivanov, that "energy diplomacy" is becoming a new direction of foreign policy, is also applicable in ECE: www.strana.ru/state/foerign/2001/05/23/990626595.html.

22. For a detailed analysis, see Margarita M. Balmaceda (ed.), *On the Edge: Ukrainian-Central-European-Russian Security Triangle* (Budapest: CEU Press, 2000).

23. See Prime Minister Kasyanov's statement at a press conference in Stockholm: "There is no cooling down of relations between Russia and the United States, but Russia intends to reinforce its relations with its European neighbors.... [This] does not mean the reorientation of the Russian interests toward Europe." Available at: www.strana.ru/print/988116138.html.

24. March 2000 marked the first trilateral U.S.-EU-Russian meeting. It was held in Lisbon, where the sides discussed a wide range of issues of international politics.

25. *Diplomat`icheskiy Vestn`ik,* no. 4 (2000), p. 5.

26. *Alexander's Gas & Oil Connections,* vol. 6, no. 7 (April 5, 2001) www.gasandoil.com/goc/news.

27. See www.strana.ru/worldwide/press/2001/02/15/982247749.html.

28. The essence of the visa-free regime is to enter another country with a valid passport for a given time without any additional pre-arranged documents. However, this was not the case in Russian-ECE relations. In order to enter Russia—and vice versa—one needed either a "voucher" (an official document, e.g., from a tourist agency), attesting that the bearer was entering the country in an orderly way, or an invitation legalized by notary public. It is also telling that of the approximately 20 million foreigners visiting Hungary annually, Russians account for approximately 12,000.

29. There exists a nonspecified list of Russian desires that was officially handed over to the European Union in 1999. See www.strana.ru/state/foreign /2001/03/21/985195824.html.

# 10

# Russia and NATO Enlargement

*Aleksander Duleba*

Russia's attitude toward the eastward enlargement of the North Atlantic Treaty Organization (NATO) has been unequivocal since NATO's mid-1990s decision to open the door to the central and east European post-communist countries. Russia has opposed the process, considering it to be a fatal mistake on the part of the West and a lost historical opportunity for building a new and fair European security system in the post–Cold War period. Nevertheless, Russia and NATO did manage to achieve agreement over the first wave of enlargement in 1996–97.[1] This chapter will analyze the prospects of Russia's attitude toward the next wave of NATO enlargement through the assessment of Russia's arguments and policies in this regard.

The chapter begins by evaluating Russian arguments, bargaining positions, responses, and policies in order to analyze Russia's approach to the first wave of NATO enlargement. Special attention is given to consequences that could have an impact on future NATO expansion. Then follows an examination of changes in Moscow's strategy toward NATO since the Yugoslav crisis of 1999, which was a turning point in NATO-Russia relations. This includes an assessment of the security and military strategy adopted by Russia in 1999–2000 after the Yugoslav crisis in order to prevent creation of a NATO-centric security system in Europe. The following section examines Russian debate on the second wave of enlargement and evaluates potential "response actions" from Russian leaders, officials, and security experts. It also discusses feelings that NATO's expansion ignores Russian interests, especially by inviting one or more Baltic countries into the alliance. This is followed by the assessment of Russia's response potential with an attempt to mold basic scenarios of Russia's behavior concerning what types of response actions Russia might implement, depending on the geographical scope of the next round of NATO enlargement.

The end of the chapter attempts to formulate a long-term solution in the Russia-NATO relationship, focusing on the enlargement process and Russia's role in global security. The study also examines significant shifts in Russia-U.S.-NATO relations following the September 2001 terrorist attacks against the United States.

## FIRST WAVE OF NATO ENLARGEMENT

According to Russia's expectations from the first half of the 1990s, NATO should disintegrate in the same way the Warsaw Pact did. The other acceptable scenario from the Russian perspective is the transformation of NATO from an exclusive, and mainly military, organization to a Europe-wide, open political structure. As long as the political transformation of NATO would end in its subordination to the Organization for Security and Cooperation in Europe (OSCE), Russia could even accept the accession of the central European countries, except for the Baltic republics.[2] However, NATO's evolution has not met these Russian expectations.

NATO's success during the Cold War went far beyond its accomplishments as an effective military organization for the collective defense of Western democracies and deterrence of the former Soviet Union and Warsaw Pact countries. Member states opted to continue NATO, as the functions it fulfills remain relevant. Thus, NATO's adaptation to the new post–Cold War conditions has been developing contrary to Russia's expectations. Moreover, the Western allies considered NATO enlargement to be part of a broad and long-term strategy supporting the evolution of a peaceful, undivided, and democratic Europe expanding the zone of stability and security eastward. The decision to enlarge NATO was, for the first time, officially signaled by then U.S. President Bill Clinton during his January 1994 visit to Europe, when he stated that enlargement was no longer a question of "whether" but "when."[3]

NATO proved its declared commitment to build a strategic partnership with a democratic Russia. Parallel to the enlargement, NATO proposed a series of initiatives, including a document on NATO-Russia relations and a permanent consultative mechanism that assured Russia an active role in the efforts to build and participate in a new European security system. Even though Russian leaders still perceive NATO enlargement as an approach of military machinery to Russia's borders rather than as an expansion of the zone of stability and security eastward, NATO and Russia managed to come to an agreement in the first half of 1997.

The Founding Act on Mutual Relations, Cooperation, and Security between NATO and the Russian Federation was signed on May 27, 1997, in Paris. At the Madrid summit in July 1997, the Czech Republic, Poland, and Hungary were invited to become members. The first three post-communist countries, also former Moscow satellites, formally joined NATO on March 12, 1999.

Russian arguments against NATO enlargement, formulated at the beginning of the 1990s, are twofold: military-strategic and political. The military-strategic argument followed the fact that Russian troops withdrew from more than 1,500 kilometers of central Europe, from Magdeburg, Germany, to Smolensk, Russia. After that came the development of the strategic central European corridor, which kept NATO and Russian forces at a safe distance. Moreover, Russian territory was inaccessible even to the most modern tactical air weapon systems of west European NATO member countries. Russian security planners wanted the central European countries (CEC)—which created this new strategic corridor between NATO and Russia—to be neutral.[4] NATO enlargement into this central European corridor would mean a breach of the new, post–Cold War strategic stability and a radical change in the European military-operational theater.

In the early 1990s, Russia's security strategy focused on legal endorsement of the CEC's neutral status, a global partnership with the United States in the sphere of strategic stability and nuclear weapons, and the establishment of a European security system via the OSCE. NATO's decision to open the door to the CEC from the strategic corridor was perceived by Russia as a diplomatic failure and a serious blow to Russia's strategic interests.

The political argument followed an old-fashioned Russian perception about NATO. Russian leaders did not change their opinion that NATO is a relic of the bipolar conflict, and thus should dissolve as the Warsaw Pact did. According to this logic, NATO expansion will lead to the international isolation of Russia. If not, NATO should be subordinated to the OSCE, as the only pan-European security structure in which Russia is on equal footing with the NATO countries. Moreover, Russian leadership still perceives NATO enlargement as a deception of the West and an international abasement of Russia. This perception followed the fact that Soviet leadership, namely the first and last Soviet president, Mikhail Gorbachev, was promised by Western counterparts that there would be no NATO expansion if the Soviet Union approved the reunification of Germany and withdrew its troops from central Europe.[5]

Another indirect domestic political effect of NATO enlargement is the strengthening of radical leftist, nationalistic, antidemocratic, and anti-Western forces in Russia, which consequently means the weakening of the democratic and pro-Western political camp and the hampering of the post-communist democratic transformation. Ultimately, an authoritarian and anti-Western Russia would be a less cooperative partner in international security and that is the reason why the price of European, and even global, security would be incomparably higher with NATO expansion.

Minister of Foreign Affairs Andrei Kozyrev (1992–95) based Russian diplomacy on the strategic premise that Russia could avoid international isolation only by joining Western security and integration structures simultaneously with the Central European countries. Kozyrev thought Russia needed to ensure that the CEC did not get preferential treatment in the process of integration.[6]

In the mid-1990s it became clear that NATO enlargement would continue regardless of Russia's disagreement and that the first period of Russia's post–Cold War foreign policy was finished. In January 1996, Kozyrev was replaced with a new minister of foreign affairs, Yevgeni Primakov, who did not share his predecessor's vision on the subject. Both NATO and Russia came to an understanding that a realistic agreement on the enlargement of NATO would be better than no agreement at all.

For Yevgeni Primakov, who was responsible for negotiations during the first phase of NATO enlargement, there were three options open to Russia:

1. Oppose the enlargement and renounce all relations with NATO;
2. Recognize, or at least do not protest, NATO enlargement, and on this basis define Russia's relations with the alliance; and
3. Continue to oppose NATO enlargement but try to minimize the drawbacks for Russia's security and interests.

Primakov felt the first option would be a road to nowhere, essentially a return to the Cold War. The second option smacked of capitulation and would have been quite unacceptable to Russian society. And that is the reason, in Primakov's view, why Russian leadership agreed on the third scenario, considering it to be the best suited to the situation. In other words, Russian diplomacy decided to focus on influencing the process of enlargement.[7]

During the end of 1996 and the first half of 1997, six rounds of negotiations were held between NATO Secretary General Javier Solana and Russian Foreign Minister Yevgeni Primakov, as well as two rounds between Primakov and U.S. Secretary of State Madeleine Albright. At the beginning of the discussions, Russia proposed ten main requirements vis-à-vis its role in NATO enlargement. The requirements may be classified according to the following three categories.

*Legal Form of NATO-Russia Relationship.* Russia requires the NATO-Russia document on the adjustment of their future relationship to be legally binding. According to Russia's proposal at the end of 1996, a NATO-Russia treaty would have to be ratified by all parliaments of the NATO member states, as well as Russia's Federal Assembly. New members would be allowed to enter the alliance only after completion of the process of ratification.

*Military and Strategic Requirements.* The key to the negotiations is Russia's urging of NATO to accept the following military and strategic requirements. First, Russia would be given a veto on NATO decision-making about important issues of European security. Second, the first wave of NATO enlargement would be the last one, whereupon the alliance would close its doors. Third, NATO would not deploy nuclear weapons to the territories of new member states. Fourth, strict limits would be fixed for the NATO conventional forces, which might be deployed to the territories of new members. Fifth, restrictions would be stated for the alliance's accession to military infrastructure on the territory of new members. Sixth, the Treaty on Conventional Forces in Europe (CFE Treaty) would be revised with the aim of meeting Russia's requirements.

*Political and Economic Requests.* In addition to the above-mentioned military requirements, Russia raised three political-economic requests during the negotiations: Russia's membership in G-7 and its transformation to G-8, Russia's membership in the World Trade Organization (WTO), and Russia's membership in the Paris Club of creditors and the restructuring of Russian foreign debt.

In order to strengthen its bargaining position, Russian diplomatic efforts have put forth a series of response actions and policies in case NATO does not take Russia's interests seriously. The following actions and policies in this respect are considered most relevant:

1 Suspension of START I implementation and refusal to ratify the START II Treaty on nuclear warhead reduction;
2. Postponement of the withdrawal of tactical nuclear missiles from the western borders of Belarus and the resumption of their deployment, there;
3. Formation of a military pact among the Commonwealth of Independent States (CIS) countries on the basis of the Tashkent Treaty;
4. Unilateral revision of the CFE Treaty and withdrawal from the international monitoring system on conventional forces, their deployment and movement;
5. Continuation of military and technological cooperation with Iran and other "problematic" countries with anti-Western regimes;
6. Building a strategic partnership with China in order to build a security counterbalance to the West;
7. Independent policy in crisis areas important to European security, e.g., the Balkans and the Middle East;
8. Offering security guarantees under the security-for-neutrality model (to include Russia's "nuclear umbrella") to those CEC that do not choose to join NATO;

9. Threatening economic sanctions on CEC that neglect Russian security interests, using their dependence on Russia's oil and natural gas
   imports; and
10. Favoring certain key European countries, such as France and
    Germany, over the United States and NATO in dealing with the
    European security agenda.

Two years after the first NATO enlargement, it is clear that most of the
above-mentioned response actions and policies can be considered part of
Russian diplomatic folklore. Russians would say that this is true only
thanks to the compromise achieved in May 1997 when the Founding Act
was signed. Russia could not stop NATO's enlargement, and it would be
difficult to believe that Primakov's diplomats did not understand this. On
the other hand, Russia is a country with military potential, which does
allow her to raise the price of European security. Some of the Russian
countermeasures are back on the agenda in the context of the NATO
enlargement.

Russia has not succeeded in concluding a binding document with NATO
equivalent to an international treaty. However, NATO has not managed to
sign a charter with Russia either, although the alliance originally proposed
to prepare a common non-commitment declaration. Compromise has been
found in the form of the Founding Act, which was neither a standard binding international treaty nor a noncommitment declaration. Rather, it resembles the Helsinki Act of 1975. The heads of NATO member states and
Russian President Boris Yeltsin signed the Founding Act on May 27, 1997,
in Paris.

What Russia did not achieve from the requirements instead raised its bargaining position. At first, Russia failed to force NATO to make the first
wave of enlargement the last one. Second, Russia was not granted a veto
over NATO decision-making. And third, Russia is still not a member of the
WTO and the Paris Club. Instead of granting Russia the right to veto NATO
decision-making, both sides agreed to create the Joint Permanent Council
(JPC) as a venue for permanent consultations and a "no surprise" policy
and relationship between NATO and Russia. As far as other points of
Russia's bargaining position are concerned, Russian diplomacy enjoyed a
certain success. First, NATO agreed that it would not deploy nuclear
weapons to the territories of its new members. Second, NATO met Russia's
requirements concerning the deployment of conventional forces and use
of the new member countries' infrastructure through the revision of the
CFE Treaty. And finally, Russia has been invited to take a part in the regular G-7 meetings, which have become known since then as the G-8.

Thus, the signing of the Founding Act in May 1997 did not end the talks
between NATO and Russia on eastward enlargement. Negotiations contin-

ued in the form of talks about revisions to the CFE Treaty, which was completed de facto, on March 8, 1999, three days before the official entry of the Czech Republic, Hungary, and Poland into NATO. The new CFE Treaty was officially adopted at the November 1999 OSCE summit in Istanbul. The revised CFE established new, lower national ceilings on conventional forces for the three new NATO members, thanks to which a limit has been set on the aggregate total of all types of NATO conventional weaponry deployable on their territory. This refers also to the military infrastructure of the new member states, as limits established by the adopted CFE Treaty do not allow NATO to deploy on a permanent basis significant combat forces to the territory of new member countries.

Thus, it is possible to conclude that although NATO managed to obtain the indirect consent of Russia for the first enlargement, it also met some of Russia's important military requirements for Russia. In sum, NATO met the Russian requirement concerning the non-nuclear status of the CEC, as well as the limits for NATO conventional forces and infrastructure in the territory of the former Moscow satellites. One could interpret this, in a certain way, as NATO's acceptance of a special buffer status of the post–Cold War central Europe strategic corridor as Russian security planners define it, even though the first three CEC joined the alliance.[8]

The first wave of enlargement has left the following legacy to the eventual second wave: if NATO plans to continue its eastward enlargement with Russia's consent, it must deal at least once more with the new adaptation of the CFE Treaty. The next NATO enlargement will take place in a much more complex web of European security obligations than before, even without the kind of Yugoslav crisis that happened in the first half of 1999.

## THE SECOND WAVE OF NATO ENLARGEMENT

On March 24, 1999, two weeks after the Czech Republic, Poland, and Hungary formally became members, NATO launched its military action against Yugoslavia to halt ethnic cleansing in Kosovo and to handle the Balkan crisis. NATO's April 1999 Washington summit adopted the new Strategic Concept of the alliance, which envisioned the possibility of conducting "non–Article 5 crisis response operations."

The Yugoslav crisis became a turning point in NATO-Russia relations. Russia had cut off relations with NATO, declaring that the use of military force against a sovereign state without the U.N. Security Council's sanction undermined the basic principles of international law and the European security system as created after World War II. As Russian leaders and security experts allegorically pointed out, the Founding Act after Yugoslavia became only a "tatter." Furthermore, their view was that NATO had completely ignored Russia as a strategic partner in the European security system and that no transformation of the alliance into a less military and more political structure had taken place. And finally, the new Strategic Concept with its "non–Article 5 crisis response operations" meant that NATO was changing from an organization whose purpose was collective defense of its members into an arbitrary and aggressive pact using military force beyond the borders of the member states.[9]

There were three main approaches identifiable in Russia in response to the NATO intervention in Yugoslavia:

1. *Radical (nationalist and communist):* called for immediate retaliatory action against NATO "aggression" in order to help the Slavic and Orthodox brothers of Serbia and form the so-called Slavic Union of Russia, Belarus, and Yugoslavia;
2. *Pragmatic-official (official representatives)*: requested that the NATO military operation cease immediately, stay away from the conflict, act as a mediator for peace, and thus restore Russia's already feeble international reputation and importance; and
3. *Pragmatic-unofficial (security and military circles):* same as above, plus "kept fingers crossed for Serbs" and undertook steps that would help Serbs to "carry on as long as possible" without Russia's direct involvement in the conflict. This approach counted on procrastination to end the conflict, without visible success for NATO, which would eventually erode the whole of NATO and bring it to extinction.

Another effect of the Yugoslav crisis was a radical shift in Russia's public perception of NATO. According to the Russian VCIOM agency (Vserossiyskiy Centr Izucheniya Obschstvennogo Mneniya), in the course of NATO intervention against Yugoslavia in March–May 1999, Russia's anti-Western sentiments had not run higher since the Caribbean crisis in the 1960s. For the first time since the Cold War, 63 percent of Russian respondents indicated that they considered NATO a direct threat to Russia's national security. Before the Yugoslav crisis this indicator hovered around 31 percent but never exceeded 48 percent. The percentage of Russian respondents who unequivocally condemned the NATO military operation against Yugoslavia ranged from 86 percent to 92 percent (in Moscow from 67–75 percent).[10] Moreover, it seems reasonable to assume that the Russian public will be far more focused on Russia-NATO relations during the second wave of NATO enlargement than during the first. In addition, the Yugoslav crisis revived the Russian public's image of NATO as a Cold War institution. Thus, new domestic limits on the maneuverability of Russia's leadership in developing a relationship with NATO were created after the Yugoslav crisis of 1999.

Otherwise, the Joint Permanent Council (JPC) resumed its functions in May 2000, a year after the end of the NATO military operation against

Slobodan Milosevic's regime. NATO-Russian relations after the Yugoslav crisis regressed to their pre-1997 state, when consent on the first wave of enlargement had been managed. Both NATO and Russia have changed their strategic security planning. Thus, the second wave of NATO enlargement will take place under the new international juncture and qualitatively different shape of NATO-Russia relations than did the first wave.

Within a year of Vladimir Putin's assuming the presidency in 2000, Russia revised the basic security strategy and defense planning documents. The revisions covered the National Security Concept, the Military Doctrine, and the Foreign Policy Concept. In addition, a new document called the Information Security Doctrine of the Russian Federation was authorized.[11]

Of the eight factors determining the main threats to Russia's national security under the National Security Concept, the following five (at least) reflect the Yugoslav crisis and NATO military operation of 1999:

1. The struggle of some nations and international alliances to diminish the role of existing international security mechanisms, mainly the United Nations and OSCE;
2. The weakening of Russia's political, economic, and military influence in world affairs;
3. The reinforcement of military and political blocs and alliances, especially NATO's eastward expansion;
4. The possibility of deploying foreign military bases and large-scale combat forces at close distance to Russia's borders; and
5. The escalation of conflicts near the Russian border and external borders of the CIS member states.

What is new in these basic security documents is the treatment of NATO enlargement as a threat to the national security of the Russian Federation. The 1993 Basic Principles of Military Doctrine of the Russian Federation defined a military threat as "an approach of military blocs and alliances to the Russian borders."[12] The revised 2000 Military Doctrine states that "an enlargement of military blocs and alliances at the expense of military security of the Russian Federation" presents one of the main military threats. Both the emphasis on nuclear deterrence and on nuclear first-use as the principal pillars of Russian security are new, as are a robust conventional defense against a "Balkan-type" attack by NATO, and regular employment of the armed forces to deal with local—including domestic—conflicts. Accordingly, Russian military spending is expected to rise from 2.8 percent of gross domestic product (GDP) in 2000 to about 3.5 percent in the next years.[13]

Russia's foreign policy concept under President Vladimir Putin and Minister of Foreign Affairs Igor Ivanov does not differ significantly from that formulated by Primakov on the eve of negotiating with NATO over the first wave of the enlargement in 1996 and 1997. The concept is based upon the premise that even though Russia cannot recapture its leading position in world politics on a par with the United States, it can still contribute significantly to the creation of the so-called multipolar world. This will restore the position of Russia as one of the centers of world politics. What is new in the Foreign Policy Concept from 2000 is also a "post-Yugoslav" emphasis on the need to prevent a weakening of the U.N. Security Council and the OSCE role in ensuring international security. In other words, the main goal of Russia's foreign and security strategy is to prevent both the formation of a new U.S. unilateralist world order and the building of a European security system on the basis of NATO.

These pains overlap the issue of NATO enlargement in Russian security policy and debate over the course of the last two years following the Yugoslav crisis. This is a new moment in comparison with the situation before the first wave of enlargement in 1996–97. What policies does Russia now undertake in this context?

The first priority is to reform the U.N. Security Council in order to boost the effectiveness of the United Nations in dealing with international crises while the expected effect is twofold: to reduce U.S. unilateralism in the post-bipolar world and to limit NATO "wantonness" in conducting "non–Article 5 crisis response operations." The reform involves an enlargement of the U.N. Security Council through the inclusion of new permanent members. This is an instructive idea mainly for such countries as Germany, Japan, India, and Brazil.

Second, Russia seeks to develop a security and defense partnership with the European Union. At first Russia was suspicious of the European Union's plans for developing the European Security and Defense Policy (ESDP). However, this changed once Russia realized that the purpose of the ESDP was to take over NATO's European peacekeeping functions. At the Munich 2000 Security Forum, the Russian Security Council secretary and minister of defense, Sergei Ivanov, proclaimed that Russia considered the European Union a preferred security partner in Europe.[14] A turning point in the EU-Russia relationship was the October 2000 summit in Paris, when both sides agreed to build a consultative mechanism on security and defense issues and develop cooperation in the field of crisis management. According to Russian expectations, the ESDP could gradually decrease the role of NATO in European security.

A third priority defined in the Foreign Policy Concept is the formation of an anti-U.S. National Missile Defense (NMD) coalition. The U.S. plan for developing an NMD system and the revision of the 1972 Anti-Ballistic Missile (ABM) Treaty was announced after the new George W. Bush administration came to power in the United States under the spotlight of the Russian security debate. Originally, Russia was ready to accept the U.S. proposal to revise the ABM Treaty, but underwent a change of opinion after several European powers (with the first being Germany in the summer of 2000) raised objections to the U.S. NMD system.[15] Russia appealed to key European countries during President Putin's visit to Italy, the United Kingdom, Germany, and France in 2000, to create a so-called Pan-European Non-Strategic Anti-Missile Defense (EUROPRO) as a European response to the U.S. NMD. Only after February 2001, during NATO Secretary General Lord Robertson's visit to Moscow, did Russia address its proposal to NATO. The ABM/NMD issue became another reason for Russian efforts to reduce U.S. unilateralism in world affairs and to decrease the role of NATO in European security. While Russian diplomacy under Yeltsin was seeking a multi-polarized world above all in cooperation with China, India, etc., Putin's diplomacy shifted its focus on western Europe as well.

Fourth, Russia seeks to expand its relationship with China. In June 2001 Russia, China, Kazakhstan, Tajikistan, Kyrgyzstan, and Uzbekistan created the Shanghai Cooperation Organization (SCO) to strengthen their ties in the field of security and economic collaboration. This is considered in Russia to be a qualitatively new level of cooperation within the grouping previously known as the "Shanghai Five" established in April 1996. This forum from the beginning has been viewed in Russia as an alternative center of world politics counterbalancing U.S. influence in Eurasia.[16] In addition, Russia's view of the SCO is that it could be a tool for preventing a possible NATO peacekeeping mission in Central Asia and the former Soviet territory.

Finally, the Foreign Policy Concept focuses on deepening collective security and defense cooperation within the CIS. There is a plan in 2001 to create three so-called coalition military units in Central Asia, the Caucasus, and Belarus, as well as a united headquarters in Moscow, within the CIS Treaty on Collective Security. The purpose is to develop a common strategy for peacekeeping missions conducted by CIS member countries within the CIS area. Russia has recently begun to increase security and defense cooperation within the CIS, as well as to change the focus on peacekeeping planning and creating special military units under common command.

The points mentioned above are the most relevant moves within Russian foreign and security policy aiming to reduce U.S. unilateralism in world affairs generally, and especially the role of NATO in European security, as defined by Russia after the Yugoslav crisis. However, it would be too simplistic to view them as a part of Russia's response policies against the next wave of NATO enlargement. If we look over Russia's response actions and policies announced during the first wave, it is possible to find some of them on the list. At the moment, Russia's responses to the first wave of enlargement are actually understood in broad terms as "anti-U.S." and "anti-NATO," not only "anti-enlargement" responses. Russia's "post-Yugoslav" understanding presents policies worthy of attention for themselves and not only because NATO is going to expand once again. In other words, during the first wave of enlargement Russia voiced potential response actions against the *process* of NATO enlargement. After Yugoslavia, response policies criticized NATO as an *organization*.

Nevertheless, it would be a mistake to conclude that Russia's current anti-U.S. attitude means that Moscow wants to remove the United States from the European security system entirely. The Russian perception is that U.S. security policy ignores Russia's interests first in the sphere of global stability (nuclear weapons) by questioning the ABM Treaty, and second in European security by changing NATO's strategic concept (i.e., the Washington summit), which pushes Russia out of the European security system. Both of these factors designate the size and measurement of Russia's current anti-U.S. perception and attitude, which would be changed when consent on both issues has been managed. Actually, these topics overshadow the next wave of NATO enlargement in the current Russian security debate.

## RUSSIA'S INTERNAL DEBATE

NATO enlargement is the issue over which Russian leaders, political parties, security experts, intellectuals, the business elite, and the public reached an unequivocal consensus. According to the ROMIR public poll agency (Rossiyskoye Obshchestvennoye Mneniye i Issledovaniye Rynka), which in September 2000 interviewed members of the Russian political and business elite, 93.6 percent of respondents indicated that NATO's eastward enlargement presents a threat to Russia's national security. As for perceptions of security threats, 99.1 percent of respondents pointed to "Russia's inability to solve its internal problems," while 96.5 were concerned about "interethnic conflicts in Russia and CIS countries."[17] Thus, even two years after the Yugoslav crisis, the Russian elite's negative attitude toward NATO and its eastward enlargement has not changed. This is a constant premise that needs to be taken into account when assessing Russia's willingness and readiness to respond to the second wave.

During the first wave of enlargement Russian debate focused on central Europe as a whole region; however, it has currently shifted to the Baltic countries as the hot candidates for NATO membership. This is also a new moment in the Russian attitude toward the issue, which is explainable by fact that the first wave was to give a principal answer to the question "if yes at all," while the question about "what countries" played a secondary role from Russia's perspective at that time. NATO enlargement was the most important issue for the Russian establishment. However, the eventual NATO expansion into the area of the former Soviet Union, including the accession of the former Soviet republics, is viewed as greatly overstepping the "red borderline," which would mean no chance for normal relations with NATO. Other hot NATO candidate countries for the next wave of enlargement, such as Slovenia and Slovakia, are far afield of Russian debate and concerns.

There are still two main relevant arguments in the Russian debate formulated during the first wave of NATO enlargement. In addition, new arguments have evolved from the Russian assessment of the 1999 Yugoslav crisis and its consequences for European security. The character of Russian arguments could be divided into two main groups: general arguments of the strategic security character, based on Russia's accusations against NATO regarding infringement of the principles of the Founding Act, and a group of military arguments interlocking with so-called Baltic and/or CIS arguments.

The strategic security arguments against further NATO enlargement are fivefold. First, the continuing crisis in Yugoslavia (Kosovo, Macedonia) proves that NATO's concept of "humanitarian intervention" failed and that NATO is not an adequate structure able to meet the new challenges of European security. Consequently, NATO enlargement is not a contribution to European security, and therefore plans for enlargement contradict the provision of the Founding Act from 1997, which envisages that the next NATO enlargement will take place only in the case of strengthening European security.

Second, both NATO and Russia, in the Founding Act, committed themselves not to undermine the primary responsibility of the U.N. Security Council for maintaining international peace and security, or the role of the OSCE as the only inclusive and comprehensive pan-European security organization. The Yugoslav crisis shows that NATO ignored both the U.N. Security Council and the OSCE, and thus it has challenged the basic principles of European security. Under the post-Yugoslav international juncture, the next wave of NATO enlargement could be regarded only as an act ignoring Russia's legitimate interests. Consequently, any NATO enlargement would mean a threat to Russia's security and will destabilize the whole of Europe.

Third, the NATO-centric architecture of European security excluding Russia is unacceptable from Russia's perspective. In other words, the current NATO-centric security system for Europe is unacceptable for Russia because Russia is not a member of NATO, which means that Russia is left out of decision-making. NATO enlargement will deepen this tendency and Russia has no choice other than an adequate response aiming to protect national interests and security. The future NATO-Russia relationship will depend upon whether NATO will enlarge eastward or not.

Fourth, there is a need to clearly differentiate NATO's proclaimed "good intentions" from the growth of its military and geopolitical potential through accession of new members. "Intentions" is a temporary category, while "potential" is a constant one. If NATO will not change its strategic

concept with the "non–Article 5 crisis response operation," then it cannot
be regarded as a "defensive pact." This is why NATO's eastward enlargement presents an objective threat to Russia's national security.

Fifth, the U.S. goal is to cause problems in the Russian-EU relationship,
which is the only strategic partnership able to ensure long-term security
and prosperity for all of Europe. By initiating the process of NATO expansion, Washington aims to create a rift between Moscow and the western
European capitals. Such a move divides Europe and makes it dependent
on the United States.

New issues arise concerning the military-operational aspects of the second wave of enlargement. After approaching the Russian borders, NATO
will try to "proofread Russia's policies" in the CIS area, which represents a
zone of vital Russian interests. Therefore, the probability of new NATO-
Russia conflicts will be very high. In addition, NATO enlargement will
change the military-strategic theater of Europe and will launch a new wave
of armament races that will consequently undermine European security.
Further, the admission of small states into NATO, especially the Baltic
countries, will mean the strengthening of NATO's anti-Russian character.
NATO enlargement will reduce the CFE Treaty to nothing, especially if the
Baltic countries enter the alliance. The agreed northern flank ceilings
would be utterly broken. The Baltic countries would strengthen their secu-
rity at the expense of diminishing Russia's security and undermining the
CFE Treaty, which is unacceptable from a Russian—but also from a
European-wide—viewpoint. Provided that the Baltic and Black Sea coun-
tries will join NATO, the Russian navy's maneuvering capacities will be cur-
tailed, and the Kaliningrad region will be isolated from Russia. Last, the
Baltic countries, except for Lithuania, have not settled their relations with
Russia concerning the status of Russian ethnic minorities and borders.
NATO has declared that only countries that have adjusted their relations
with neighbors may be admitted to the alliance. Thus, if NATO invites the
Baltic countries it proves that its policy is a double standard.

There are two main groups of Russian elites, and each has a different
view of NATO. The first is the old-fashioned "revanchist school" (nationalist and radical leftist), which refuses potential agreement with NATO on
anything. The second group is the "pragmatist school" (modern Russian
*gosudarstvenniki*), which is open to negotiation and potential agreement.
The latter have formulated their ideal vision of NATO as follows:

1. NATO is not a hostile organization, but it remains a military pact that
   changed its security strategy and plans to approach Russian borders,
   which challenges Russia's interests;
2. If NATO remains a defensive pact without any eastward expansion,
   with its military supporting collective security in Europe and peacekeeping and peace-enforcing operations under U.N. and OSCE regu-

lations, Russia would like to cooperate and become a NATO member in the future; and

3. Meanwhile, in view of the Yugoslav conflict, NATO and Russia need to sign a new binding treaty, which would renew trust in the Balkans, as well as set rules for cooperation and coexistence.

However, Russian "pragmatists" also believe that if NATO develops in a way that is not acceptable from the Russian perspective, Russia must respond as she sees fit.

## MOSCOW'S RESPONSES TO ENLARGEMENT

Some of the principal trends of Russian foreign policy directed at preventing a formation of a NATO-centric security system in Europe are mentioned above. Moreover, many response actions formulated during the first wave of enlargement remain relevant, as the Russian security debate has shown us. Here we will try to briefly summarize the potential response actions that have been emerging or have been repeated during Russia's recent debate over the second enlargement.

The first such group of actions is connected with discussion about the NMD/ABM issue. Russia's perception is that both NATO enlargement and the revision of the ABM treaty are taking place concurrently. If Russia's interests are not given approval or consideration, Russia would have to respond as follows:

1. End implementation of START I;
2. START II would not be enacted;
3. START III would become impossible;
4. The ongoing implementation of Russia's unilateral nuclear initiatives from 1991–92 would be stopped and reviewed;
5. The Intermediate-range Nuclear Forces (INF) Treaty would be scrapped;
6. Negotiations with China and Europe on antimissile defense would be initiated; and
7. Military cooperation with Iran would be expanded.

The second group of announced response actions pertain to European security and relations with NATO:

1. Relations with NATO would be disrupted, which would heighten general risks to European security in terms of its transparency and predictability;
2. Russian peacekeeping units would leave the Balkans; and

3. The CFE Treaty would be placed in doubt, especially if the Baltic countries were to be admitted to NATO.

The last group of response actions focuses on the case of eventual admission of the Baltic countries into NATO:[18]

1. Russia would unleash economic retribution against the Baltic countries, namely a reduction in transit of Russia's goods and energy sources. This currently represents an important source for those countries' incomes; and
2. The new joint Russia-Belarus 300,000-strong military corps would be created and deployed to the Baltic countries' borders and would be able to occupy Baltic countries in short order. It would be quite hard for NATO to find an adequate response to this military challenge and to ensure the security of the Baltic countries in accordance with Article 5 of the Washington Treaty.

These are the main security-related response actions to a second wave of NATO enlargement that were raised during the Russian security debate over the Yugoslav crisis. During the 1990s, foreign policy under Yeltsin was characterized as a "policy of strong words but moderate actions."[19] Putin's administration, however, is working hard to change this image. The second wave of NATO enlargement is one of the challenges that it must simply deal with.

The first question is whether Russia would implement response actions against the second wave of NATO enlargement. There are some domestic, as well as external, factors that support answering "yes."

The first wave of NATO enlargement was not an important issue for the Russian public. Russia's elite was very concerned about NATO enlargement, but the Russian public was not. This changed significantly after the Yugoslav crisis in 1999. Russia's elite and the public reached a broad national consensus on the perception of security threats and the character of response policies that Russia should implement. The 1990s are generally perceived in Russia as a decade of foreign policy defeats—Russia's weakness, craftiness on the part of the West, ignorance of Russia's legitimate interests, etc. In addition to the call for changes in Russia's foreign and security policies, the following factors were key in forming the national consensus during the 1990s: the Yugoslav crisis, wars in Chechnya, the status of Russian minorities in the CIS (especially in the Baltic countries), and finally, NATO's eastward enlargement. Therefore, the decision-making power of Russia's leaders in the context of the second wave has been significantly reduced by the broad national consensus that has emerged during the past two years. This is the reason why Russia is likely to respond far more strongly to the second wave than to the first wave.

The CIS area is defined in all strategic security documents as a zone of Russia's primary interests. The former Soviet republics along the Russian borders are not only defined but are also perceived as areas of vital Russian interests due to the ethnic Russian minority population of 25 million living there, the transit connections with other countries, common history, cultural heritage, etc. Security experts and people close to the power structures in Russia use the common name "red borderline" for the Baltic countries, Ukraine, and Georgia. It is true that nationalist, leftist, and Soviet nostalgists (the "revering school" of Russian foreign policy) are not psychologically ready to allow the former Soviet satellite countries of central Europe into NATO. However, the same is true of the new Russian pragmatists when it regards countries from the red borderline. In the case of invitations to the Baltic countries to join NATO, the probability measure of Russia's response to the second wave would increase.

The VCIOM public polling agency reported that at the beginning of April 2001 the first signals appeared that the Russian public's trust in Putin's presidency was decreasing slightly.[20] This is a new challenge for Putin, one he faces for the first time since the 1999 presidential elections. It must be emphasized here that an enormous level of public support is a key factor in Putin's strong political position in Russia. Without such public support Putin could not take domestic political initiatives quickly nor would he be able to successfully enforce important power changes, administrative reforms, anticorruption measures, etc. The Russian public is easily mobilized in political terms through the NATO card. That is why Putin cannot neglect NATO's agenda and let the opposition handle it. Moreover, the Duma already initiated a resolution on May 15, 2001, appealing to the president and the government to elaborate and implement the "Complex Program of Measures against the NATO Enlargement."[21]

The Russian security and political establishment considers the new Russian diplomacy under Putin a success story, especially in comparison with the Yeltsin period. Many Russian experts think that the diplomatic tactics chosen for negotiating the ABM/NMD issue proved that Russia is capable of enforcing and protecting her interests. In this case, Russia clearly defined her interests, developed allies, demonstrated her response actions in order to safeguard her interests, and implemented an offensive and hard-line position. The effect was a revised U.S. position on the subject, which became more moderate in response to Russia's diplomatic pressure. Russian experts agree that the same resolve must be shown concerning the second wave of NATO enlargement as well. Russia has to concentrate her resources on defending her vital interests. The eventual admission of the Baltic countries into NATO represents a challenge to Russia's vital interests. Therefore, Russia must respond even at the expense of breaking relations with NATO and an increase in defense spending.

There are three main groups of domestic actors in Russia who could profit from a worsening relationship between Russia, the United States, and NATO. The Ministry of Defense and the Russian army, who depend on state financing, represent the first group. The ministry and the army already gained some benefits from the Yugoslav crisis and the change of security and defense planning that followed. Russia's defense spending increased 43 percent in 2000 as compared to 1999.[22] The second group is represented by the military-industrial complex (VPK) that benefited from the Russia-NATO confrontation during the Yugoslav crisis, followed by Russia's rapprochement with China. This has opened a huge market in China for Russian military exports, thus creating a new and important source of income for the VPK. The last group comprises Russia's criminal business elite. This group is not interested in too close of a relationship with the West because of Western requirements for business transparency, which do not fit with the venal interests of these individuals.[23]

NATO's success in solving the crisis in the Balkans is crucial for its ability to implement the Strategic Concept adopted at the Washington summit in 1999. However, if the NATO's policy regarding the Balkans proves unsuccessful and the conflicts flare up (e.g., in Macedonia), this will encourage Russia to decide in favor of response actions against the second wave of NATO enlargement. The following two extreme scenarios are possible in this context:

1. NATO peacekeeping missions and the subsequent restoration of democracy in the Balkans achieve success; the regimes in the Balkan countries commit to building democratic and tolerant societies; armed conflicts do not break out again; and the alliance involves Russia to the extent of the country's resources and potential in arriving at a political solution to the postwar situation in the Balkans. This scenario would restore Russia's own view of its the international position to where it was during the first wave of NATO enlargement when the parties were able to arrive at consent.

2. The NATO peacekeeping mission fails; the new democratic regimes in the Balkans are fragile and tend to autocracy and ethnic intolerance; new armed conflicts flare up; new military interventions of NATO are needed; Russia terminates her peacekeeping cooperation with NATO and sides against NATO with traditional allies in the Balkans, meaning the Serbs, Orthodox, Slavs in Macedonia, etc., against NATO; consequently, no consent over the next wave of NATO enlargement is possible. NATO enlarges and Russia responds to the extent of the country's military resources and potential.

Of course, there are possible scenarios in between, but only the first one is the most appropriate for the second round of NATO enlargement. However, the relationship between the NATO mission in the Balkans and NATO enlargement, including Russia's attitude in this respect, is a subject of great importance and is worthy of a special analysis.

The Joint Permanent Council (JPC) began functioning again in May 2000. Up until now no serious shift in NATO-Russian relations concerning the second wave of the enlargement has been visible, not to mention a consent reminiscent of that managed in the course of the first wave. The talks have not even started yet. If one takes into account that the bargaining on the CFE Treaty adaptation in the context of the first wave lasted almost two years, it is time to initiate negotiations again with Russia. Provided that an essential dialogue on the topic with Russia is absent, the likelihood of Russia's response will grow.

The next question is "when" would Russia implement response actions to enlargement, which depends primarily on the regional scope of the second wave of NATO enlargement and on the choice of the countries invited to become members. Following the Russian debate on the topic, it is possible to outline the following three levels of Russia's response actions according to their probability: low, middle, and high.

NATO will invite Slovenia and Slovakia to become members. Both of these countries are small as far as military capacity is concerned and their admission would not require significant changes in the CFE Treaty. Both are geographically far enough from Russia, and their NATO membership would not be reflected as a challenge to Russia's security in an ongoing Russian security debate. In fact, a "Slo-Slo" scenario would be received in Russia as something that has more to do with the completion of the first "central European wave" of enlargement than with the new second one.

Admission of the Balkan countries, like Romania and Bulgaria, would make the probability of Russia's response more likely than in the case of Slovenia and Slovakia. Provided that the Balkan crisis flares up again over Kosovo and Macedonia and no visible positive shift in the NATO-Russia agenda occurs, admission of the Balkan countries will challenge Russia's interests. From the perspective of the Russian security debate the Balkans is a decisive region for the building of a post–Cold War European security system, and that is why Russia must be strongly involved there.

The likelihood of Russia's response will be high when NATO admits one or more of the Baltic countries for reasons mentioned above. The same is applicable for a "big bang" scenario of the next wave of enlargement if NATO decides to invite all nine candidate countries at once. If NATO decides for a gradual expansion, it could follow the logic of a "regional cascade" admitting first central Europe, second the Balkans, and third the Baltics. The likelihood of Russia's response would be significantly lower with the regional cascade expansion in comparison to the big bang scenario. In any case, Russia's attitude in any scenario will depend upon the state of NATO-Russian relations and the availability of consent in this regard. From this point of view, the agenda for negotiating admission of the central European countries of Slovenia and Slovakia will barely be contested by Russia. Russia's response action will significantly expand in the case of the Balkan countries (Bulgaria and Romania) and will increase dramatically in the case of the Baltic countries (Lithuania, Latvia, and Estonia). At the same time a "Balkan agenda" is more easily manageable as it represents an "external" agenda for Russia, while a "Baltic agenda" plays an important role in Russia's domestic politics and security planning.

The last question is "what" actions Russia could implement as her response to the second wave of NATO enlargement. Here follows an evaluation of the probability of implementation for the list of potential response actions cited earlier:

1. Response actions regarding treaties on nuclear armaments and non-proliferation would theoretically be implemented only if Russia and the United States do not achieve rapprochement on the ABM/NMD issue, as well as if NATO enlargement and the disagreement on ABM/NMD become a "one package" challenge for Russia. The most likely scenario is that this would not happen and that both issues will be tackled separately;
2. The enactment of the second radius of potential response actions, as mentioned above, would be probable if Russia and NATO do not achieve agreement over the second wave of the enlargement. Furthermore, this would be least probable when NATO admits Slovenia and Slovakia, more probable when NATO admits Romania and Bulgaria, and most probable when NATO admits one or more of the Baltic republics; and
3. The implementation of the third radius of Russia's potential responses would take place only in the case of a NATO invitation to one or more of the Baltic countries. Finally, economic response is less probable than a military one in terms of creating a new joint Russian-Belarusian military unit on the borders of the Baltic republics.

Altogether, the whole package of Russia's anti-NATO arguments can be reduced to one basic view, which was excellently voiced by President Vladimir Putin during the press conference at the end of the Ljubljana summit with U.S. President George W. Bush. Putin stated the following: "We do not consider NATO to be a hostile organization. But, is it a military organization? Yes, it is. Do they want to have us in? They don't. Is it approaching our borders? Why?" These words express the quintessence of Russia's understanding and attitude toward NATO. Does NATO indeed not want to have Russia in? Would eventual Russian membership provide a long-term solution to the NATO enlargement process?

It is clear that Russia's NATO membership is not a question of tomorrow or today. The issue, however, is whether or not NATO in principle could provide Russia with a clear—at least political—vision of prospects for eventual membership. One possible solution would be to develop an "open-door policy for Russia" with a ten- to fifteen-year timeline for entry into the alliance. The timeline would have clearly stated conditions and rules for monitoring accession, and it could be shortened or expanded depending on compliance. A serious discussion of the possibility of Russia's membership in NATO started recently in the context of new positive shifts in the U.S.-Russia relationship. There are three basic arguments against Russia's membership: 1) Russia's entry would undermine the operational capability of NATO and radically change its character; 2) NATO never could take over responsibility for guaranteeing Russia's national security (Article 5) because of Russia's geographical size, her active engagement in Central Asia, the Middle East, and Far East, and her problematic relations with China, etc.; and 3) Russia has a deficit as far as basic NATO values is concerned, i.e., democracy, the rule of law, and a market economy.

All these principal arguments are relevant. Nevertheless, there is no doubt that the West is interested in a democratic and stable Russia, which is a part of the civilized world, and there is no question that such a Russia would mean a significant contribution to global security. Western assistance to Russia's post-communist political and economic transformation was extremely important, but it did not include a strategy on how to get Russia into the key Euro-Atlantic institutions such as NATO and the European Union. The Founding Act of 1997 was first of all about managing the first wave of NATO enlargement and building a strategic NATO-Russia relationship in which both partners are treated like external entities. Neither the Founding Act of 1997 nor the EU strategy on Russia adopted by the EU summit of June 1999 addressed how to involve Russia in the alliance or the European Union. Once again, we are not dealing with whether to admit Russia to NATO tomorrow. We are just considering the challenge faced by NATO and the European Union as the key Euro-Atlantic institutions in building a strategic relationship with Russia.

While Russian membership in NATO remains a question of the future, its participation in key Euro-Atlantic institutions and the development of a new strategic relationship suited to the realities of the 21st century must be considered carefully by Russia, the United States, and Europe. Specifically, what is the strategic goal of a NATO relationship with Russia? For example, is the goal either to have good relations with Russia as an external partner? Or is the strategic goal to provide Russia with a clear vision that the long-term process of post-communist transformation would end in Russia's joining the West as an insider and an inherent part of it? Regardless of the answers to these questions, both NATO and the European Union could provide Russia with a clear and political vision. This would be beneficial for both Russia and the West, because Russia would obtain a Western perspective of her transformation as well as be pressed to become more open to the West.

The least that this solution would accomplish is that Russia could never repeat the arguments that NATO does not want to have Russia in the alliance nor that Russia is excluded from the European security system. On the other hand, NATO would demonstrate that it has done its best to show good political will to arrive at consent with Russia and improve mutual relations and strengthen European security. Russia has the right to refuse such a proposal. Yet afterward, Russia must assume political responsibility for the possible results of such a refusal.

Giving Russia the opportunity to become involved in the NATO enlargement process, within the terms mentioned above, would undermine the actual grounds of the government's arguments and policies on this subject. It is possible that the central European countries would first react negatively to an eventual NATO "open door policy for Russia." But it must be made clear that Russia has to qualify for NATO membership in the same way the central European countries did. From this point of view, there is no guarantee that a NATO open-door policy for Russia would result in Russia's admission. If Russia accepts the terms and conditions for eventual NATO membership and will meet them within the next decade or decades, there would be no relevant and rational reason for a negative reaction of the CEC.

## RUSSIA-NATO RELATIONSHIP AFTER SEPTEMBER 11

The terrorist attacks against the World Trade Center in New York and the Pentagon in Washington, D.C., on September 11, 2001, challenged the existing system of international relations and patterns of behavior of international actors. The Russia-NATO relationship is no exception. On September 24, 2001, Russian President Vladimir Putin made a public statement in which he declared that Russia would support the U.S.-led campaign against international terrorism and the response operation against Osama bin Laden's al-Qaeda network. Putin stated that Russia would share intelligence, provide airspace for humanitarian flights, participate in search-and-rescue missions in Afghanistan, and supply arms to the Northern Alliance fighting the Taliban. Moreover, he said that Russia had coordinated this position with her allies in Central Asia and that they shared this position with Russia.[24]

The last decision in particular represents an unprecedented change in Russia's security and defense strategy formulated in the aftermath of the

Yugoslav crisis in 1999. The main goal of this post-Yugoslav strategy is not only to prevent the possibility of a Balkan-type operation by the West or NATO in the post-Soviet area (especially in the northern Caucasus and Central Asia), but also to restrain any Western or NATO military presence in these areas. Russia made the crucial decision to join the antiterrorist alliance, which meant it had to change one of the basic premises of its security and defense concept.[25] The alternative option would have been strict adherence to Russia's national security tenets of 2000, which would mean closing airspace for U.S. or any NATO country flights and pressing Central Asian states to do the same. A decision to limit cooperation with the West to sharing intelligence would have been the most that could have been expected from Russia under the post-Yugoslav international juncture and the "pre-September" character of the Russia-U.S. and Russia-NATO relationship. Russia's offer to open its own and its Central Asian neighbors' airspace, participate in search-and-rescue missions, and supply arms to the Northern Alliance went far beyond what Russia was expected to undertake to protect its interests in Afghanistan and Central Asia in accordance with her national security and defense doctrine.

The Russian decision followed intense diplomatic consultations with the U.S. administration and sharp domestic debate. Especially, conservative military circles were strongly opposed to such a radical shift in post-Yugoslav security policy because of recently adopted national security tenets followed by a growth in defense spending. Putin's decision to join the antiterrorist alliance in the form announced on September 24, 2001, has challenged post-Yugoslav defense planning in Russia. In addition, it requires some redirection and reallocation "on the go" of resources within previously adopted defense spending. All those in the Russian military who are affected by such decisions as well as those security planners who consider Russia's relationship with the West in post-Yugoslav terms were strongly against this shift in security policy. Putin's presidency successfully passed a crucial test in this regard.[26]

To many observers Russia and the United States started to create an entirely new framework for bilateral relations by putting the battle against terrorism at the top of their agendas. This has opened the possibility of collaboration in other areas that would have seemed impossible before September 11, 2001.[27] Naturally, one of them is Russia and NATO's relationship. As much as NATO expansion concerns President Putin, he voiced a significant shift in Russia's attitude during his visits to Germany at the end of September and to Brussels at the beginning of October 2001, where he negotiated with leading representatives of both NATO and the European Union. At a press conference with senior EU officials Putin said:

As for NATO expansion, one can take another, an entirely new look at this ...
if NATO takes on a different shade and is becoming a political organization.

Of course we would reconsider our position with regard to such expansion if we were to feel involved in such processes. They keep saying that NATO is becoming more political than military. We are looking at this (and) watching this process. If this is to be so, it would change things considerably.[28]

During his visit to Germany, Putin was asked whether Russia might ask to join NATO. "Everything depends on what is on offer," Putin responded. "There is no longer a reason for the West not to conduct such talks."[29] NATO Secretary General Lord Robertson told reporters at the joint press conference with President Putin that their discussions marked a major milestone in the NATO-Russia relationship. "We have identified a number of new areas where NATO and Russia can work together," he said. Putin added, "NATO and Russia agreed to initiate creation of a new working body that will examine the possibility of widening, deepening, and qualitatively changing the Russia-NATO relationship."[30]

It would be an exaggeration to conclude that Russia's position on NATO enlargement was dramatically changed in the aftermath of September 11. Russia has not tabled a new bargaining position on the subject since the terrorist attacks against the United States. Rather, Russia has signaled that the window of opportunity for improving the Russia-NATO relationship would be wider if NATO becomes a more political organization as well as involving Russia in the process of enlargement. What could that mean?

First of all, the military phase of the antiterrorist campaign is being carried out by U.S. and some other Western forces, but not by NATO as was the case in Yugoslavia in 1999. This fact is highly welcomed by Russian leadership, as it appears to predetermine a political role for NATO in the antiterrorist war, which will frame the international juncture for a long-term period. And a nonmilitary role is what Russia—and especially the Russian "pragmatist school"—wants for NATO to have for as long as possible. Following this logic, excellently voiced by President Putin as quoted above:

NATO's nonmilitary role in the war against terrorism—in particular its absence from the current operation in Afghanistan—starts the process of the alliance's transformation de facto into a more political and less military organization.

As already mentioned, if NATO were to remain a defense pact without geographical expansion, with a military capable of protecting collective security only in the European theater, and conducting peacekeeping and peace-enforcing operations under U.N. and OSCE sanctions, Russia would wish to cooperate. Russia is an equal partner of the NATO countries in both the United Nations and the OSCE; thus, this option does not need a special Russian-NATO relationship, because NATO would be de facto subordinated to the United Nations and OSCE. Another option is a European security system based on a NATO in which NATO remains responsible for peacekeeping and peace-endorsing operations and Russia is involved. In any case, Russian involvement in such a NATO-centric security system would mean redefinition of the post-Yugoslav Russia-NATO relationship so that Russia would be an integral member of it. In other words Russia would participate in NATO decision-making as an insider, not as an outsider who can only comment on it.

Provided that NATO plans to continue its territorial expansion—which consequently means that it will remain a building block of any future European security system—it has to address how Russia will participate in Europe's security architecture. There are two basic options on how to address this issue: 1) A new binding treaty with Russia, in which Russia's participation in NATO decision-making would be agreed upon and defined as to the scope and forms with Russia remaining an external partner; and 2) Russia's NATO membership.

While evaluating Russian arguments and policies with respect to a potential second wave of NATO enlargement before September 11, 2001, one conclusion was that NATO would have to develop an "open door policy for Russia." After September 11, we can conclude that NATO would have to develop such a policy even if it decides that only one or two countries— not to include any Baltic countries—will be invited to the Prague summit. In order to meet Russian expectations, NATO would have to develop a practical way of looking at its relationship with Russia, which will define the scope and forms of Russia's participation in NATO's decision-making, including the enlargement process. It would also provide Russia with a clear political vision concerning prospects for her eventual membership in the future. Russia's expectations in this regard are predictable, given Russian security policies and attitudes over the last decade, especially after the Yugoslav crisis of 1999. Both these tasks could be combined, as NATO could ask Russia first to accept conditions for a ten- to fifteen-year timeline leading to membership, and then to negotiate the scope and forms of participation in decision-making. Actually, the proverbial ball is in NATO's court, which means NATO must now develop a long-term strategy on Russia and how to involve Russia in a European security system

An agreement reached by President Putin of Russia and NATO Secretary General Lord Robertson in Brussels at the beginning of October 2001 on the creation of a new NATO-Russia working body, which will deal with "widening, deepening and qualitative changing" their relationship, confirms another conclusion of this analysis made before September 11. And that is that the JPC is unable to meet the current NATO-Russia agenda and that both sides need a new political start in their relations. The talks between President Putin and President Bush of the United States in Washington, D.C., in November 2001 confirmed that both sides agree that the NATO-Russia relationship should evolve into an increased alliance between Russia and NATO members against international terrorism, regional instability, and other contemporary threats. Both presidents declared that the United States and Russia will work, together with NATO and other NATO members, to include Russia in the European-Atlantic community, develop new effective NATO-Russia mechanisms for consultation, cooperation, coordinated joint actions, and—what is especially important to stress in the context of this analysis—joint decision-making.[31]

## CONCLUSIONS AND RECOMMENDATIONS

Russia cannot stop NATO's eastward enlargement, and it is clear that NATO will enlarge. This fact was well understood in Russian foreign policy circles under former President Yeltsin and former Premier Primakov before the first wave of enlargement. And it is well understood under President Putin and Defense Minister Sergei Ivanov prior to the second round.

There are two basic scenarios for NATO enlargement in the context of its relationship with Russia. NATO will enlarge eastward with or without Russia's consent. Both scenarios are relevant and differ from each other mainly regarding the price of future European security. Russia cannot stop NATO enlargement, but it can increase the price of European security. The European security system, without or against Russia, will be more expensive than the European security system with or at least in cooperation with Russia. Russia's ability to hike the price of European security is limited by her economic weakness. Russia could pay less for her security than the NATO countries, yet it is very probable that both sides will pay more if no consensus is reached over the second wave of NATO enlargement.

Both NATO and Russia need a new post-Yugoslav start for their relationship, or at least they need to attempt to overcome misunderstandings that appeared in the recent past. The JPC mechanism is a good forum for doing that, but it is not enough for restoring mutual trust from the pre-Yugoslav period. The JPC is about military-to-military cooperation; meanwhile, NATO and Russia need to deal with the political dimension of their relationship.

Following the Russian security debate it is clear that the biggest concern regarding the second wave of enlargement is connected with any invitation to one or more of the Baltic countries to become NATO members. It would be an elegant solution if, at the same NATO summit during which an invitation to join was extended to the Baltic countries, the alliance would adopt, as well, a similar "open door policy for Russia" within the terms mentioned above. Of course, Russia has the right to refuse such a proposal. However, a refusal will force Russia to accept political responsibility for the effects that might result.

While evaluating Russian arguments and policies with respect to a potential second wave of NATO enlargement before September 11, 2001, a conclusion was that NATO would have to develop such a concept especially if it were inviting one or more Baltic countries. After September 11 we can conclude that NATO would have to develop such a concept even if it theoretically decides that the Prague summit will invite only one or two countries, not to include any Baltic countries.

NATO would have to develop a practical concept of its relationship with Russia, which would define the scope and forms of Russia's participation in NATO decision-making, including the enlargement process. It would provide Russia with a clear political vision concerning prospects for eventual membership. At least such Russian expectations after September 11 could be predicted following Russian policies and attitudes toward European security and the relationship with NATO over the last decade, especially after the 1999 Yugoslav crisis.

Finally, if Russia and NATO would reach an agreement on the structure and nature of their strategic relationship—a less probable but not an entirely excludable scenario, especially under the new post–September 11 international juncture—then this chapter's topic would become a subject for historians, not for political scientists or security experts.

## NOTES

1. During the conference discussion, an argument was raised that President Boris Yeltsin of Russia was in his heart a Westernizer and he fundamentally did not believe that NATO enlargement was a threat to Russia. However, even if we agree that "Yeltsin was key at each crucial juncture in steering Russia away from confrontation with the West over this issue [NATO enlargement] and toward a soft landing," it does not mean that it would be correct to interpret his attitude as favorable to NATO enlargement. Russian foreign policy was headed at that time by another leading Westernizer, Foreign Minister Andrei Kozyrev (1992–95), who operated on the premise that Russia can avoid international isolation only if she joins the security structures of the West simultaneously with the central European countries, and that she must make sure that CEC are not given preference in the process of integration. At the same time, Russian Westernizers believed it was necessary to create a pan-European security system stretching from the Atlantic to the Urals and standing above NATO. In other words, Russia must seek to become an integral part of any institutionalized security system in Europe. Both Russian Westernizers and hardliners always viewed NATO enlargement without Russia as conflicting with Russia's interests. This was true at the beginning of 1990s and is true at the beginning of first decade of the new century. By the same token it does not disqualify a positive diplomatic role for leading Russian Westernizers in finding consent with NATO over the first wave of enlargement. For Kozyrev's foreign policy doctrine, see *Kontseptsiya vneshney politiki Rossiyskoy Federatsiyi* (Moscow: Ministerstvo Vneshnikh Del Rossiyskoy Federatsiyi, 1993).

2. For more about the Russian attitude at the start of serious discussions about prospects for NATO enlargement in 1993, see *Perspektivy rasshireniya NATO i interesy Rossiyi* (Moscow: Sluzhba Vneshney Razvedki Rossiyskoy Federatsiyi, 1993); *Programma povysheniya effektivnosti SBSYe* (Moscow: Ministerstvo Inostrannykh Del Rossijskoy Federatsiyi, 1994); etc.

3. James M. Goldgeier, "NATO Expansion: The Anatomy of a Decision," *Washington Quarterly,* vol. 21, no. 1 (Winter 1998), pp. 85–102.

4. Alexei Arbatov, "Rossiya: natsional'naya bezopasnost' v 90-ye gody," *Mirovaya ekonomika i mezhdunarodnyye otnosheniya,* no. 7 (1994), pp. 5–15; no. 8–9 (1994), pp. 5–18.

5. Yevgeni Primakov quotes in his book *Gody v bol'shoy politike* (Moscow: Sovershenno Sekretno, 2000) the following Western leaders who "promised" Gorbachev that there would be no NATO enlargement: James Baker, Helmut Kohl, John Major, Douglas Hurd, and François Mitterrand. Quoted here from Yevgeni Primakov, *Years in Big Politics,* trans. and abridged J.B.K. Lough, available at: http://www.ppc.pism.org/Projects/csrc/f70-jbkl.htm, p. 1 (ch. 2: "NATO—In the Center of Attention").

6. See note 2 above.

7. Primakov, *Gody v bol'shoy politike,* p. 3.

8. Within the conference discussion, a point concerning the Founding Act and NATO-Russian negotiations over the first wave of enlargement was raised that "Russia never agreed to NATO enlargement, nor did (NATO) ever ask Russia to agree to NATO enlargement. NATO's goal was to negotiate a NATO-Russia relationship that in the short term prevented a train wreck over the issue of enlargement and in the long term launched a process which would lead to a very different kind of strategic relationship with Russia over time." In addition, an argument was stressed that "NATO gave up nothing from the point of NATO criteria when negotiating the text of the Founding Act with Russia." Indeed the Founding Act sustained prospects for an open door policy, did not give up Russia's veto on NATO decision-making, and opened the window for building a strategic relationship with Russia. But, from a central European point of view, there are some implications, which are simply not negligible in terms of security and defense planning. First of all, it concerns non-nuclear status for new members agreed by NATO and Russia, as well as limitations for NATO conventional forces and infrastructure on the territory of new members through revision of the CFE Treaty. However, the last issue is not explicitly treated in the Founding Act, but it is pre-negotiated there and at the end it is a direct consequence of NATO-Russia negotiations over the first wave. Both the above-mentioned limitations for central and east European countries correspond with an idea of special buffer status of the post–Cold-War central European strategic corridor as Russian security planners defined it after the breakup of the Warsaw Pact. In diplomatic terms the question does not address who was a winner or loser of the Founding Act or whether new NATO members should be allowed to have nuclear weapons, etc. However, it seems correct to conclude that, to a certain extent, both NATO and Russia had to revise their original bargaining positions during the process of negotiations over the first wave of enlargement.

9. For an example of the official Russian view, see: Zayavleniye Ofitsial'nogo Predstavitelya MID Rossiyi, *V Vashingtone proshli meropriyatiya po sluchayu 50-letiya NATO,* from April 27, 1999.

10. Vserossiyskiy Centr Izucheniya Obschstvennogo Mneniya (VCIOM), public polls conducted from March to May 1999.

11. *Kontseptsiya Natsional'noy Bezopasnosti Rossiyskoy Federatsiyi* ot 10 yanvariya 2000 g. (Presidential Decree No. 24); *Voyennaya Doktrina Rossiyskoy Federatsiyi* ot 21 aprelya 2000 g. (Presidential Decree No. 706); *Kontseptsiya Vneshney Politiki Rossiyskoy Federatsiyi* (approved by the President of the Russian Federation on June 28, 2000); *Doktrina Informatsionnoy Bezopasnosti* ot 9 sentyabrya 2000 g. (Presidential Decree No. 1895).

12. *Osnovnyye Polozheniya Voyennoy Doktriny Rossiyskoy Federatsiyi*, 1993.

13. Alexei G. Arbatov, *The Transformation of Russian Military Doctrine: Lessons Learned from Kosovo and Chechnya* (Marshall Center Papers, no. 2), p. 12.

14. Vystupleniye Sekretariya Soveta Bezopasnosti Rossiyi S.B. Ivanova na 37-y konferentsiyi po problemam mezhdunarodnoy bezopasnosti po teme: "Global'naya i regional'naya bezopasnost' v nachale XXI veka," 4 fevralya 2001 goda, Myunkhen (Moscow: Soobscheniya Press-Sluzhby Soveta Bezopasnosti Rossiyskoy Federatsiyi, February 13, 2001).

15. Andrei Piontkovskiy and Vitaliy Tsygichko, "Tango s Rossiyey," *Nezavisimaya gazeta* (February 14, 2001).

16. Andranik Migranyan, "Shankhayskiy forum kak protivoves dominirovaniyu Vashingtona," June 14, 2001, www.strana.ru/992522358.html.

17. *Rossiyskoye Obshchestvennoye Mneniye i Issledovaniye Rynka* (ROMIR), 2000.

18. For more about the Russian-Baltic security dialogue see *Rossiya—Baltiya* (Moscow: Doklady SVOP, 2001).

19. Nikolay Sokov, *Russia's Relations with NATO: Lessons from the History of the Entente Cordiale* (PONARS, Policy Memo Series No. 29, 1998).

20. VCIOM, April 2001.

21. *O merakh po protivodeystviyu rasshireniyu Organizatsiyi Severoatlanticheskogo dogovora* (Moscow: Soobshcheniya Press-Sluzhby Godudarstvennoy Dumy Federal'nogo Sobraniya Rossiyskoy Federatsisiyi, May 16, 2001).

22. Interview given by Stockholm International Peace Research Institute Director Adam D. Rothfeld, *Nezavisimaya gazeta*, June 5, 2001.

23. See Vitaliy Tsygichko, "S Amerikoy—vmeste ili porozn," *Nezavisimaya gazeta*, June 9, 2001.

24. *Zayavleniye Prezidenta Rossiyskoy Federatsiyi V.V. Putina.* Administratsiya Prezidenta Rossiyskoy Federatsiyi, Moskva 24 sentyabriya 2001 goda, www.president.kremlin.ru/events/311.html.

25. For a Russian discussion on relations with the West after the terrorist attacks against the United States and Russia's attitude to the U.S.-led antiterrorist campaign see, e.g., Sergey Sokut and Vladimir Muchin, "Vojna otkryvajet put' k peredelu mira. Rossiya stremitsiya usilit' svoye vliyaniye v Tsentral'noy Aziyi i reshit' problemu agressivnogo separatizma," *Nezavisimoye voyennoye obozreniye*, September 28, 2001; Yuliya Petrovskaya and Lyudmila Romanova, "Sblizheniye—da, smyagcheniye—net. Protivorechiya mezhdu Rossiyey i NATO ostayutsia prezhnimi, khotya i otteneny diskusiyami o borbe s obshchim vragom," *Nezavisimaya gazeta*, October 3, 2001; etc.

26. Ibid.

27. Alan Sipress, "U.S., Russia Recast Their Relationship," *Washington Post,* October 4, 2001.

28. Quoted from Gareth Jones, "Putin Softens Opposition to NATO Expansion" Reuters, October 3, 2001.

29. Quoted from Megan Twohey, "Russia Waits for NATO's Embrace," *Moscow Times,* October 2, 2001.

30. *Vystupleniye Prezidenta Rossiyskoy Federatsiyi V.V. Putina i otvety na voprosy zhurnalistov v khode sovmestnoy press-konferentsiyi po okonchaniyu besedy s General'nym sekretarem NATO Dzh. Robertsonom,* Administratsiya Prezidenta Rossiyskoy Federatsiyi, Bryussel', 3 oktyabrya 2001 g.

31. *Joint Statement by President George W. Bush and President Vladimir V. Putin on a New Relationship Between the United States and Russia* (Washington, D.C.: White House, Office of the Press Secretary, November 13, 2001). The following part of the joint statement deals with the Russia-NATO relationship: "We support the building of a European-Atlantic community whole, free, and at peace, *excluding no one,* and respecting the independence, sovereignty, and territorial integrity of all nations. To this end, the United States and Russia will work, together with NATO and other NATO members, to improve, strengthen, and enhance the relationship between NATO and Russia, with a view to *developing new,* effective mechanisms for consultation, cooperation, *joint decision-making,* and coordinated/joint action. We believe that these mechanisms should reflect the fact that the *members of NATO and Russia are increasingly allied* against terrorism, regional instability, and other contemporary threats, and that the *NATO-Russia relationship should therefore evolve accordingly"* [Italics and breaks are those of author].

# 11

# Russia and the United States

*Vladimir Votapek*

This chapter deals with two problems influencing U.S.-Russian relations. First is the origin of the relatively unsatisfactory character of relations between Washington and Moscow and—more generally—between Russia and the West. Then follow recommendations for possible approaches in developing cooperation with Russia. The chapter ends with some policy recommendations.

The answers to the historical questions and the recommendations for the future depend heavily on being able to assess the current situation within Russia. One cause for the difficult state of relations between the West and Russia is the serious cultural disparity between the two regions. As a result, Russia's potential for being able to solve problems early is often overestimated; disillusion arises from its inability to meet expectations and obligations later on.

Another manifestation of cultural disparity is Russia's perception of international security as a zero-sum game. It should come as no surprise that from such a standpoint certain Western steps could be misunderstood.[1]

Second, Russia has begun to exercise stronger influence on the status of bilateral relations. Although the United States is clearly a stronger partner, Russia is more in control of the ups and downs of relations between Washington and Moscow. The internal stability of the West, its understanding of global responsibility in combination with Western efforts to keep Russia on the track of reform, and its readiness to help solve a broad spectrum of problems in Russian society significantly restricts the available American (and Western) approaches to Russia. The range of Russian approaches is distinctively broader, partly because Westernization is not a generally accepted goal for the reforms currently targeted by the Russian elite. Thus, the Russian government is also freer, at times, to play a card of confrontation with the West.

Third, having considered the pros and cons of cooperation with Russia, we can conclude that it is in the very interest of the United States, and the West as a whole, to cooperate with Russia as broadly as possible. In general, all types of cooperation are welcome. On the governmental level, cooperation in the field of security risk reduction is much more profitable than regular economic cooperation. This holds true even for cooperation that is in reality merely direct assistance. Russian problems may seriously threaten the well-being of the Western nations. The West should not be miserly with its financial assistance, for it will only pay more in the future. One can only imagine what could have taken place if a terrorist like Osama bin Laden had access to Russian nuclear, chemical, or bacteriological materials.

Fourth, shock from the September 11 terrorist attacks changed the scale of values in international affairs. The desirability of Russian cooperation in the antiterrorist offensive of the United States and other Western nations gives Moscow a unique possibility to prove its reliability to the developed world. At the same time it also creates some risk.

The author hopes that the U.S. government will not broker stronger Russian participation in the antiterrorist war by, for example, postponing the eastward enlargement of NATO. All deals with Russia, which may explicitly or implicitly recognize eastern Europe as a Russian sphere of influence, may impede stability in this region and in some cases even threaten the statehood of some newly formed countries.

## RUSSIA'S ECONOMIC AND POLITICAL STATUS

From the outside it looks as though Russia has, after ten years of muddle-headed economic and political reforms, reached a phase of relative stabilization. Due to the interaction of a number of favorable circumstances, Russia's economic decline has come to a halt, and during the last two years it has even registered some economic growth. The political situation has also calmed down.

Among commentators and policymakers, opinion is divided on whether the above-mentioned stabilization reflects fundamental (qualitative) changes in Russian society and thus lays a foundation for undisturbed future development, or whether it is the result of a combination of factors that will expire over time and open up room for a new crisis. The analysis presented in this chapter tends toward the latter point of view, and holds that the stabilization of Russian society is only temporary.

Russia limps behind the developed world both in absolute figures and, more importantly, in the rate of development. Russia is grievously behind in the quality of production, services, and quality of life. Even if the

Russian government were successful in combating the day-to-day problems, it would be difficult to imagine how they would cope with the challenges of the future. The Russian social system is inadequate[2] and thus unable to meet the demands of the beginning of the third millennium. Russian society is mismanaged, and its wealth and human potential are wasted without sufficient returns.

To lead a society successfully today requires that it be managed in a systematic and transparent way. Success can result from the implementation of a management system that is designed to continually improve performance by addressing the needs of all interested parties. However, this is not the case for Russia. The pseudo-democratic and pseudo-market nature of the Russian administration is not up to dealing effectively with today's problems and is even less prepared to face the challenges of the future.[3] The most probable scenario is that the country will continue to suffer from internal disorder, and sooner or later Russia will find itself up against a profound and multifaceted crisis.

Russia's economy is growing for the third consecutive year. Industrial production and wages are up, while inflation is down.[4] Russia's trade surplus is huge and Central Bank reserves exceeded U.S.$36 billion. The government's legislative agenda is impressive.[5] The Duma adopted the second part of the Tax Code, a very important step that may become a landmark in the process of the economic transformation. The strong limitations placed on the number and type of taxes imposed on the various levels of government should clear the Russian tax system, which is still plagued by an excessive number of continually changing tax rates, regulations, exemptions, and local interpretations.

Alongside these positive factors, many negative factors that weakened the Russian economy throughout the 1990s remain in force. Price distortion supporting energy-intensive manufacturing persists. Although investment activity has increased to some extent,[6] it has still not reached a level reflecting the simple reproduction of industrial capacity.[7] The reconstruction of Russia's commercial banking sector remains a major challenge for the Central Bank and the government. Corruption and capital flight, along with the close connection between the economy and politics, have crippled the entire Russian economy.[8]

Stabilization is based mainly on two factors. The first and less significant factor has been imports substituting for industrial growth, which is induced by the weak (undervalued) ruble. The second and decisive factor is export revenue caused by historically high prices that are unprecedented on the whole spectrum of energy and raw materials exported from Russia.[9] It is hard to deny that both factors will sooner or later fade away.[10] In fact, recent statistics have suggested that Russian economic growth is slowing, partly because inflation has begun biting into the competitiveness of industry.[11]

There is no need to dispute that the Russian political system under President Boris Yeltsin was ineffective and contributed to the paralysis of the country. However, the new president dramatically reshaped the power structure in Russia and created a top-down model of governance. He has not broken the constitutional framework, but his changes are enormous— executive power dominates absolutely; the Council of Federation (upper chamber of the Russian parliament) was dissolved; the Duma (lower chamber) works as a rubber stamp; the independence of the courts is restricted;[12] local authorities are more submissive; and freedom of the press is far more limited than it was three years ago.

The authoritarian policies of President Vladimir Putin respond to the desire of many Russians for a stronger state, order, and cohesiveness in public life. His durable popularity stems from this "authoritarianism" buttressed by his very effective public relations.

The electorate is disappointed both with the ideas of democratic reform and the tenets of socialism (communism). This ideological stalemate opens the door for the accession of a non-ideological state authoritarianism. The top leaders of the political and economic elite have taken advantage of their de facto control over the electronic media and actively manipulate the mood of the majority of the electorate. Although elections are supposed to adhere to a series of democratic rules, unequal access to the media, finance, and different forms of state support create a de facto inequality of opportunity. It fictionalizes the results of the contest and deforms the nominally democratic process into a mere caricature.

Image makers, sociologists, and media advisers are working strenuously in Russia and are effectively manipulating the average Russian voter as a result. The last two presidential campaigns provide excellent examples of this effectiveness. In 1996, Boris Yeltsin won despite a dismal approval rating of around 5 percent only five months before the election. In the year 2000, Vladimir Putin was the victor, even though only one year earlier he was unknown to the population.

This situation completely conforms to the Russian tradition of a strong state holding the masses in passivity and provides the political and administrative elites with a secure career and a privileged position. For a large part of the Russian elite, it is thus very attractive to try to limit reforms in a way that would not threaten their comfortable status quo.[13]

The development of both of the basic parameters—the economic situation and the internal political developments—can move within a relatively wide spectrum. Thus, the political and economic outlook ranges from Russia dealing with its problems and becoming a democratic country with a developed market economy, all the way to an economically devastated Russia breaking apart into several smaller entities based on territorial or cultural (religious) proximity. The following are three possible scenarios.

*The Miracle.* Pursuing democratic and economic reforms, launching sustainable growth, and gradually catching up to the pace of development of the advanced world will all lead to the creation of an advanced and democratic Russia. Such a Russia will gradually reconcile itself with its post-imperial legacy and step-by-step will become an integrative core for the former Soviet republics. The probability of further territorial divisions in Russia is very slight, the armed forces are under reliable civilian control, and foreign policy is founded upon broad social consensus. Thus, Russia will stop being a source of instability.

*The Stumble.* An authoritative regime and an ineffective economy nevertheless ensure the ruling elite a sufficiently comfortable lifestyle. This phase is the transition variant between the Miracle and the Crisis. Depending on the favorability of external conditions and other random factors, Russia could swing between the two following variants: 1) an economically stabilized Russia with an authoritative government taking advantage of democratic attributes; or 2) an economically weak Russia with a weak central government. The first choice, an economically stabilized Russia with an authoritative government taking advantage of democratic attributes, is most likely the aim of the present ruling elite in Russia. The economy widely exploits Russia's potential in the realm of raw materials. The foreign trade balance is heavily dependent on price fluctuations in the global commodity markets. The standard of living of the population falls ever farther behind the advanced world. The social division follows the model of a very exclusive and wealthy elite and a relatively small middle class, from which new members of the elite are occasionally recruited. The vast majority of the population has a very low standard of living and negligible influence in public life. The results of elections are decided by the degree of influence of the state-controlled electronic media and financial groups linked with the government. Government retains the capability to falsify results of elections. The influence of the regions is marginal as power is concentrated in Moscow and in a few other cities.

The second choice is an economically weak Russia with a weak central government. Decisive influence is in the hands of political-financial groups and regional elites, which is the model of the 1990s. The stability of Russia, as a united state, is threatened by the greed of interest groups. Regional elites capitalize on their own interests under the political banner of regionalism and resistance against "parasitic" Moscow. Political-financial groups living as parasites off of the central power often use the rhetoric of Greater Russian chauvinism and anti-Westernism. Such a model could likely take effect if the present government's economic model proves ineffective (i.e., after the fall of the presently high prices for commodities on the world markets).

*The Crisis.* The increasing regression of Russia behind the advanced world raises tension both inside Russian society and in external relations. A fall in the global prices of commodities, a military defeat in the Caucasus, an extensive technological catastrophe, the effect of an external economic crisis, or any other more or less random occurrence could cause a breakdown in the unstable system, which could result in a chain-reaction crisis. If the government is not capable of stabilizing the situation, Russia will first economically, and then formally, disintegrate into several different parts.

The West has to reconcile itself with the unpleasant fact that, after ten years of reform, one-seventh of the world is still very far from the model of democracy and market economics achieved in the advanced countries. But does this mean that the West has lost Russia? Definitely not. The West has not lost Russia, because it never had Russia. The beautiful vision of Russia throwing off its totalitarian ways and integrating among the democratic and advanced countries was simply a mistake, an illusion, a fata morgana.

All of the Western countries, including the United States, have looked upon Russia with a good bit of naiveté and an unwillingness to be rational.[14] The developed world has shown an ability to see what it wants to see in Russia and to overlook anything that would ruin its beautiful picture of a country transforming itself. The West was prepared to accept President Yeltsin in the role of fervent defender of democracy even though he had dissolved the legitimate parliament and carried out genocide upon one of the nations of his own country. The case of President Putin is quite similar. Once again we override embarrassing facts. For example, it was Putin who returned Russia to the path of Chechen war. It is Putin who is backing the return of the FSB (the former KGB) and who is limiting freedom of the press.

Time and time again, plans and intentions have diverged from reality. However, the world has demonstrated an extraordinary ability to believe Russian announcements and ignore the Russian reality.[15] The Russian leadership has been granted undeserved trust repeatedly. It can fulfill the West's expectations to about the same extent that it can pay back all of its previous financial loans.

The United States should realize the fundamental cultural disparity between itself and Russia. Russia is in another period of modernization.[16] Russia is under pressure to accept core Western institutions, values, habits, and attitudes. Naturally, these institutions are modified by the society in which they are placed, as they are influenced by modern and traditional elements. Nominally, they are the same as in the core countries, but in fact their functioning is different. This is why the internal logic of social, political, and economic life in Russia and in the West is dissimilar.[17]

Many observers emphasize the "strange" behavior of Russia's masses and their attitude toward the government. They reject the Western model of life, but do not want to lose political and economic freedoms. They accept the idea of a market economy but are in favor of regulations on prices and income levels. They see the United States as an enemy, yet they like Americans. They look to the communist past as a Golden Age, but do not advocate its return. Almost all Russians despise Yeltsin, yet they support Putin, who is Yeltsin's chosen successor. These contradictions are hardly explained by classical sociological models. Sociologist Vladimir Shlapentokh uses three different models for describing the Russian masses.[18] The first model suggests that post-Soviet Russians have extremely eclectic minds that border on schizophrenia. The second model describes Russians as uncivilized people who are unable to live under democracy and whose opinions have no value for those who are trying to build a normal society. Though the basic data used to support these models cannot be disputed, both models are problematic. It is not possible to work with a model that describes some nations as schizophrenic or lazy drunkards and thieves. This is why the third model, working with the rational behavior of the masses in a concrete historical context, is needed.

Understanding the historical context and cultural disparity enables us to comprehend the differences in the social contract between the government and people in Russia and in the West. Western governments are supposed to do something positive for their citizens. The Russian citizen fears that his government will harm his life or well-being and is quite content to have his government leave him alone. This is why Russians are so patient with their irresponsible elites and governments.

As was discussed above, Russian institutions may have a different content and words may have different meanings than in the Anglo-Saxon world. When dealing with Russia one should constantly compare every piece of information and confirm every word. Otherwise, even an astute analyst will be probably misled.

## RUSSIAN MODERNIZATION

Efforts to catch up with the modernization spreading from the West are a permanent feature of Russian history since the end of the seventeenth century. Like many other nations, Russia has been responding to the assertiveness of modernization with a mixture of ambition, anger, and horror at the possibility of losing the values that it has grown accustomed to over the course of centuries.[19] The problem is that the Russian elite was never united in its attitude toward modernization. Russia was not able to activate the necessary mechanisms—neither in the social structure, nor in cultural tradition—that could have provided the basis for a rapid industrial leap. Repeated steps backward postponed Russia's modernization. During the period of the industrial revolution Russia was still handling problems of the Renaissance. The Russians have been working to solve the challenges of industrialization throughout the course of the twentieth century, but in some ways have still not completed the task.

Similar situations have been observed during the ten years following the collapse of the Soviet Union. Once more in its history, Russia came up against the challenge of modernization. And once again, the Russian elite did not succeed in the correct implementation of foreign patterns. The Russians were given political freedom, but it did not change them into citizens in the Western sense. Despite the fact that the Ministry of Justice has registered almost 238,000 nongovernmental organizations, the institutions of civil society are very weak and vulnerable.

More than 70 percent of Russia's economy is in private hands, but this does not mean that companies are managed in a systematic and transparent way. Also, it does not mean that the influence of bureaucracy has diminished. The golden rule of Russian bureaucracy, formulated more than 150 years ago by Count Speranskyi, is still in use: "No one state decision should be formulated in a way allowing its implementation without participation of bureaucracy."[20] For example, an ordinary Russian company is inspected almost daily by one of the sixty-seven different Russian government agencies that regulate businesses. However, the real interest of these agencies lies in extorting bribes. Their ubiquitous interference has limited the number of legally registered enterprises to just one per fifty-five persons, whereas Western countries have about one per every ten persons.[21] No wonder present-day Russia is incapable of coping with the challenges of globalization.[22]

The Russian government and the Russian people are combating everyday problems. They are fighting floods and fires, unemployment and corruption, disasters and diseases. They do their best, but the results are poor. This is not only due to mismanagement on the government level. The authoritarian management style at the level of enterprises also has a pernicious effect.[23]

The only remedy for Russia is a comprehensive reformation of its political system and economy. Although the success of reform is primarily in the interest of the Russian people and government, prospective Russian achievements might be important for other states as well. The advancement of the Russian economy can contribute to global growth. Failure can hit some weaker states in the Russian neighborhood. Crises or even the collapse of the Russian state may lead to the eruption of different threats—from military and security perils to ecological, economic, and humanitarian hazards.

The developed countries are fully aware of the hopes and threats arising from Russian reforms. The United States and other G-8 members are doing their best to help Russia cope with its enormous problems and prevent most danger risks.

## RUSSIAN FOREIGN POLICY

Two main tasks lie before Russian foreign policymakers. The first is to preserve as much as possible of the superpower status inherited by Russia from the former Soviet Union. The second task is to contribute to the creation of the most favorable possible conditions for the stabilization and further development of Russia. These tasks are sometimes in conflict.

The current international situation gives Moscow time to concentrate on domestic problems because Russia does not face any significant threat from abroad. Other countries in deep crisis and in need of reformation, e.g., post–World War II Germany and Japan, successfully tested this kind of "silent" foreign policy. Unfortunately, it looks like such foreign policy is not attractive for Russia's leadership. Permanent and visible efforts to keep at least some elements of superpower status may lead Russia down the path toward confrontation with the West. Such a threat is strengthened by the practice of deciding significant issues within a small circle of advisers around the president, which opens the door to some subjective and poorly thought out decisions.

Moscow is trying to counterbalance its deficiencies in its relations with the advanced countries by strengthening its cooperation with a number of other, often problematic states. The concept of a multipolar world places more emphasis upon their technological and arms capacities. Through this cooperation, Russia accomplishes two goals: it improves its balance of trade and also adds to the dispersal of sources for military and security threats, as well as potential targets for missions by the United States and other advanced countries.

Russia's multipolar world policy is one of the factors reducing the effectiveness of the bans on proliferating weapons of mass destruction and their delivery systems. Even though this does not necessarily mean direct sales to rogue states, such actions as cooperating with Iran contribute to a relativization of the nonproliferation regime.

U.S.-Russian relations are obviously dependent on the positions and behavior of both subjects. The United States is the stronger partner; however, it is a democratic, transparent society. Moreover, U.S. foreign policy tends to be similar: stable, rational, and predictable. Even if we take into account the differences between the rotating Washington administrations, we can observe that all U.S. governments are aware of the importance to cooperate with and help Russia to become a democratic country with an efficient market economy, as well as a constructive member of the international community and not a threatening pariah. It corresponds with a stable and permanently positive attitude toward Russia. Such an attitude is only partly reciprocated by Moscow.

Russia's government understands that it depends on good relations with developed countries, investment inflow, and access to cheap loans. The problem is that, simultaneously with cooperative steps, Russia is playing with a card of confrontation. Consequences of their own weaknesses and unwise deeds are often presented as a result of a machination of external powers. The factor of irrationality in Russia's internal development and foreign policymaking process induces the paradoxical fact that the quality of bilateral relations is influenced more by Russian instability than American reliability.[24]

The Russians have more motives to resist National Missile Defense (NMD) than they normally admit in public statements. Russia is conscious of the economic, technological, and scientific backwardness that keeps it behind the United States. Russia still has enormous potential in missile and weapon related technologies. Yet it is quite difficult to imagine that Russia will be able to develop and deploy her own NMD. If the United States succeeds in deploying NMD, it will be a heavy blow for Russia's ability to keep a credible nuclear deterrent and in turn a blow to what is left of its superpower status.

Russia is evidently unable to adopt another possible response to NMD— an expansion of her nuclear arsenal. Even in the area of existing nuclear missiles and warheads, Moscow probably will not be capable of maintaining a strategic balance with the United States. It is difficult to estimate exactly how many nuclear warheads and missiles the Russian economy can afford. Some analysts claim that it is even less than the potential limit of 1,200 warheads which shall be, according to preliminary information, established in the future third Strategic Arms Reduction Treaty.

The last development in Russia's position toward NMD shows that President Putin has tried to exchange his consent with NMD for the further lessening of warhead limits, in order to keep strategic balance with the United States. If that is true, it might be understood as a demonstration of common sense by Russian leadership. It is still questionable whether NMD will be successfully deployed. The whole business may fail during tests, or it may be buried in the U.S. Senate. Even if deployed, it will take a long time to significantly reduce Russia's nuclear deterrent. And during this time Moscow will be able to enjoy a strategic nuclear balance with Washington.

The second reason for resistance to the U.S. administration's plans is the attempt to make political use of NMD. Moscow may be hoping that the discussion surrounding missile defense will exacerbate the security discrepancy between the United States and the European Union. The same holds true for the expansion of NATO, concerning which the Kremlin hopes to make a security-related tradeoff.

Finally, there are even more possibilities for tradeoffs related to NMD. Russia may try to work out a financial or technological deal, or negotiate a way to gain access to the American (European) market with armaments.

## THE ANTITERRORIST OFFENSIVE AND RUSSIAN FOREIGN POLICY

The terrorist attacks on September 11, 2001, changed many countries' viewpoints on many questions, including international relations and security affairs. The need for joint efforts in the civilized world to combat terrorism has changed relations between many countries. One of the most significant shifts has taken place in the relationship between the United States and Russia. Moscow can provide substantial assistance in an international effort to capture Osama bin Laden, to destroy the capacity of his organization to spread terror, and in the long run to diminish the influence of terrorism as a factor in international relations.

There are two principal questions. The first is whether Russia is really prepared for full-fledged cooperation with the West. The second is the price of such cooperation. Russian participation in an antiterrorist offensive, together with only moderate demands in return, might be a substantial indication of Russian preparedness to become a reliable partner of the West. It is exam time and we can only hope that Russia will not fail. From the very beginning Moscow has been trying to capitalize on the new situation for its own interests.

On the basis of the mass media's analysis and information,[25] we can draw a preliminary sketch of Russia's attitude toward the antiterrorist offensive. In general, Russia has tried to slip its war against the Chechen separatists into the international antiterrorist agenda. A chronological analysis shows that on September 21, President Putin offered cooperation in five areas: active cooperation among intelligence agencies, the opening of Russian airspace for humanitarian missions, agreement with Central Asian allies on flyovers, participation in search and rescue operations, and expanded cooperation with Afghanistan's Northern Alliance. The same day he requested a quid pro quo for such moderate cooperation when, in an interview with the German TV network ARD, he said that Moscow continues to view Washington's withdrawal from the 1972 Anti-Ballistic Missile (ABM) Treaty as an "erroneous" step, because "the present international security system is based to a considerable degree on the 1972 ABM Treaty." He said that the current situation in the world suggests that all parties should be careful about doing anything that might undermine the existing arrangements.

According to information from September 24–25, Russia had denied open airspace for U.S. military flights (except humanitarian flights) first and pretended to have agreed on such a position with its Central Asian allies. However, the presidents of Kazakhstan and Kyrgyzstan offered to open their airspace for the needs of U.S. military on those same dates. Also on September 25, Russian defense minister Sergei Ivanov said that Moscow had agreed to allow U.S. forces to use a Russian air base near Dushanbe to conduct retaliatory strikes. With Russia having lost control over its Central

Asian allies, Ivanov made an offer to open Russian airspace to American and allied aviation for any attacks on Afghanistan on September 26. The same day, President Putin said that the North Atlantic Treaty Organization (NATO) should admit Russia as a full member.

Russian behavior up to mid-October shows that Moscow has chosen a step-by-step approach, searching for more benefits by holding out the carrot of providing assistance to the Western antiterrorist offensive. However, Russia's payback demands are considerable: In addition to predictable efforts to defend the ABM Treaty and thus block U.S. plans for NMD, Russia asked to join NATO. This is a more serious threat to NATO than Russia's traditional resistance to the plans of NATO enlargement. Russia's ambition to become a NATO member without substantive internal changes is absurd. Moreover, Russia is demanding to alter NATO by reducing its military component. Such a NATO would be a weaker version of the Organization for Security and Cooperation in Europe (OSCE). If Russia, in its present form, gains membership in NATO, it would threaten the effectiveness of the only operational military structure that can provide security for the Northern Hemisphere and abroad.

One may ask what is wrong with giving Russia a larger role in security policy? The answer is quite short: keeping in mind both Russia's level of reliability and the possible consequences of Russian participation, the conclusion is that Russia already has too large a role in European security. We all know very well that Russia is not the Soviet Union. We also know that the Cold War is over. But Russia has not changed much from Soviet times. It might be useful to reexamine the Russian role in European security policy over the course of the 1990s. What did Russia do in the so-called Transdniester Republic? How much did Russia help to solve the Abkhazian-Georgian conflict? Why are Armenia and Azerbaijan still on the edge of war? What was the Russian position toward conflicts in Bosnia and Kosovo? We should not forget that if Russia had its wish, there would be no NATO presence in the Balkans and the whole region would continue to suffer from war.

Doubts about Russian reliability are extremely significant with regard to possible Russian membership in the NATO alliance. The Russia of the last decade, with its many burdens—such as the Chechen war, an insufficiently developed civil society, the authoritarian character of its ruling regime, and its Cold War stubbornness in security affairs—is not an acceptable member. The situation would be quite different if we could consider a democratic Russia with a proven record of pro-Western commitments and a strong civil society. These features would indicate that Russia had changed significantly and could be considered as a NATO ally. In fact, the integration of Russia into the Western security architecture is the best possible scenario for the West as well as for Russia itself. But once again, the sine qua non is a thorough, trustworthy transformation in Russia, not an expedient political decision by the governments of the NATO member states.

## RUSSIA, THE UNITED STATES, AND EASTERN AND CENTRAL EUROPE

As regards the dependence of the region of Eastern and Central Europe (ECE) on Russia, the countries can be broken into three distinct groups.[26] We can observe several currents in U.S. policy vis-à-vis Russia that would be similarly welcome, or more likely unwelcome, in the entire region.

Any sort of return to the politics of spheres of influence[27] would have a devastating impact on the Baltic states and on the states of the Commonwealth of Independent States (CIS). In Russian policy, even in times of weakness, there have been very evident traces of the former imperialistic stances from the days of the Soviet Union. In periods of relative stability, Moscow becomes more interested in asserting Russian dominance over the territory of the former Soviet Union. Russia maintains military bases or border guard divisions in most of the CIS countries. Should the Baltic and CIS states lose their potential for counterbalancing Russian influence through developing relations with the West, it could dangerously strengthen nationalist circles in Russia.

Weaker, but still negative, effects can also be traced to the policy of endlessly providing Russian leadership with carte blanche. The slogan that the Russian president is doing well no matter what he does, because the communists would be even worse, is not correct. First of all, the prospect of a communist return to power is quite fanciful. Furthermore, the "democratic" Russian government has already committed enough mistakes and atrocities to be treated firmly. Examples include the first and second Chechen war, Russian peacekeeping "efforts" that have not resolved any conflicts, or Russian pressure on Central Asian CIS countries in the context of development of Caspian Basin gas and oil resources. In fact, this is an old disparity between the West and the ECE countries in assessing Russian behavior and intentions. ECE and CIS nations traditionally think that Western policy toward Russia is either naive or cynical.[28] In light of the above-mentioned arguments, one can understand why.

Tighter coordination of U.S. policy vis-à-vis Russia with the policy of the European Union (EU) would be very desirable. However, this definitely would not be easy for two reasons. First, the policies of the European Union and its member states are often internally disputed. Second, EU and U.S. relations with Russia differ naturally. The European Union is by far the most important economic partner of Russia, but in the political and security areas the main partner for Russia is the United States.

The same dichotomy applies to the central and east European countries. In the sense of economy, they are more interested in cooperation with the European Union. In the sense of security, their main partner is the United States. Thus, in regard to Russia, the countries of Eastern and Central

Europe should not be forced to choose between their relations with the United States and the European Union.

With regard to Russia, it makes no sense to give Moscow a chance to exploit any disparity between the United States and Europe. For example, within the Czech Republic there are two quite distinct schools of thought. President Vaclav Havel represents the first school, which views the possibility of cooperation with Russia quite realistically and strongly supports the right of all states to freely choose their own methods of guaranteeing their own security.[29] However, the Czech Social-Democratic government seems to be much more sensitive to Russian arguments. This group places higher value on the prospects of developing economic[30] and other relations with Russia than does the president. It could even appear that the government is willing to restrict criticism of human rights abuses in Russia in the interest of strengthening economic cooperation (just as it does in relation to China).

## DEALING WITH RUSSIA

Overall, the basic world trend today is to try to link and make use of the potential of all countries and regions. However, this does not only mean the potential offered by raw materials. What is special about the current stage of modernization is an effort to make use of human potential. From the point of view of a globalized economy, it is irrational to avoid any country with exploitable potential. And it is quite dangerous to let any country fall into disarray, thereby threatening the safety and well-being of other states. Russia is a very important country in both aforementioned aspects. It has enormous potential for participating in global growth, and equally important potential to menace. It is in the common interest of the West (or the developed world) to help Russia become an integrated part of international society.[31] The United States, as the only remaining superpower, has a special responsibility in this long-lasting and perhaps tedious process.

Despite Russia's unique character, it is quite clear where its path should lead. There is no solution to Russia's problems other than to become an integrated part of the international community of developed countries. It is Russia's responsibility to reach this goal. The West may be helpful, but it is Russia's task, not ours. The problem is that sometimes one must doubt whether the Russian government and Russian elites are aware of this basic fact. It is an old question of how to treat a sick Russia that does not take adequate care of itself and behaves like a hysterical and rather spoiled patient shifting responsibility for its health into the hands of its doctors.

The United States and other Western countries understand the Russian situation and their responsibility very well. Russia has been treated fairly after the collapse of the Soviet Union. The international environment has been favorable. Western governments and international organizations, as well as private companies, have invested heavily (in a direct and indirect sense). It is not the West's fault that these contributions have been weakened and devalued time and time again by muddled economic, legal, and political rule in Russia. It is a common experience of the West for cooperation with Russia to occasionally mutate into one-sided assistance in the name of achieving specific goals.[32]

There are two main areas of cooperation between the United States and Russia. The first deals with the lessening of threats and risks. The second is concentrated on Russia's potential to participate in global growth. Both areas are important, and there is even an effect of synergy between them. Nevertheless, the aforementioned areas have different levels of urgency for Russia and for the developed world.

Development of Russian economic relations with the West is always welcome. However, from the point of view of developed countries, the potential profit to be derived from economic cooperation is marginal. U.S.-Russian trade is about U.S.$3 billion to $5 billion per year. The above-mentioned "peace dividend" amounts to hundreds of billions of U.S. dollars per year. Moreover the realization of one or more threats or risks that derive, or could derive, from the state of Russian affairs or from faulty policy of the Russian government may have a real and negative impact on the well-being of the developed nations.

Russia's relations with the United States and other advanced countries are just the opposite. None of the advanced countries comprises any sort of direct threat to Russia. Surely Russia is threatened by the prospect of further setbacks in international relations and the prospect of getting left further behind the advanced world. These prospects, however, are not caused by any bad will on the part of the West. Rather, they are caused by Russia's inability to keep up with the pace of development in the advanced world. And Russia is well aware that it can only overcome its backwardness with the help of the United States and the other countries of the West. Only with the help of the advanced world will Russia be able to modernize its economy and escape the vicious circle of de-industrialization.

*Numerous Risks.* The spectrum of risks currently or potentially threatening the outside world is relatively wide. While more distant countries are primarily interested in military and security problems, Russia's closer neighbors are also troubled by ecological, economic, and humanitarian hazards. Serious threats to the central European region include a possible mass wave of emigration; a chemical, biological, or nuclear sort of technological catastrophe; or a major reduction of Russia's capacity to export oil and natural gas. Along with other states we also share concerns about the possibility of a random military incident, the loss of control over a weapon of mass destruction, or the illegal transfer of arms or weapon technology. Some of these even consist of combined threats (for example, the widespread contamination of residential territory could spark a wave of emigration).[33] Also troubling is the growing presence of Russian-speaking criminal groups.

In considering the issue of the appropriateness of assistance to Russia, there are two basic groups. The first adheres to the idea of "Help Russia now or face the consequences later." The other group claims the contrary, namely that assisting Russia is, at best, simply throwing money out the window and, at worst, helping Russia to fortify its army and increasing the potential threat to the United States (and other countries).

One can understand the opponents to widespread aid to Russia. We truly should expect Russia to take more responsibility and to make efforts to resolve problems that are mainly threats to Russia itself and only secondary threats to the outside world. It is also quite natural to say that the Russian government should first invest in the environment, combat AIDS, or liquidate its old weapons systems before spending money on new systems.

But we should be very clear on one matter. Russia's elite is not much interested in the fate of common people. The elite live in Moscow or in other large cities like St. Petersburg. They travel to Europe or to the United States, not to Severodvinsk. Corroded reactors in arctic ports are far away for them; such problems are not a part of their world. All problems having to do with obsolete weapons, lack of finances, and growing risks will never force the Russian government to concentrate its efforts on effective problem solving. Not even dozens of deteriorating submarine reactors floating in its harbors will deter the Kremlin from investing its limited resources in the construction of new submarines (like the *Kursk*).

If the advanced world wants to eliminate risks related to Russian weapons of mass destruction, the international community will have to provide the lion's share of the financing for the liquidation of these hazardous materials alone. In this area, it is probably not worth trying to scrimp on spending, because proper investment will reduce the threat to the security of the entire world, according to the risk equation.[34]

*Security Issues.* While the classic security threats (arising from the possibility that an armed conflict will erupt) are constantly weakening, new security risks are appearing to take their place. The first category is connected with the danger of unauthorized use or illegal sale of weapons of mass destruction and the related technology. The second category surrounds the issues involved in the safe dismantling of obsolete arms and materials.

It appears that the rise of President Putin's government has somewhat lowered the degree of chaos in Russia and also the probability of such risks as the unauthorized sale of weapons of mass destruction to irresponsible states or criminal groups.

The risks involved in the liquidation of arms and materials are a much more realistic danger today. The fundamental problem is based on Russia's inability to live up to the legacy of the Soviet armed forces. The physical aging of weapons systems, together with the commitments arising from the disarmament agreements and initiatives, place great financial, organizational, and material demands on Russia in relation to the safe liquidation of arms and materials. This includes both the nuclear area and chemical weapons.

Russia's modest budget lacks the funds needed to fulfill all these commitments. Furthermore, the management of the armed forces and companies connected with the dismantling of weapons of mass destruction is far from optimal. Thus, Western assistance in eliminating these risks is absolutely essential.

The advanced world is aware of this, and much has been done in the security field in recent years. But the results of the joint efforts of Russia and the advanced countries are still insufficient. For the future it will be deemed necessary to continue some individual activities and possibly expand them, while focusing on the factors that have been limiting their effectiveness. One example is the Cooperative Threat Reduction Program initiated by U.S. Senators Sam Nunn (D-Ga.) and Richard Lugar (R-Ind.) in 1993. This program was designed to help Russia and other countries of the former Soviet Union destroy nuclear, chemical, and biological weapons of mass destruction and associated infrastructure, and establish verifiable safeguards against the proliferation of those weapons. Since its inception, the program has substantially reduced the threat posed by weapons of mass destruction by helping to better account for weapons previously aimed at the United States and reduce their delivery systems.

Another question has to do with financial efficiency. During the realization of the program, several factors appeared that reduced the overall effectiveness of U.S. assistance. One of the problems was that the United States did not provide financial assistance in cash, but rather in the form of equipment produced in the United States and transported by American ships. In many cases, the same equipment could have been produced in Russia at a much lower price. The money saved could have been directed toward, for example, financing the use of the dismantled equipment, which was often left idle due to internal Russian problems with financing.

On the other hand, the emphasis placed on quick progress in deactivating missile compartments highlighted the problems involved in dismantling reactors and even entire submarines. That is why there are dozens of Russian submarines floating (or sunken) in ports with missile compartments cut out and a reactor still on board. Similarly unresolved is the problem of liquidating the solid and liquid radioactive waste arising from the dismantling of submarines.

Russian also faces problems in meeting their commitments in the area of chemical disarmament. Moscow inherited 40,000 tons of chemical weapons from the Soviet Union and committed itself to getting rid of them by 2009. The first stage was in 2000, when Russia was required to dispose of one percent of its stock. It did not meet this commitment and asked for it to be postponed until 2001, just as it asked for the final deadline to be moved from 2009 to 2012. In the area of chemical weapons as well, the problems related to lack of funds mix with the consequences of mismanagement.

In the spring of 2000, in a scientific institute under Moscow, a laboratory for perfecting techniques used in the liquidation of chemical weapons was ceremoniously opened. The facility was constructed at an expense of U.S.\$21 million, provided by the United States and Russia. By May 2001, however, the laboratory was still not operational—partly due to unexpected construction problems and partly due to the expected problem of financing its services.

The total cost of disposing of Russia's chemical weapons supplies is estimated to be U.S.\$7 billion to \$8 billion. Russia claims that it is capable of freeing up only a small fraction of this sum from its budget. Although Western donors justifiably question why Russia is not willing to dedicate more substantial sums to disposing of weapons that pose a great risk to Russia and its citizens, the fact remains that if the West wants to get rid of the Russian chemical arsenal it will have to pay for it.

The Western allies are well aware of this. At present, along with the United States, which is providing the largest financial contribution, Canada, the European Union, Finland, Germany, Italy, the Netherlands, Norway, and Sweden have also decided to share the costs of eliminating Russia's chemical weapons.

*International Cooperation.* Although generous assistance is needed in the field of risk and crisis prevention, this does not mean it makes no sense to cooperate with Russia in other areas. Despite its backwardness, Russia is a very attractive market of 146 million consumers. Its vast territory and natural resources could become a significant factor in the global economy. It is therefore in the common interest of the developed countries to integrate Russia into the advanced world.

Strengthening economic and commercial ties should provide a stable element in Russian-American bilateral relations. High-level government support is essential for further reducing risks that threaten private sector investments. We can already see some positive examples of changes in Russia influenced by the positive engagement of Western governments and business circles (e.g., the adoption of two parts of the tax code). But there are still many problems where Western engagement may be very helpful, including inconsistent and arbitrary application of tax laws, currency control laws, complicated and unclear custom procedures, investor protection, and intellectual property rights violations.[35]

Many of these questions might be part of the negotiations on Russian accession to the World Trade Organization (WTO). The Russian government has already identified membership in the WTO as one of its top priorities. The U.S. government should support Russia's aspirations and transform this long-lasting process into an important element of U.S. engagement.[36]

Another chance for strengthening economic ties might be the expansion of microcredit programs to support small and micro businesses. It would be natural to coordinate the U.S. position with that of other important members, especially the European Union and Japan. A partnership between Russia and the European Union also has a lot of potential to change Russia's economy.

Programs of cooperation should also be targeted toward the development of nongovernmental organizations and the human sector. The Russian social system is so poor that any form of cooperation and assistance would be helpful. The U.S. government, as well as private agencies, may address problems like the spread of infectious diseases (tuberculosis, AIDS, etc.).

Another important goal for the future of Russia and U.S.-Russian relations is investment in educational activities. It is obvious that the new generation of Russian elites may support more pro-Western changes. It would therefore be advantageous to help Russia's elites to gain Western-style education and experience with life in the United States.

The end of 1990 was a time of disillusionment with democracy and a return to Soviet-style culture in Russia. More important are the activities of such human rights groups as the Helsinki Group or Committee of Soldiers' Mothers of Russia. These people are often subjected to harassment from official circles. It would be good if these groups did not experience problems in financing their activities.

It is not clear how to support democracy on Russia's domestic scene. There are few democratic parties with real influence in the Russian political system except perhaps for the Yabloko Party. And even Yabloko would be terrified to be considered a pro-American party. Thus, possible assistance should be indirect and prudent. It might be targeted to support the free media, organizations for youth, or to support nongovernmental organizations advocating democracy and liberties in general but not the United States or the West. In addition, there are opportunities to exploit official "twinning" programs of cities and institutions and to invite U.S. officials from middle management levels. Despite all precautions, direct assistance will remain an easy target for anti-Western circles.

The Russian government has already demonstrated an amazing ability not to make good use of an entire series of loans and assistance provided during the 1990s. Therefore, Russia's partners should think about how they can contribute to Russia's development: to the promotion of democracy and market economy in a country with such deep nondemocratic roots and with such a degree of mistrust toward foreigners in general, and the West in particular. It was explained above that such mistrust is in some way natural. However, mistrust can be seen in developing countries throughout the world, all of which are trying to catch up with the latest wave of modernization.

Another argument in favor of cooperation is the fact that without Western assistance Russia will probably remain a source of instability and risk for a long time to come. The form and urgency of these risks will change as individual development scenarios are realized. One very troubling possibility is the risk that the Russian state will continue to deteriorate. That would have a number of unpleasant consequences, such as weakening of Russian fuel exports and the end of geopolitical control over the vast lands of Siberia and the northern Caucasus.

In fact, there are numerous areas in which Moscow's influence has already been weakened. Obsolete railway infrastructure and high transport tariffs played a role in the weakening of Russia's economic ties with many Siberian and Far Eastern provinces. There have also been significant demographic changes. The total population of Russia's Far East decreased during the 1990s from 8.1 million to 7.4 million inhabitants (8.6 percent).[37] Demographic pressure from the Chinese side is enormous. The size and scope of illegal Chinese immigration to Russia's Far East is unknown, and estimates differ greatly. Extreme estimates go as far as 2 million Chinese illegally staying in Russia, of which 1 million are said to have settled in the Russian Far East.

Even if such estimates are exaggerated, the general tendency is quite clear: Russia is losing and China is gaining. And in the event that Russia weakens or even implodes, it is China that will gain. It appears that the West is ill prepared to face such challenges. Nonetheless, since Washington had the foresight to understand that China could grow into a rival of the United States, it should also have the imagination to envision the consequences of China's rule over Siberia or the Russian Far East.

## CONCLUSIONS AND RECOMMENDATIONS

Russia is going through a difficult period. The end of twentieth century showed clearly that Russia is desperately behind in developing its society. After the collapse of the Soviet Union, Russia is seeking the best way to improve both its internal situation and international status. The developed world is looking toward Russia with a mixture of hopes and qualms.

The only good solution is for Russia to become an integrated part of the community of developed countries. The basic question is whether, and how, the West can help Russia in this process. Examples of Russian inefficiency and mismanagement abound. But that does not mean cooperation with Russia should be terminated or emasculated. The process of accommodation and adaptation to Western standards can be only piecemeal. Western nations should be patient as well as demanding.

The U.S. government will face two basic problems in its relations with Russia. First, there is a principal cultural disparity between Russia and the United States. The Russian government's priorities are different than those of the Western governments. The suffering of Russian citizens is not reason enough to stop a Chechen war. Hazards and risks are not reason to concentrate efforts on the effective solution of the hundreds of problems that plague Russia. Unfortunately, it is not possible to solve all problems from the outside. The United States and other developed countries should concentrate on handling the problems that can be solved, such as military-security threats or environmental hazards that endanger Russia's neighbors or the global environment. There is no need to be frugal here. Second, in international affairs, the main task is to restrain imperialistic Russian nostalgia and at the same time not puncture Russian security fears. The problem is that the Russian understanding of international security is based on a zero-sum game approach. If somebody gains, Russians are sure that they are in the red. Such understanding of security is untenable not only in small Europe, but throughout the planet.

It is true that Russia is in the process of a complex transformation. However, the difference is that this process of transformation, with unclear social structures and unstable rules, should not be seen as a temporary phenomenon. According to all indicators, Russia's current state of disorder is a typical and natural characteristic of its development in the present era. The international community should accept the unpleasant fact that the process of reform in Russia will probably be very long and tedious. That does not mean it makes no sense to cooperate and assist Russia. In the case of success, profits might be high. In the case of failure, losses will be painful. The West should cooperate with Russia, but also should be conscious that the process is complex and knotty.[38]

There is a broad spectrum of threats and risks that can be addressed only on a governmental level. Cooperation can often take the form of simple unilateral Western aid. Despite this, it is proper and advantageous to help Russia in every way that might reduce global and transborder threats. Resources allocated to the dismantling and utilization of Russia's weapons of mass destruction should increase significantly. An inseparable part of cooperation should be the observation and scrutiny of Russian actions, the inspection of effectiveness, and an audit of financial flows according to the motto "trust but verify."

Governmental cooperation should not be focused only on risk-reducing issues. The engagement of the U.S. government can be helpful in solving many of the economic and commercial relations problems. The U.S. government should be tough and should not give the Russian leadership any carte blanche in their activities of post-imperial nostalgia, like the semi-genocidal Chechen war. Such activities of the Russian government should be addressed by harsh criticism.

Russia is a sovereign country and it is not possible to judge and micromanage every twist and turn in Russia's reforms. Nevertheless, the U.S. administration should stress that the preservation of democracy is a basic condition for political and economic cooperation. Areas of cooperation and opposition should be tightly coordinated with the European Union and other allies to minimize the possibility that Moscow would be able to take advantage of mutual disputes.

The main emphasis should be placed on the nongovernmental sector to support the process of the pro-Western transformation of Russian society. It would be counterproductive to openly support some of the political parties, because to be labeled pro-American is deadly for any political party. It makes more sense to support institutions of the emerging citizen society. Very helpful can be support for human rights organizations, like the Committee of Soldiers' Mothers of Russia, the Helsinki Group, or Memorial. In general, what Russian society needs is greater access to information.

Most promising is support of students of all levels, especially in the social sciences. The goal should be to provide them with Western knowledge, but to keep them living and working in Russia. Support for a broader connection of schools and libraries on the Internet will result in a significant improvement.

Support for prodemocratic changes and the firm opposition to post-imperial nostalgia will help all ECE countries. For example, the general declaration that Russia has no right to veto the future enlargement of NATO should be supported not only by the integration of "unproblematic" countries like Slovakia into the alliance, but also by the integration of at least some of the Baltic states, such as Estonia. The enlargement of NATO will help the ECE region immediately and will help Russia in the future. Firm support for the independence of the Baltic states and Ukraine helps to promote security and stability in the ECE region.

A U.S. policy of taking Russian problems into consideration, evaluating Russian promises realistically, and fundamentally refusing any attempts at fixing so-called spheres of influence could make a significant contribution to the stabilization of the region.

However, although Russian participation in the antiterrorist offensive is very desirable, the West should be aware of the balance of Russian assets and rewards. Full-fledged cooperation with the West might be a first step on the long road toward Russian integration into the Western security system. Such an evolution would be the best possible scenario for the West as well as for Russia itself. But this would require profound reformation in

Russia. Unfortunately, current analysis of Russian behavior shows that Russia has chosen a step-by-step approach, providing very limited assistance and asking for immoderate concessions in return. In fact, Russia is still holding out the carrot in search of more benefits. Finally, Russia's joining NATO before realizing certain key reforms would inevitably lead to the paralysis of the only operational military structure that can provide security for the Northern Hemisphere and beyond.

## NOTES

1. A classic example of such misunderstanding is the Russian approach to the enlargement of NATO.

2. Such assessment depends on the basis used for benchmarking. Russian social figures would be very good for Sierra Leone, but for a member of the G-8 the figures are quite poor. Forty percent of citizens live under the poverty line. Male life expectancy declined from 65.4 to 57.6 years between 1989 and 1994. Although there has been some improvement (60.8 years in 1997), the situation is still very poor. Incidence of infectious disease, alcohol and drug abuse, cancer and heart disease, as well as mortality on external causes, is on the rise. U.N. projections suggest that population decline will reach 28 percent in the next 50 years.

3. Problems connected with a dramatic increase in competition on the international market during the next decades are traditionally undervalued in international studies. According to trustworthy estimations, in each sector of industry and services only a handful of international companies will survive, which will cover a huge majority of world consumption of given products. Success of a company will depend on its ability to continually improve the level of quality. At present, Russian companies do not follow this general trend of quality management.

4. It is a relative observation. Inflation in the year 2000 reached 20 percent and almost the same figure is predicted for the year 2001.

5. A comprehensive list of legislative intentions includes tax reform, a new state budget, pension and social welfare reform, housing and utility subsidies, regulation of natural monopolies, property rights, bankruptcy legislation, privatization, and product-sharing agreement legislation can be found in: *Toward the Common Good: Building a New U.S.-Russian Relationship* (Washington, D.C.: East-West Institute, July 2001), p. 26.

6. As of January 2001, cumulative foreign direct investment (FDI) in Russia amounted to U.S.$16.1 billion. By comparison, Poland, as the most successful transition economy in central Europe, attracted an estimated U.S.$35.5 billion in FDI from 1991 through the end of 2000. Last year Poland enjoyed a record FDI of U.S.$9.3 billion, whereas the equivalent figure for Russia was U.S.$4.4 billion. *Ibid.*

7. Lack of investment remains critical even in the oil and gas industry. Russian oil production fell to less than 5.9 million barrels per day (mb/d) in 1999, down from 12 mb/d in the late 1980s. In 2000 it rebounded by 4.7 percent, following a 25 percent increase in investment in 1999 and doubling of total investment in 2000. Nevertheless, investments needed to keep Russian oil output increasing are estimated at some U.S.$140 billion during 2000–2020. Amy Myers Jaffe and Robert A. Manning, "Russia, Energy, and the West," *Survival*, vol. 2, no. 43 (Summer 2001), pp. 133–52.

8. For a description of factors that caused the 1998 crisis and influenced later recovery, see *OECD Economic Surveys: Russian Federation* (OECD, 2000), www.oecd.org/pdf/M00002000/M00002720.pdf.

9. Oil, gas, and metal account for roughly 75 percent of Russian export revenues (Sabrina Tavernise, "A Stable Economy, but for How Long," *New York Times,* June 17, 2001). Even more striking are data about growth of Russian exports. The 100 biggest Russian exporting companies (exports above U.S.$20 million) exported U.S.$37.727 billion in 1999 and U.S.$62.096 billion in 2000. Export growth represents U.S.$24.369 billion, or 64.6 percent. U.S.$20.983 billion of this enlargement had been made by the 22 largest companies (exports above U.S.$500 million). With the exception of one, the 22 largest companies export gas, oil, or metal. From Russian magazine *Expert,* no. 27 (287), July 16, 2001.

10. Quite sure about future lessening of oil prices are A. M. Jaffe and R. A. Manning, "The Shocks of a World of Cheap Oil," *Foreign Affairs,* vol. 79, no. 1 (January/February 2000), pp. 16, 29.

11. Sabrina Tavernise, *op. cit.*

12. As usual, Putin has a very good explanation. Courts in Russia are indeed corrupt (as is the entire society). But making a judge punishable for his decision is hardly the right way to a secure rule of law.

13. This is evidenced by the fact that Russia's leadership has not been willing (and may not even be able) to take advantage of the favorable climate in international relations and high trade surplus during the last two years to pursue qualitative changes (e.g., a thorough reduction of the Russian army, investments into promising sectors of the economy, or the modernization of education and health care).

14. Stephen Cohen, *The Failed Crusade: America and the Tragedy of Post-communist Russia* (New York: Norton, 2000). The author here details the criticism of the majority of leaders who dealt with the status of Russia and its reforms in the first decade.

15. This is not the first time this blindness has appeared in relation to Russia. Let us think back to the positive information about the Soviet Union received in the 1920s, when a great number of humanists and undeniably decent people simply did not see or did not want to see the horrors of the developing Soviet system.

16. The definition of modernization in this paper is broad. Modernization as an aggregate of rational attitudes and practices began to spread from the countries of northern and western Europe in the early sixteenth century. The concept of modernization divided the world into two distinctive parts—the core and the periphery.

17. Jerzy Gierus, *Russia's Road to Modernity* (Warsaw: Institute of Political Studies, Polish Academy of Science, 1998).

18. Vladimir Shlapentokh, "Russian Society: The View from Below," in *Russia in the International System,* conference report, National Intelligence Council, February 2001, www.odci.gov/nic.

19. Jerzy Gierus, *op. cit.*

20. Michail Michailovich, Count Speransky (1772–1839), council of Tsar Aleksander I and author of the "great codification" of Russian law.

21. Anders Aslund, "Winners Take All," *Foreign Affairs,* vol. 78, no. 5 (September/October 1999), pp. 64–77.

22. A valuable account of present-day Russia can be found in the report *Russia—Facing the Future* (New York: Carnegie Corporation, 2001).

23. The authoritarianism of the current directors has become even stronger than in the Soviet period, since they are no longer subject to restraint by the Communist Party or ministerial structures. At the same time, it is rare for outside shareholders to exert effective control. Veronika Kabalina and Simon Clark, *Innovation in Post-Soviet Industrial Enterprises,* report from the EU INCO-COPERNICUS program, www.warwick.ac.uk/fac/soc/complabstuds/russia/innovation.html.

24. This stance corresponds to the experiences of the countries of central Europe. Despite all the problems and failures on their path to reform, the countries of the Visegrád group have been markedly more successful and, in the sense of foreign policy, more stable than Russia. However, in their relations with Russia, it has been primarily Moscow who has decided on the quality of mutual ties. We can see this in the example of relations between the Czech Republic and the Russian Federation, which due to an ostensible lack of interest on the Russian side somehow went into a sort of hibernation in the late 1990s. (Cf. L. Dobrovsky [former Czech ambassador in Moscow]), "Cesko ruske vztahy" (Czech-Russian relations), *Mezinarodni politika,* no. 1 (2001), Institute of International Relations, Prague.

25. Analysis made on the basis of RFE/RE *Newsline* (September/October 2001), www.rferl.org/newsline.

26. The region of Central and Eastern Europe can be broken into at least three groups in regard to security issues in their relations with Russia:

    a) Czech Republic, Hungary, Poland, Slovakia, and Slovenia—none of these states shares a border with Russia (with the exception of Poland, which shares a border with Kaliningrad). Three of them are NATO members and the other two are on the way to joining the alliance. All of them should become EU members relatively soon. Their security problems with Russia are the same or similar to those of the West European countries.

    b) The Baltic states—as a part of the former Soviet Union, they are regarded by Russia as an area of vital interest. Their membership in NATO would undoubtedly provoke a very negative reaction from Russia. Along with amending the ABM Treaty, they could be a significant factor leading to changes in Russian stances toward the United States and NATO. Even though they are trying to distance themselves from the former Soviet Union, they are heavily dependent economically on Russia and the other countries of the CIS. The resolution of security issues is minimally related to the situation in Russia. Their advantage is undeniable progress in economic and political reforms. Estonia and, to a certain degree, the other two states are becoming real candidates for EU accession. Their possible membership in the European Union would stabilize them economically and in the area of security, and it would clearly divide them from the Russian zone.

    c) The CIS countries—they are tied to Russia with tight bonds in economic, humanitarian, security, and other areas. Social reforms often develop even slower and with more difficulties than in Russia itself. The development of Russian-American relations has a direct effect upon them. The support of the United States and other advanced countries could be vital for the maintenance and construction of their statehood.

27. The author is speaking about the sphere of influence in the sense of the Yalta arrangement. About spheres of influence, where the stronger is allowed publicly to threaten the weaker with the use of military force, the free will of people is restricted by external power. Such a sphere of influence may be created if Russia is granted the right to veto membership of the Baltic states in NATO.

28. Ronald Asmus, "Central Europe's Perspective," in *Russia in the International System,* conference report, National Intelligence Council, February 2001, www.odci.gov/nic.

29. Speech by President Vaclav Havel of the Czech Republic at the conference, "Europe's New Democracies: Leadership and Responsibility," Bratislava, May 11, 2001.

30. The last step in this direction was a Czech-Russian consent to sell a large part of Russian debt for 22 percent only.

31. The United States (as well other Western countries) has benefited enormously from the "peace dividend" that came with the disappearance of the Soviet military threat. The United States saves 50 percent of its military budget (U.S.$300 billion) per year. Anders Aslund, "Russia," *Foreign Affairs,* vol. 80, no. 4 (July/August 2001).

32. It is worth noting that the quality and alacrity of Western assistance differs. Huge amounts of money are spent on Western specialists. Organizational structure is cumbersome and absorbs too many resources sometimes. The U.K. Know How Fund keeps organizational structure as light and flexible as possible and is able to deliver projects quickly and responsively. The EU TACIS program is bound by Brussels procedures and thus rarely succeeds in striking while the iron is hot. David Gowan, *How the EU Can Help Russia* (London: Center for European Reform, 2000).

33. An interesting view of the changes in security risks is presented in an essay by Richard H. Ullman, *Russia, the West, and the Redefinition of Security* (New York: M.E. Sharpe and the East/West Institute, 1999).

34. There is no general consensus on how to evaluate the level of risks in the relations between states. The author was inspired by the method of risk evaluation in industry production. The degree of risk of a certain threat [R] can be expressed as the product of the degree of harm [H], the probability of its occurrence [P], divided by the probability that it will be detected in time and eliminated [E].

$$R(x) = \frac{H(x) \cdot P(x)}{E(x)}$$

Even in this very simple formula we can understand that the positive impact of evolution in one factor might be depreciated by the negative impact of another factor. Our efforts in the reduction of the Russian nuclear arsenal (lessening of H) should not provoke suspicion in Russia and thus increase its willingness to use its remaining warheads (heightening of P).

35. A large list of problems remaining in economic and business relations is found in *Commercial Engagement with Russia: Policy Recommendations for the Bush Administration* (Washington, D.C.: U.S.-Russia Business Council, March 2001).

36. The problem is that existing Russian legislation and practice currently falls short of many WTO requirements. There is a danger that Russian membership will be treated politically and conditions for Russian admission might be significantly weakened. Cf. remarks of WTO Director-General Mike Moore, during his visit to Moscow at the end of March 2001, that the "WTO will not be a truly World Trade Organization until Russia ... takes her rightful place at our table," www.wto.org/english/news_e/pres01_e/pr216_e.htm.

37. "Current Economic and Political Situation in the Russian Far East," *NIRA Research Output,* vol. 14, no. 1 (Tokyo, 2001).

38. Zbigniew Brzezinski, "Living With Russia," *National Interest,* no. 61 (Fall 2000), pp. 5–16.

# About the Contributors

**Janusz Bugajski** is the director of the Eastern Europe Project at the Center for Strategic and International Studies in Washington, D.C. Bugajski runs the South-Central Europe area studies program at the Foreign Service Institute (FSI), U.S. Department of State. He has served as a consultant for the U.S. Department of Defense, the U.S. Agency for International Development (USAID), the International Research and Exchanges Board (IREX), the International Republican Institute (IRI), and several private organizations and foundations. He has testified before various congressional committees and in 1998 was the recipient of the Distinguished Public Service. His books include *Political Parties of Eastern Europe: A Guide to Politics in the Post-Communist Era; Ethnic Politics in Eastern Europe: A Guide to Nationality Policies, Organizations, and Parties; Nations in Turmoil: Conflict and Cooperation in Eastern Europe; East European Fault Lines: Dissent, Opposition, and Social Activism;* and *Czechoslovakia: Charter 77's Decade of Dissent.* He is a regular contributor to various U.S. newspapers, publishes in international journals, and is a columnist for several East European newspapers, including *Nacional* in Croatia, *Koha Ditore* in Kosova, *Albania* in Albania, and *Kapital* in Bulgaria.

**László Csaba** graduated from the Budapest University of Economics (BUES) in 1976 and received his Ph.D. in 1984. From 1976 to 1987, Dr. Csaba was associated with the Institute for World Economy and from 1998 to 2000 with the Kopint-Datorg Economic Research Center, both in Budapest. Between 1991 and 1997, he was honorary professor of international economics at the College of Foreign Trade in Budapest, and was named full professor of comparative economics. Dr. Csaba has been a visiting professor at various universities, including Bocconi University, Milan; University of Helsinki; Europa Universitat Viadrina, Frankfurt; and the Free University of Berlin. Dr. Csaba also serves on the editorial board of several scholarly journals, including *Intereconomics* (Germany), *Europe-Asia Studies* (United Kingdom), *Voprosy Ekonomiki* (Russia), *Russian and East European Finance and Trade* (United States), and *Acta Oeconomica, Közgazdasági Szemle,* and *Külgazdaság* (Hungary). He has written 170 articles and chapters in books published in 18 countries, and he is also the author and editor of ten books, including *Eastern Europe in the World Economy* and *Small Economies' Adjustment to Global Challenges.*

**Aleksander Duleba** is director of the Research Center of the Slovak Foreign Policy Association (SFPA). A graduate of Comenius University in the Slovak Republic, Dr. Duleba received a Ph.D. in political science from the Slovak Academy of Sciences, Bratislava, in 1998. Throughout his career, he has published a variety of books and articles, which include forty-four completed field studies on Eastern Europe. His latest books include *Russia at the End of Yeltsin's Era: Foreign and Domestic Politics, NATO Enlargement, and Slovakia's Interests; Ukraine and Slovakia: Geopolitical Characteristics of State-Building;* and *International Position of Ukraine: Implications for Slovakia.* In addition, Dr. Duleba has contributed to several books, including *The EU Accession States and Their Eastern Neighbors* and *On the Edge: Ukrainian–Central European–Russian Security Triangle.*

**Marko Mihkelson** is director of the Baltic Center for Russian Studies, where he monitors current political, economic, and military developments in Russia, with the goal of improving overall understanding of Russia's impact on the Baltic region. He graduated from the University of Tartu in Estonia where his thesis was entitled "Russian Political Development in 1990–96." Mr. Mihkelson worked for an eminent Estonian daily newspaper, *Postimees,* from 1994 to 1997 as its Moscow correspondent, and from 1997–2000 as its editor-in-chief. He has also published columns and analyses on Russia in various international outlets, including *Economic Trends* (Finland), *Radio Free Europe, Postimees, Internatum* (University of Helsinki), and the *Baltic Times.*

**Hryhoriy Nemyria** is director of the Center for European and International Studies (CEIS) at the Institute of International Relations of Taras Shevchenko University in Kyiv. He is also chairman of the Department for European Integration at the Ukrainian Academy of Public Administration; chairman of the board, Ukrainian International Studies Association; and editor, *New Security: Ukrainian Journal on World Affairs.* He is an expert on European integration, regionalism, and Ukrainian foreign policy. In

1992 he founded the Center for Political Studies, a policy institute in Donetsk, Ukraine. In 1996–98, Dr. Nemyria was Dean of the Graduate School at the National University of Kyiv Mohyla Academy. In 1994 he was a National Forum Foundation Fellow at the Center for Strategic and International Studies (CSIS), Washington, D.C. Since that time he has been a CSIS Adjunct Fellow. Dr. Nemyria is the Chairman of the International Renaissance (Soros) Foundation in Ukraine and a member of Freedom House's Central and Eastern Europe Advisory Committee.

**Katarzyna Pełczyńska-Nałęcz** is head of the Russian Department at the Center for Eastern Studies (CES) and assistant professor at the Institute of Philosophy and Sociology at the Polish Academy of Science in Warsaw. Dr. Pelczyńska-Nałęcz graduated from the Sociology Department of Warsaw University in 1994. She received her Ph.D. in 1999 at the Institute of Philosophy and Sociology, Polish Academy of Science. Her thesis was entitled "Dynamics of Political Participation under Systemic Transformation: Poland 1989–99." Her research work focuses on two topics: the analysis of the social and political situation in the Russian Federation and analysis of political transformation in Poland and the other central European countries. Her publications include "Oil and Natural Gas in the Russian Federation"; "Center-Regions: The Division of Incomes in the Russian Federation"; "The Dynamics of Systemic Preferences of Poles 1990–95"; "Political Participation under Systemic Transformation"; "The Russian Federation: The Return of the State"; "The Russian Federation—Characteristics of the Political System"; and "The Kaliningrad Oblast in the Context of EU Enlargement."

**Marcin A. Piotrowski** is a member of the editorial board of *Strategic Yearbook* published by the University of Warsaw. He holds an M.A. in International Relations (thesis entitled "Commonwealth of Independent States 1991–98") and an M.A. in Political and Social Sciences from the University of Warsaw. He has also been a student in the Postgraduate National Security Faculty in Warsaw. Currently he is working on his Ph.D. thesis at the Institute of Foreign Relations at the University of Warsaw on the problems of Caspian regional security. He has conducted field research in Iran and several Central Asian countries. He has published analytical articles about Ukraine, Russia, and other CIS countries in *Strategic Yearbook*. He also contributed the chapter "Poland: Returning to Europe" in *Enlarging NATO: The National Debates,* and to the *Yearbook of Polish Foreign Policy.*

**Leonid Polyakov** is director of Military Programs at the Ukrainian Center for Economic and Political Studies (UCEPS) in Kyiv. Previously he served as state expert at the National Security and Defense Council Staff, Ukraine. His previous assignments included a combat tour as company commander in Afghanistan, two years of military service in Russia's Kaliningrad *oblast,* three years of military service in the Russian Far East, and group chief (U.S./Ukraine military contacts) and senior research fellow in the General Staff of Ukraine's armed forces. He is a graduate of the U.S. Army War College and Frunze Military Academy (Moscow). He guided the development of UCEPS 2000 analytical reports, including "Military Reform in Ukraine: START, or Another False Start?" "Democratic Civilian Control over the Military in Ukraine: On the Path From Form to Substance," "Ukraine's Relations with NATO within the Context of European Security," and "Development of an Export Control System in Ukraine in the Context of Regional Security." His numerous publications cover a broad range of Ukrainian and regional security issues.

**László Póti** is senior researcher at the Strategic and Defense Research Institute in Budapest. His field of research includes post-Soviet foreign policy, post-Soviet–East European relations, and Hungarian foreign policy. Dr. Póti graduated from the Moscow State Institute of International Relations in 1984 and received his Ph.D. in International Relations at the Budapest University of Economic Science in 2000. He was also a research fellow at the Hungarian Institute of International Affairs from 1987 to 1997. His publications include *Les aspirations et dilemmes de la politique exterieure hongroise face a la crise yougoslave; Relations with the Former Socialist Countries,* (ed. Bela K. Kiraly); *Lawful Revolution in Hungary, 1989–95; The Land of Doctrines: Russia's Policy in the Post-Soviet Region and in East Central Europe;* and *From Subordination to Partnership: Hungarian–Russian Relations, 1990–1997.*

**Krzysztof Strachota** is director of the Central Asia and Caucasus Section at the Center for Eastern Studies (CES) in Warsaw. He specializes in security problems of the Caspian region (including Central Asia and the Caucasus), Afghanistan, Iran, and contemporary Islam in the post-Soviet area. He graduated from the Department of Ethnology and Cultural Anthropology at Warsaw University in Poland. His studies included the cultural aspects of war in the former Yugoslavia and problems of exporting Islamic revolution in Iran (with field research in Qur'anic schools, Qom, Iran). He is also affiliated with the Stefan Batory Foundation (Warsaw) and the Institute for Democracy in Eastern Europe (Washington, D.C.). His recent publications include *Islamic Fundamentalism in Central Asia; Uzbekistan in the Regional Political and Security System;* and *New Regional In-security System in Central Asia.*

**Jurgis Vilemas** is director of the Lithuanian Energy Institute (LEI), a position he has held since 1981. He graduated from the Moscow Energy Institute in 1962 and completed his Ph.D. thesis on thermonuclear energy in 1966. Dr. Vilemas is also a member of the Lithuanian Academy of Sciences, member of the European Atomic Energy Society, chairman of the Lithuanian Association of Energy Economics, member of the Senate of the Kaunas University of Technology, chairman of the Board of Lietuvos Energija, chairman of the National Nuclear Safety Consulting Committee, foreign member of the Royal Swedish Academy of Engineering Sciences, and executive committee member of the International Energy Agency (IEA) Hydrogen Program. Dr. Vilemas was also a member of the Strategy Committee for Energy Strategy of the Soviet Union in the Academy of Sciences from 1986 to 1990, and rector of Vytautas at Magnus University. Between 1991 and 2000, he served as an adviser to the Lithuanian government on energy policy.

**Vladimir Votapek** is a Czech political scientist and diplomat. He has also been principal researcher on Russia at the Czech Institute for International Relations since 2001. Mr. Votapek graduated from the Czech Technical University (Prague) and studied at Moscow State University, Oslo University, Charles University (Prague), and the Clingendael Institute (The Hague). During 1986–90, he taught social sciences at the Czech Technical University. In 1992, he joined the Czech Foreign Ministry. During the 1990s, he served as secretary at the Czech Embassy in Moscow and as consul general in St. Petersburg, Russia. His publications include *Russian Presidential Elections; Phases of Russian Foreign Policy; Russian Crisis;* and *Russia and Religion.*